UNSTOPPABLE

Conquering the storms of life by
The Power of God

Dr. Jerome D. Jordan, *D.B.A., M.M.*

Unstoppable by Dr. Jerome D. Jordan
Published by Dr. Jordan Ministries (DJM)
P.O. Box 10535
St. Petersburg, Florida 33733

www.facebook.com/drjeromejordan

Cover photograph and design by Kendra Jordan and Keona Jordan

ISBN 13: 978-1544992105

Dedicated To

MY AMAZING WIFE, the remarkable Pastor Kisha Jordan, whose love and prayers have been paramount to our family's success: Your understanding from the moment we started dating in middle-school and as our lives have unfolded together has been exceptional, thank you. As we have journeyed together you have remained steadfast and unmovable, a true friend, companion, and soul mate for life. I love you. I will always love you, thank you from the bottom of my heart.

My three beautiful daughters, Kendra, Keona, and Kenya Jordan: You have provided joy and special moments of laughter that have made my life so enjoyable. You are truly gifts from God and you have made being a father to easy. I pray that as you pursue your hopes and dreams the favor of God will be on your lives. Always remember, hard work rewards itself.

My hero, my superman, my father, James D. Jordan, Sr., and the world's greatest mother, Delores Jordan: Their love, guidance and unwavering support provided the foundation for the wonderful life I have enjoyed. I cannot thank them enough. They taught me the importance of perseverance, to love all men and most of all they taught me that I could do all things through Christ, who strengthens me. Looking forward to the day when we meet again.

My brothers, James *"Salty Dog"* Jordan and Jason Jordan, and to my sister, Jada Jordan: You will never know how much of a blessing you will always be to me. Although we are separated by time and place, we are and forever will be a family.

My mother-in-law Grace Thompson *"Gracie-Pooh"*: I am forever grateful for the special person you have been in my life and for treating me as your son.

My relatives: I am appreciative of your thoughts and prayers. I pray that God will pour His blessing upon your life. To my church family and friends in the body of Christ who witnessed my journey over the years, you have inspired me with words of encouragement and wisdom.

My mother and father in the Lord, Bishop Joseph and Pastor Jeweline Stallings: Your unwavering support, prayers and love are invaluable. Your exceptional leadership, wisdom of God's Word and command of the anointing have help my family and I experience the breath of God in ways we would have never dreamed were possible. You are awesome.

Finally, to all my friends, colleagues, associates, coworkers, cohorts and even my enemies I have met along life's journey: I dedicate this book to you. I simply would not be who I am today without you.

Table of Contents

First Things First

You Must Be Born Again
(John 3:7)

FIRST AND FOREMOST, Jesus said we must be born again (John 3:3). It is a non-negotiable requirement for walking in the benefits of the Kingdom. You see everything begins with salvation. Without it, nothing else really matters.

Furthermore, I must admit to you dear reader that the principles of this book will not work to their fullest for those who have not accepted Jesus as their Lord and Savior. If you have not done so, now is the perfect time to make Jesus the Lord and Savior of your life.

It's simple, Romans 10:9-10 *"If you confess with your mouth, Jesus is Lord, and believe in your heart that God raised him from the dead, you will be saved."*

If you made Jesus the Lord of your life, welcome to the family of God. Even the heavens rejoice at the saving of one soul (Luke 15:7). Your life will never be the same again. As Ellicott's Commentary for English Readers tells us:

> *"God has given us all we need for salvation; let us profit by it, and show ourselves worthy of it."*

We're Saved!

In October 1989, with my grandmother *"Inez Brooks"* standing by my side at Travelers' Rest Missionary Baptist Church, I surrendered my life to the Lord. I accepted Jesus as my Lord and Savior. Let me tell you, my life has never been the same again.

What is so amazing is God protected us with His power until we received His salvation (See 1 Peter 1:5, New Living Translation). He did not have to do it. But, I am so glad that He did.

Once we accept Jesus as our Lord and Savior, we are covered under the blood and His word starts taking root within us. By God's grace we are now more than conquerors and ain't nobody mad but the devil. With joy, we can draw life-giving water from the wells of salvation and my, my, my, it sure tastes good (See (See Isaiah 12:3).

As children of God, God strengthens and protects us from the evil one (2 Thessalonians 3:3). In addition, He will cause us to triumph in all things in Christ Jesus (2 Corinthians 2:14). But, the key words in the scripture are *"in Christ."*

Thus, as a child of God, I encourage you to walk in truth, follow peace with all men, stand in faith, study the Word, commit to a life of prayer, and be watchful (See Ephesians 6:11-19). If you do, the Apostle Paul says you will be able to stand firm against the tricks of the devil.

Let the Church say
AMEN!

Unfortunately, so many people are missing the great opportunity to join the family of God. The Prophet Jeremiah said it best in Jeremiah 8:20, *"The harvest has past, the summer has ended, and we are not saved"*. Thankfully, this scripture no longer applies to me. It is my prayer that it no longer applies to you.

If you have accepted Jesus Christ as your Savior, then we can proudly say we are born again and to Satan's chagrin our minds, bodies, souls and spirits are now submitted to God. Satan should have gotten us when he had the chance.

Now, it's too late!

Introduction: My Test and Testimony

UNSTOPPABLE

"God has protected me right up to this present time so I can testify to everyone"
(Acts 26:22, NLT)

I WOKE UP lying on my back in the middle of a busy highway. My body was in excruciating pain from the crown of my head to the sole of my feet. Cold, shivering and unable to move I wondered what had happened.

In what felt like an eternity, but was only a few moments in time, I laid motionless in the street. Dazed and disoriented, I knew something horrific had taken place. I could hear sirens blasting and indiscriminate voices in a crowd that was gathering.

Everything around me was spinning. Like a marching band, I could feel the pounding of my heart like a drum in my chest. I tried to sit up, but I could not. I felt weak. I

felt faint and try as I might, I could not catch my breath. Something was wrong. Something was different. Something was not right.

Then, I heard a voice from the crowd say:

> *"Sir, please relax. Try not to move. You have been in a terrible car accident. Help is on the way. Over here, hurry, hurry! O' my God, I think he's going into shock!"*

With those words, I knew my life would never be the same. That's just…

How Fast Things Change

Matthew 14:22-33 tells of one of the greatest events in human history, the Apostle Peter walking on the water in the middle of the sea. It was amazing, it was powerful, and it was something that no one had ever done before. But, in the blink of an eye, he went from walking on the water to sinking in the middle of the storm in the middle of the sea.

That's just how fast things can change. One word from your spouse, one diagnosis from the doctor, one phone call from your child's school, one knock on the door by the police and you can go from having a great day to wondering will you make it through the night.

Peter walking on the water was an impressive act of faith. However, some question Peter's confidence in Christ when he took his eyes off Jesus and focused his attention on the storm. It was at that moment, he began to sink. But the truth of the matter is:

> *We have all taken our eyes off Jesus and like Peter, we have all sunk in the storms of life.*

Yet, seconds later, after Peter took his eyes off the Lord the saving power of God is revealed. As Peter started to sink, he regained his focus and called out *"Lord save me!"* The Bible says immediately the Lord lifted him up and kept him from drowning.

Isn't this a powerful illustration of our life in Christ?

*Sinking in a world of sin, we call out to the Lord and He
saves us when we cannot save ourselves.*

This thin, tenuous line between success and failure, life
and death, good and bad, victory and defeat seems unfair.
Nevertheless, it is what it is and everyone must walk this
line.

I Still Believe

There is an important facet of Peter's walk on the
water that is not written in Matthew 14:22-33. It is an
aspect of this amazing event that I have preached for
years. After Peter walked on the water, after he had started
to sink, after he had cried out to the Lord and the Lord
lifted him up:

> *Peter had to walk on the water a second time to get back
> to the boat.*

Yes, Peter walked on the water not once, but twice.
How else did he get back to the boat? When the Lord
revealed it unto me, it revolutionized my walk with Him. It
is this second walk on the water that is central to my
message to you in this book *"Unstoppable"*.

With the Lord's help, Peter had to get back up in the
place he had previously fallen and walk on the water again.
With the help of the Lord Peter conquered the storm that
nearly conquered him. That's the spirit of being
unstoppable.

Just as there are storms at sea when Peter walked on
the water, there are storms in our lives. The songwriter
said:

> *"There's a storm cloud over the ocean and it's moving this
> way. If your soul is not anchored in Jesus you will surely
> drift away."*

Just as Peter walked on the water in the middle of a
storm, we must also walk on the water in the middle of the

storms of life. This book is my clarion call to you to do as the songwriter said:

> *"Come on and walk on the water with me. Don't be afraid, you will not fail."*

The writer did not say you would not fall, the writer said you would not fail. Fall means to come down or go down. To fail or failure on the other hand implies that it is over, that you will never be successful or rise again. But, the devil is a liar and failure is not your lot in life.

> *We all fall down, we all fail, we all make mistakes, we all miss the mark, we all fall short of the glory of God (See Romans 6:23).*

The Bible says *a righteous man will fall (See Proverbs 24:16).* Expect it, prepare for it, it is inevitable. We all fall down. But falling down is not failure. However, refusing to get up is. Don't be mistaken, there will be moments when you get knock down or fall down. But, do not fret over it. You may be down today. But, you won't be down always.

Ironically, getting knocked down, falling down and failure are not the issues at hand. Neither is the issue the tricks and schemes of Satan mounted against you to knock you down. The issues at hand are you getting back up after you have fallen and continuing on the path that God has you on.

We all fall. We all deal with failure. Unfortunately, many people make the destiny damaging decision to stay down, to quit, to give up. Not the Apostle Peter and the Apostle Paul, they got back up again and you should too.

The questions that I have for you are:

- *Will you get back up again?*

- *Will you trust God after defeat?*

- *Will you follow God after failure?*

This is critical because in order to fulfill the destiny that God has purposed for your life your answer to these questions must be *"Yes, Lord Yes!"* Like Peter, you must be willing to walk on the water a second time. It is my prayer that you are because it was not until *"after"* Peter walked on the water a second time that the storm winds ceased (See Matthew 14:32).

After all, anyone can step out of the boat the first time. They do not know what they are getting into. But, after you have fallen, failed, made a mistake, or missed the mark, do you still believe enough in God to get back up and try again.

You did not get the promotion. Get back up again. Your friends, coworkers, or boss has pulled you down. Get back up again. You did not get the loan. Get back up again. Your marriage did not work. Get back up again. The doctor says there is nothing more he can do for you. Get back up again.

WORDS TO THE WISE

You are not defined by what knocks you down; but by your willingness to get back up again and again.

You lost a loved one. Get back up again. Your heart has been broken in a relationship. Get back up again. Life can hurt you. People can hurt you. You owe it to yourself to get back up again.

The Apostle Paul after being stoned, shipwrecked, beaten on several occasions, jailed, bitten by a snake, rejected, and isolated said it best:

> *Having therefore obtained help from God, I have continued unto this day"* (Acts 26:22).

In spite of all that he went through *"he still believed"* in God and he trusted God to be there to deliver him in the time of trouble. That, my friend, is what I call the unstoppable spirit!

BACK TO MY TEST AND TESTIMONY
Without Warning

Our horrific car accident happened on Christmas Day of 1989. I was driving, my wife was in the front passenger seat, and our daughter, Kendra was tucked comfortably in her baby seat in the back seat. We were on our way to my grandmother's house for the family Christmas dinner. Less than a mile from our destination tragedy struck.

Our car was blindsided by another vehicle. A 13-year-old boy had stolen a car from the mall nearly 10 miles from the site of the accident. The officer attempted to stop the car thief at the mall. However, a high-speed car chase through the city ensued and ended when the stolen car slammed into ours. The police estimated the car hit us traveling in excess of 90 miles per hour.

Those that witnessed the car accident assumed we were dead on impact. I was somehow removed from the vehicle and thank God that I was. The collision was so violent that the steering wheel had been smashed straight through the driver's seat like a harpoon. Had I remained in the seat I would have been impaled and killed instantly.

Lying on the street with neither the strength nor the wherewithal to get up, I felt defeated. My mind was ablaze. My wife was trapped in the car surrounded by twisted metal. The paramedics had to use the *"Jaws of Life"* to remove her from the vehicle. My daughter was lying helplessly in her baby seat covered in glass. Only God knew if they were alive.

The accident came without warning. There were no screeching tires, no blasting sirens or blaring car horns, and no roaring engines. One moment my wife, my daughter and I are enjoying a Christmas Day, the next moment we are battling for life. One moment we were sitting on top of the world and in the blink of an eye, the whole universe was sitting on top of us.

This Could Not Be Real

When I finally regained consciousness, it felt like I was trapped in a bad dream. It all looked like a scene from an action movie or a horror film. I must have been watching a fatal scene from *"Final Destination"*.

Instead of *"The Nightmare Before Christmas"*, this was *"My Nightmare On Christmas"*. This was an awful accident in *"Fast and the Furious"* in 4D. This was a NASCAR race gone terribly wrong.

Bones were broken, blood was lost, and lives were torn asunder. Young love seemingly gone too soon and a child's life had been apparently cut short before she even had a chance to live. This could not be real.

This was Christmas Day and I can assure you we did not put imminent death, sudden destruction, and total dismay on our Christmas list. Maybe Santa has a warped since of humor and he moved our names from the nice list to the naughty list.

Maybe this was all just another misadventure of Jack Skellington and I had somehow awakened in Halloweentown. Unfortunately, this was by no means a fictional story, in a mythical land. This was real. The reality of the moment suggested instead of celebrating a Merry Christmas and a Happy New Year, our families would be planning wakes, funerals and graveside services.

We Did Not Ask For This

At the hospital, the magnitude of the moment had not fully sunk in. My wife now lay motionless, almost lifeless, in a hospital bed. Her body had ballooned beyond recognition and by all accounts, she had only a few hours or moments to live. The machines and medication were barely keeping her alive.

The look on everyone's face suggested she was already dead. Her heart had already stopped twice in route to the hospital and the doctors feared she had suffered some brain damage. She was given less than 24 hours to live.

Death was imminent. The vultures were circling overhead. The grim reaper was closing in. Like an ominous cloud, death was looming on the horizon. You could feel it. You could sense it. You could almost taste it.

We did not ask for death, destruction, and the end of the road. Who in their right mind would ask for something like this? We were praying and believing God for the opposite. We asked for life, liberty and His favor as we pursued happiness. We asked God for His protection, His provisions, and His presence. We asked Santa for gifts, goodies, and all those things that make for a good Christmas.

For us, all signs were pointing up. Life was only going to get better. I was in college with dreams of making it to the NFL, law school or medical school. We were not married at the time of the accident but it was certainly in our plan for the near future.

From the moment we met and started dating in middle school, I was hooked. We married less than a year after the accident. The Bible says *when a man finds a wife he has found a good thing and obtains favor from God (Proverbs 18:22).* Furthermore, *marriage is honorable, and the bed is undefiled (Hebrews 13:4).* I say when a man loves a woman, put a ring on it.

Can I get an
AMEN!

At the time of the accident, my wife was a stay at home mom who was eagerly formulating her plan for the future. She has always had an indomitable entrepreneurial spirit and that tough, invincible mindset would pave the way for mighty moves of God.

God had blessed us with the first of three beautiful daughters. Life was looking good. As four-time Olympic gold medalist Jessie Owens would say, we found the good.

It was all around us. We found it, we were showcasing it, and we really started believing it. The Word of God was manifesting in our lives:

> He holds success in store for the upright, and He is a shield to those whose walk is blameless." (Proverbs 2:7).

We were on our way to achieving the American dream and to grabbing a big piece of the pie. We were moving on up. Young and ambitious our plans for life were coming together. Having just dedicated my life to the Lord, we were living Psalms 1:1-3:

> Blessed is the man who walks not in the counsel of the wicked, nor stands in the way of sinners, nor sits in the seat of scoffers; but his delight is in the law of the Lord, and on his law he meditates day and night. He is like a tree planted by streams of water that yields its fruit in its season, and its leaf does not wither. In all that he does, he prospers.

It All Came Crumbling Down

With one swat of Satan's hand, my family's hopes and dreams came crumbling down. Using a stolen car like a misguided missile, he struck our car with tremendous force. With our lives laid to waste like an enemy target decimated by a direct strike from a nuclear bomb, all hope should have been lost. Who could survive such an attack?

What could I do? I was on the verge of losing my wonder woman and given the circumstances, I was unable to be her superman. Now we both look like forgotten heroes defeated by an unlikely enemy – a 13-year-old boy.

Now the fulfillment of our hopes and dreams looked impossible. Conventional wisdom said turn off the machine and let her die. To borrow a verse from Willie Nelson, it was time to *"Turn off the lights, the party's over."*

Now, I hate to be captain obvious but we have a common enemy - the devil! The Apostle Paul calls him in

Ephesians 2:2 *the prince of the power of the air and the spirit that is now at work in this world.*

He is *roaming the earth looking for lives he can destroy (1 Peter 5:8).* He is hell bent on destroying our well-being and our will to live. True to his modus operandi he wants *to steal, kill and destroy (John 10:10).*

Ephesians 6:12 tells us because of Satan's handiwork we are *wrestling against the rulers, against the authorities, against the powers over this present darkness, against the spiritual forces of evil in high places.*

Illustrations – Reclaimed, Revived, Restored

Now our goals for life lay in a pile like broken pieces of unwanted pottery. Now our dreams of success were fading faster than a puff of smoke on a windy day. Now our aspirations were in desperate need of emergency resuscitation. Now our lives were in ruin and ready to be tossed into the world's landfill.

Fortunately, our God is like a *"Potter".* He takes broken people in broken circumstances and molds them back together again. He takes people who may be in broken relationships and situations, and are left with broken promises and shattered dreams, and gives them hope and a future. Society would typically throw such people away and move on without them. Not our God.

Fortunately, our God is like a *"Garbage Man".* He collects the trash the world is throwing away and takes it back to his factory of healing and redemption. He does not toss us into hell's trash compactor. He does not dispose of us like unwanted waste.

Instead, He makes us brand new and sanctifies us by the Blood. He fills us with the power of the Holy Spirit. Who would not praise a God like that?

Illustration Application

I realize these are vivid illustrations. But, they provide a tremendous opportunity to gain deeper insight into the

hand of God in our lives. He reclaims, He restores, and He revives. He makes all things new. Just as a potter takes a useless pile of clay or a garbage man who collects the trash society has thrown away, each is analogous to God's life-saving touch in our lives.

Remember without Christ, we are not just broken; we are dead in our sin (Ephesians 2:1). We are bound for a devil's hell (See Matthew 25:46, Revelations 21:8, and 2 Thessalonians 1:9). But in Christ, we are new creatures (See 2 Corinthians 5:17), we are brought from death to life (See Acts 17:28) and we are bound for glory (Proverbs 15:24, John 14:2, Revelations 5:9-13).

After the car accident, instead of being crushed physically, emotionally and spiritually under the weight of Satan's attack, God used it as an opportunity to mold us in His hand. Instead of our lives spiraling out of control, He picked us up and placed us safely upon His Potter's Wheel.

Dear reader this is one of the many blessings of being a child of God. God redeems, restores, and renews us by His Hand. As referenced in Jeremiah 18, broken in His Hand, He was reforming me and my family as it seemed best to Him (See Jeremiah 18:4).

Satan should realize by now that God will use our brokenness to perfect us, to bring us to a place of spiritual maturity and to prepare us for the next level in life. Smith Wigglesworth, a British evangelist and faith healer who was a significant figure in early Pentecostalism said:

> *Before God could bring me to this place I was broken a thousand times.*

You see for all of Satan's efforts to break you and me the Bible says *God healeth the broken in heart, and bindeth up their wounds (Psalms 147:2).* Therefore, in these moments of gloom and doom I could feel God's hand and hear His voice speaking to my heart saying, *"It ain't over until God says it's over."*

With His Stripes

At the time of the accident, I had only been born again for three months. The deeper concepts of Christianity were still foreign to me. But even as a young Christian I was already convinced that by Jesus' stripes we are healed (See Isaiah 53).

Yes, we are healed spiritually by the finish work of Jesus Christ on the cross. But, I believe the broader application of the word is that we can be healed physically, socially, emotionally and in every area of our lives. Jeremiah 17:14 says Heal me, *God* and I will be healed. Save me, and I will be saved."

In other words, the healing we received is guaranteed and it covers every area of our lives. Saved from sin, saved from hell, save from destruction, saved from all that stands in the way of the blessings of God for our lives.

Satan had hit my family with his best shot. He was hell bent on making us fully understand that he came to steal, kill, and destroy (John 10:10). But Satan was not satisfied with just attacking our bodies.

If we survived, and we did, then he wanted to destroy our mindset. He wanted to ruin our outlook on life. If he could not stop us physically, then he wanted to stop us mentally and spiritually.

Satan was on the attack against my family. As a result, my family was now deeply entrenched in the fight of our lives. It is a fight that continues to this day.

In this fight, I discovered two things that I want to share with you my friend. First, Satan has the same destructive, insatiable desire to ruin everyone's life. Second, while Satan is attacking God is steadily releasing His revelations into our lives.

Divine Messages

Regardless of Satan's attacks, God is always speaking to us (Job 33:14). The Bible says He speaks in so many ways (Hebrews 1:1). Joel 2:28 says it will come to pass that God will give men and women prophecies, dreams and visions.

Prophecies are divinely inspired predictions, instructions, or exhortations, words spoken or revelations. Visions are the experiences of seeing someone or something in a dream, trance, or supernaturally. Dreams are thoughts, images, and sensations from God that occur in a person's mind during sleep.

Prophecies, visions and dreams give us divine instruction, inspiration and insight. These revelations from God snatch us out of the doldrums, depression, and despair that can loom in our lives. They push us past the obstacles that stand in the way, they keep us on the right course when our lives are shrouded in darkness and they give us the *"pick-me-up"* we need when we feel like throwing in the towel.

> *The revelations of God are so powerful and important for life that without them we will perish (See Proverbs 29:18).*

After the accident, it was the prophecies, visions and dreams from God that inspired me. Like Michael Jackson, there were days that *"Made me want to scream"*. But these continuous revelations from God quieted my spirit, they kept me moving forward and they rekindled the dream within me.

The Power of Your Dreams

Do not underestimate the power of your dreams. It is an inborn desire or passion to do something, to accomplish something, or to have something. Dreams revitalize our outlook on life and they strengthen our resolve. Dreams help us deal with stress and they recharge the mind. Dreams give us a picturesque view of our greatness before it manifest.

Harriet Tubman, an African American abolitionist and humanitarian said:

> *Every great dream begins with a dreamer. Always remember, you have within you the strength, the patience, and the passion to reach for the stars to change the world.*

I am a dreamer. Always have been and always will be. The good news is we all have dreams. For some the dream is to be the greatest performer, for others it is to be an astronaut and fly among the stars. Still for others, it is to be independently wealthy, or to be a doctor, a lawyer, or a famous professional football, baseball, or basketball player.

The pursuit of dreams gives life meaning, purpose, value and direction. The moment you stop dreaming and pursuing your dreams, is the moment your life becomes mundane, undefined and unfulfilling. Your vitality and zest for life starts to decline. The key is keeping your dreams ever before you and trusting in God to bring them to pass.

Dreams are the fuel of visionary people. Dreams are the octane of optimism. Dreams keep us brimming with confidence and it keeps the optimism flowing in our veins.

Speaking about Optimism American Author Seth Godin said:

> *Optimism is the most important human trait, because it allows us to evolve our ideas, to improve our situation, and to hope for a better tomorrow.*

Optimism is seen as the sparkle in your eyes and the bounce in your steps. It fuels your passions, makes all things look possible, it is the wind beneath your wings. Optimistic people are better at shaking off defeat. Optimistic people believe they can fly, believe they can touch the sky, they dream about such grandiose accomplishments both night and day.

When you are optimistic, every day is a new day to spread your wings and fly away. When you are optimistic, the possibilities are endless and the sky is the limit. Like Superman optimism makes us feel as if we are faster than a speeding bullet, more powerful than a locomotive, an able to leap tall buildings in a single bound.

Then Life Happens...

What do you do when the optimistic twinkle in your eye turns into tears of pessimism, when the bounce in your step becomes a noticeable limp, when you no longer feel like superman and you lack the confidence, dexterity and tenacity to be Clarke Kent.

> *When the wind beneath your wings starts blowing like a hurricane? When calamity overtakes you like a storm, when disaster sweeps over you like a whirlwind, when distress and trouble overwhelm you (Proverbs 1:27)*

The reality of life is dreams are frequently interrupted by nightmares. Visions are blurred by an endless stream of negativity. Our goals are confronted by seemingly insurmountable odds. Our outlook on life is distorted and frequently all we have left are pieces of a dream. Life happens, things happen. But do not be alarmed, it is just the...

School Of Hard Knocks

The phrase, School of Hard Knocks, is just another name for the storms of life. As noted in chapter 1 of this book, life is chock-full of tough times and difficult days that can knock you down. For these reasons, I am convinced that the journey of life should come with warning labels such as *"Beware"*, *"Danger Ahead"*, *"Proceed with Caution"*, or *"Enter at Your Own Risk"*.

The journey of life may be best described as a survival of the fittest, every man for himself, may the best man win, or only the strong survive. In discussing our lives in this world, the Bible gives this ominous warning in Acts 14:22:

We must go through many hardships to enter the kingdom of God.

Said differently:

You must go through, to get to!

In the School of Hard Knocks, there is no application fee, no tuition cost and no need to schedule classes. All of that has been taken care of for you when you were born. Job said:

Man born of a woman are of a few days and they are filled with trouble (John 14:1).

The School of Hard Knocks is open seven days a week and twenty-four hours a day, and there is no summer vacation or holiday breaks. Furthermore, there is no need to worry about missing class because of sickness, lack of transportation, or scheduling conflicts. If you cannot make it to class, the School of Hard Knocks will come to you. The Bible tells us in 1 Peter 5:8:

Our great enemy prowls around like a hungry, roaring lion, looking for someone to devour (New Living Translation).

Said differently, that means troubles, trials and tests will find you. But please know this. There is purpose in the troubles, trials and tests of life for the Christian. The Apostle Peter said:

The trial of your faith is much more precious than gold (See 1 Peter 1:7).

James 1:3 says:

The testing of faith produces perseverance.

But to learn from the storms of life you must educate yourself in the pain, the pressure and the problems you face. You should have a doctorate in the struggles of your life's journey, a master's degree in your disappointments,

and a bachelor's degree in all the hells and hardships you have endured.

The truth is you can learn a lot about yourself in the fires of life. In fact, if you want to know who you really are at the deepest levels of your heart, your mind and your soul, then watch your life when it is in the fire. The testing of your faith reveals important aspects of your identity.

You see trials come to make us stronger and every experience in life can teach you invaluable lessons if you are willing to learn. The Bible says *Christ learned obedience through the things He suffered (Hebrews 5:8).* The psalmist said *it was a good thing that he was afflicted so that I could learn Your statutes (Psalms 119:71).*

Learning from our experiences is the only way to get better, to do better, and to be better. The bottom line is there are no shortcuts or easy pathways to your destiny. We must go through the fires of life.

Zechariah 13:9 reads God will put us *into the fire and refine us like silver and test us like gold.* Malachi 3:3 says God is *"as a refiner and purifier of silver; he will purify his children and refine them like gold and silver."* Thus, fire and tribulation in the life of a Christian is a good thing.

Fire and tribulation will expose our issues, even those hidden, deep rooted and inconspicuous issues. God knows exactly what it takes to remove them so that we are more fruitful and productive. As Romans 5:3-4 teaches us, *tribulation produces patience; patience produces experience; and experience produces hope.*

Final Disclaimer

Being a Christian will not exempt you from the School of Hard Knocks. Even prayer warriors, worship leaders, apostles, pastors, prophets, evangelists, teachers, missionaries all must attend class. For some this may be a real downer, but it should not be.

To those that know better James 1:12 says *God blesses those who patiently endure testing and temptation. Afterward they* will receive the crown of life that God has promised to those who love him.

Some glorious day you will hear God say *well-done, good and faithful servant! You have been faithful with a few things; I will put you in charge of many things. Come and share your Master's happiness! (Matthew 25:21).*

If My People

If you are willing to give your life totally and completely to God. If you are willing to embrace the limitless possibilities of God. If you are willing to give God the praise before, during and after the storm.

If you will trust God to cover you with His great power and might. If you will courageously walk by faith and not by sight. If you are willing to stay on the path that God has for you. You will win. In fact, you have already won.

If you will make up in your mind to never give up. If you will dedicate yourself to completing the tasks God has given you. If you allow the joy of the Lord to be your strength. If you will take advantage of the opportunities that God will give you. Nothing can by any means stop you.

If you are going to be a winner. If you are going to be a champion. If you are going to make it to the place that God has purposed for you, then you must face the challenges, the unfortunate events, and the attacks of Satan head on.

If you believe in miracles, no mountain is ever too high. No problem is ever too complex. No news is ever too bad. The enemy can never win. The best is always yet to come and every round goes higher and higher.

If you believe in miracles, the sky is the limit and all things are possible. If you believe in miracles you know it only takes one mighty move of God to turn *"any"* situation around.

If you will let the light of God's goodness shine in your life at all times and in all situations. In addition, if you are willing to embrace the endless possibilities that are available to you through the power of God, you cannot be stopped.

My friend you are a child of the King and there is no doubt in my mind that you were purposed of God to be on this earth at this time. Like Queen Ester *"You have come to the kingdom for such a time as this" (Esther 4:14)*. Your life is a part of God's grand design. You have dreams to fulfill, a God to glorify and devils to defeat.

Unstoppable

What does it take to be unstoppable? It begins with salvation. Then it requires you embracing an undefeatable mentality. It requires a never-quitting, steadfast, triumphant, opportunistic, and positive mindset. It requires a passion for praising the Lord, living in the anointing, walking with boldness, long-suffering, and high expectations in God.

This mindset serves as the genesis for this book. Unstoppable was written to strengthen and encourage you in your journey with God. It was written to draw your attention to powerful truths, revelations and illustrations throughout the Bible and from my life. You see:

> *I am convinced that in spite of the trials of this life, it is a journey filled with bountiful blessings and great opportunities.*

Regardless of the storms that you and I are facing. It could be trials, ridicule, wickedness, temptation, deception, or deceit. Regardless of where we have to face them. It could be at work, in our homes, in relationships, in the store, or in the community. Regardless of the impact it may or may not have on our lives, our outlook must never change.

We are
more than conquerors!

Satan will use a montage of tactics, tricks and traps to stop you from moving forward. However, for every diabolical scheme Satan concocts, God is sending us revelations, insights and endowments to overcome them. Like the Apostle Paul, with God's help we have made it this far and I don't believe He brought us this far just to leave us.

This is your life and you only have one life to live. Therefore, I challenge you to make the most of it. I challenge you to keep moving forward. I promise you your best days are yet to come!

Never forget God's word to you *"Don't worry? I Am with you on this journey"* (Judges 18:6). I pray that you receive that word because *whoever listens to God will live safely and be at ease with no fear (Proverbs 1:33).*

In Jesus name
AMEN!

Chapter 1
Unlocking the Undefeatable Spirit
DEFEATING SATAN'S PLAN TO DEFEAT YOU
"Crush Satan under your feet"
(Romans 16:20)

OUR CRASH ON that infamous Christmas Day of 1989 was horrific. It was obvious that Satan was out to kill someone that day and it was my family and I who crossed his path. On impact, our car was folded like a sheet of paper. It was twisted like a soft pretzel. It should have been cut in half like a hot knife through butter.

Several witnesses stated they heard the collision miles away. Everyone assumed we were dead or dying. The sound was so deafening that some thought a bomb had been detonated or something had exploded. Something had in fact exploded - our lives, our dreams, and our plans.

Just moments before the accident I remember sitting at the intersection waiting for the light to turn green. The next thing I remember was waking up on my back in the middle of the street. Immobilized, dazed, and confused I knew something terrible had happened.

I could hear sirens as they approached the scene of the accident. I could hear the chatter of witnesses as they arrived on the scene. I could hear the hustle and bustle of good Samaritans eager to offer their assistance.

Struggling to get up I remember a woman's gentle touch and calming voice saying *"You have been in a terrible car accident. Try not to move. Help is on the way."*

I was appreciative of her kindness. But, given the gravity of the moment, this was a job for Jesus and thankfully, He was already on the scene. True to His word, *the present God was there in the time of trouble (Psalms 46:1).* He is *our helper* in the time of need (Psalms 54:4).

For reasons that I will never fully understand, He kept us alive! Sure, Satan thought he had killed us. But our lives are not his to take. It is the breath of the Almighty that gives us life *(See Job 33:1).*

Nevertheless, Satan had thrown down the gauntlet. The challenge had been made. The damage had been done. Our lives had been turned upside down with this vicious attack by Satan. Now hanging on to the shattered dreams and broken pieces of our lives, I had a decision to make.

Our Choices

J.K. Rowling said, *"It is our choices that show what we truly are, far more than our abilities."* Nelson Mandela said our *choices should reflect our hopes, not our fears.* With this car accident, the battle had begun and my choices were simple.

I could succumb to the pressure and the magnitude of this horrific accident. The injuries sustained by my wife in the car accident were so severe that most, if not all, in the medical community agreed death was imminent.

Her heart was weakening. Her pelvic bone was not broken; it was shattered. She was bleeding internally and her body was shutting down. All things considered, it made no sense to believe she would make it through the night.

Was it time for reality to set in, for life to take its course, for the love of my life, my wonder woman, to go down a road that I could not travel with her? Even to this day, years removed from this moment, the thought still brings tears to my eyes.

Or, I could square my shoulders, roll up my sleeves, and fight back. I could put this trial in God's hand. Given the facts, faith seemed foolish. But I had a choice to make.

What a quandary, to believe or not believe. Admittedly, I was perplexed and I did not know what to do. I was now confronted with a Goliath sized trial with nothing more than a shepherd's boy sized faith. Like Abraham *against all hope I was challenged to believe (See Romans 4:18)*.

My Choice

Satan wanted me to believe our lives were over and that it was futile to fight back. But, I chose to fight back. I chose to stay by her side. I chose to stand my ground. I chose to trust the Word of God. I chose to walk by faith and not by sight.

Thankfully, it only takes a small *"measure"* of faith to activate the power of God. Admittedly, a little bit of faith was all that I had and as I have learned over the years, it does not take a whole lot of faith to activate the power of God. However, I rather have a little faith, then no faith at all.

We had been hit with a devastating blow, but there was too much God already working in us for our spirits to be crushed. Satan had hit us and admittedly, it did hurt.

But, the God in us was just getting started. This attack that was designed to divide us had united us.

Battered physically and bamboozled mentally, we refused to be broken spiritually by Satan's attack. We had been knocked down, but we had not been knocked out. Now it was our turn to hit Satan back.

It was our turn to go on the offensive. It was our turn to crush that joker under our feet (See Romans 16:20). We took the little bit of faith we had, we put it in God's hands and by so doing, we declared to Satan...

Let's Get It Started!

Satan was on the prowl. His demonic bull's-eye was on our backs. His finger was on the trigger and our lives, our dreams, and our plans were in the crosshairs. He had taken a vicious shot at destroying us and was prepared to shoot some more.

With the car accident, he had given my family the first punch in this fight. He had drawn a line in the sand. He started a game of *"Baddest Man Hit My Hand"*.

Try as he might he could not take our lives or destroy our faith. What he could do was fight us with everything he had. But my parents taught me:

> *If someone hit me, hit them back. If someone starts a fight with me, I better do my best to finish it.*

Now, I am not advocating you being a brawler, a bully or belligerent. But, by all means when it comes to your destiny in God, you cannot be a Christian wimp, a born again chump or saved sissy. You have to boldly lift up the blood stained banner and fight for your dreams.

I grew up playing fighting games. Through my formative years, I had grown accustom to fighting for what I wanted. That same unrelenting, undefeatable and unstoppable spirit was now submitted to the will of God.

I could feel God stretching out in me. I could feel His presence working in me as He prepared me for this fight.

With a newly found *"sanctified swagger"* that flowed from the Spirit of God in my life, I was not going to back down.

The way I see it, life is precious and its days are too short and too valuable to waste time. After all, time is the most precious commodity that we have. We do not have the luxury of wasting it dancing with demons, playing with the devil or giving into his debauchery. Since Satan wanted to fight, my thought was let's get it on. Let's get it started.

Satan had hit us with all that he had, and to his dismay, we did not cower. We did not run away and hide. Maybe he assumed this would be an easy fight. But, he picked the wrong brother.

WORDS TO THE WISE

If you don't fight for your dreams, it is almost certain no one else will. It's your dream. Fight for it!

No doubt, this was going to be a tough, complex, multi-round fight and I was ready. I was ready because I know this fight is fixed and the battle has already been won. I peeked at the back of the book, I read the end of the story and in the end, we win.

Revelations 20:10 tells me *The devil that deceived them was cast into the lake of fire and brimstone…and shall be tormented day and night forever and ever.*

Just as I use to do back in the day, it was time to roll up my sleeves. It was time to take it to the alley. It was time to duke it out the old fashion way and may the best man win or should I say *"May the blessed man win!"*

I knew then, just as I know now – We are fighting a defeated enemy. If that is not enough to get you excited, reading the heading and the information in the next section certainly will.

You Are Never Alone

I am sure you would agree, the rapidly changing world we live in is complex and filled with trials. If the trials that we faced in the world were simple, and situations seldom changed for the worst, we would have little trouble managing our lives. We could simply go cavorting through life with no cares.

However, the storms of life are seldom few in number or simple in nature. If Job were here, he would tell you, *man born of a woman is of a few days, and they are full of trouble (Job 14:1).* The psalmist would tell you trouble is always near (Psalms 22:11). Jesus said, *"In this world you shall have tribulation" (John 16:33).*

Thus, it goes without saying bad things happen to God's people. It goes without saying sin is on the rise. But so is the knowledge and power of God. Habakkuk says *the knowledge of God covers the earth as water covers the see (See Habakkuk 2:14).*

Yes, the storms of life may shake you. But, knowing God is with you should give you the courage and intestinal fortitude to keep moving forward. His goodness, grace and guidance should provide the assurance that you need regardless of what is happening around you.

A central theme in Christianity is the Lord's presence in the lives of His people. In Joshua 1:5, the Lord told Joshua *I will not fail you or abandon you".* He told the disciples *"I am with you always, even until the end of the ages" (Matthew 28:20).* David wrote, "For *in the day of trouble he will keep me secretly in his pavilion (Psalms 27:5).* Psalms 46:1 reads:

> *God is our refuge and strength, a very present help in the time of trouble.*

The Apostle Paul said:

> *If you look for Him you will find Him because He is not far from every one of us" (Acts 17:27).*

Song of Solomon 2:8 says:

> *Look! Here he comes, leaping across the mountains, bounding over the hills.*

What a powerful illustration of our God, our Helper, coming to the rescue. In the Song of Solomon King Solomon is pointing out to you and me that our God knows just where we are. He is always watching us. He is always there to offer His help and God knows we need it.

The psalmist boldly said:

> *The Lord is my light and my salvation whom shall I fear? The Lord is the strength of my life of whom shall I be afraid? When the wicked advance against me to devour me, it is my enemies and my foes that will stumble and fall. Though an army besieges me, my heart will not fear; though war break out against me, even then I will be confident (Psalms 27:1-3).*

After God said to Joshua in Joshua 1:5, *"as I was with Moses so shall I be with you"* Joshua confidently conquered the land of Canaan. That promise resonates with us today since God is no respecter of persons. He is the same yesterday today and forever more and He is committed to your destiny.

Now you can choose to go it alone. I do not recommend it, but should you choose to face life without God then you must be willing to bear the consequences of your decision. Keep in mind, some decisions cannot be undone and I can assure you that doing things without God will never work in your favor.

Moses knew this when he said to God:

> *If Your Presence does not go with us, do not send us from here (Exodus 33:15).*

Moses knew his victories were dependent upon the Spirit of God being with him as he moved through life. It was by the power of God, Moses and the children of Israel passed through the Red Sea. It would have been evident to all who witnessed this event that God was on their side.

When the Lord is on your side, what can man do to you? (See Psalms 118:6). The answer is nothing. The Apostle Paul asked the question in Romans 8 *if God is for us who can be against us (See Romans 8:31)*. The answer is no one! You see *everyone born of God overcomes the world (1 John 5:4)*.

Therefore, you can tell that devil and the people he is using to stir up trouble in your life to take it up with God. After all, it is God who is sending His Word, prophecies, dreams and visions into your life (See Psalms 107:20; Joel 2:28). It is God who has filled your life and surrounded it with the power of the Holy Spirit (See John 14:26).

It is God who has connected you to a network of believers who are praying for you (See Acts 18:10). It is God who keeps lifting you up when you stumble and fall (Jude 1:24-25). So relax, God's got you covered.

If your enemies don't like it and they want to do something about it, tell them to *prepare to meet your God"* *(Amos 4:12)*. You may also want to tell them the one who argues with God is in grave danger (See Isaiah 45:9).

They should also consider the words of the Jewish leader Caiaphas to the scribes and Pharisees who were persecuting the disciples *if their work is from God, you will not be able to overthrow them. You may even find yourselves fighting against God"* *(Acts 5:39)*.

Now, there is a word for your enemies. As a child of God, your enemies must know they are not just fighting you. Your enemies are fighting the God who is working through you. That's got problems written all over it.

Let Go and Let God

We are not undefeatable because of who we are. We are undefeatable as the power of the Holy Spirit is unleashed in our lives. To unleash the Holy Spirit we must make the conscious decision to let God be God in our lives. This is important because:

God will not take from you
what you will not let go.

Therefore, if you are fighting in your own strength, if you are fighting all day every day, then you are fighting too much. If you are actively engaged in spiritual battles every minute of every day, you are doing too much. If you are always speaking in tongues, laying hands on people, and casting out devils you are doing too much.

If you are pulling down strongholds, always trying to give a word from God, interpreting dreams, and just busily engaged in everything at all times, then you are doing too much. More importantly, you are not allowing God to fight enough. If you have not done so already, you are going to burn yourself out and shorten your own life.

The bottom line is even the best, well-trained soldier must rest more than he or she fights. Because a weary soldier is a weak soldier and a weak soldier is an easily defeated soldier. Similarly,

A weary Christian is a weak Christian and a weak
Christian is an easily defeated Christian.

I cannot tell you how many Christians I have counseled over the years that were spending too much time and energy fighting someone else's battle. Or, they have exhausted themselves by working on jobs that belong to Jesus. They have two fish and five loaves of bread, and now they are frustrated to no end because they cannot feed the five-thousand.

Now that trouble is at their door, they are too battered, bruised and bewildered to fight their own battles. The Bible says one can chase a thousand and two can chase ten thousand (See Deuteronomy 32:20). Notice, it does not say *"You"* can chase ten thousand. It says *"Two"* can chase ten thousand.

Until you put this wisdom from the Word of God into practice in your life, you will spend a lot of time wrestling with problems that you should have already put in the

5

Master's hands. Make these words of wisdom apart of your mindset and allow the Holy Spirit to give you knowledge, understanding, and wisdom to walk in it.

My advice to you is,

"Just Let Go!"

Now, letting go does not mean you have the luxury of being lazy, sitting back and doing nothing. Although not all battles are

WORDS TO THE WISE

Every battle isn't yours to win, and every demon isn't yours to defeat.

yours to fight, and not every demon is yours to defeat, you do have your own battles that need your attention.

Avoiding them is not a long-term realistic solution. You cannot walk away from the storms of your life and win. You cannot stick your head in the sand like an ostrich and hope the problems of your life go away. Let me assure you that will not happen.

You have battles that need *"your"* undivided attention and God given strength. After all, some victories will not be won in your life until *"you"* pray and fast.

Overcoming Your Enemies

You can run from Satan and his evil, but you cannot hide. At some point, hell's hounds will catch up with you. At some point, you must contend with the evil in this world. At some point, you must draw a line in the sand, roll up your sleeves and fight your adversary.

The truth of the matter is:

You cannot conquer what you will not confront.

My friend, God has empowered you so you can overpower your enemies and no devil in hell can stop that.

It's just a benefit of being a child of the King. I pray that you receive this word for your life.

Illustration – Overwhelming Your Opposition

In 1916, Cumberland College Bulldogs beat Georgia Tech Engineers in a football game 222 – 0. Yes, that's right. It is not a typo. The final score was 222 – 0 (Eveleth, 2003). In the history of college football, this is one of the most lopsided, overwhelming victories. The Georgia Tech Engineers showed up for the game and put up a fight.

But, once the game started, the superior force of Cumberland College could not be matched by Georgia Tech. They were simply outmatched, overpowered and overwhelmed. This was a beat down of epic proportions. This was a good old fashion whooping.

Illustration Application

In similar fashion, Satan is outmatched because of the power of God that is at work in your life. Remember, *Greater is He that is in you, than he that is in the world (1 John 4:4)*. Remember, if God be for you who can be against you (See Romans 8:31). By faith you must believe this.

Through faith, you can see any situation as God sees it. Through faith, your ears are opened so that as God speaks to you, you are not dissuaded, but persuaded, poised and prepared to do what He says. Through faith, you'll know that even when the way seems dark, the outcome is unsure, or the prognosis is bleak, the numbers are always in your favor.

The reality of this spiritual truth is the demonic forces that are mounted against you are outmatched, overpowered and overwhelmed. When you operate in this truth you don't just defeat Satan's attacks, you annihilate them. You don't just overcome your enemies you overwhelm them

The truth of the matter is you are not just a conqueror you are *"more than a conqueror."* The Greek word for more than conqueror is *"Hupernikao".* Its denotative meaning is to gain a surpassing, lopsided victory. It means to triumph by superior force. It means to give your enemy a good old fashion beat down, whooping, thumping.

Remember, you've got help. *"Those who are with us are more than those who are with them" (See 2 Kings 6:16).* Even when you cannot see your help, even when you do not feel your help, you must believe you've got help.

That was the message from Elisha the prophet to his servant. In 2 Kings 6:14-17 Elisha found himself in a house that had been surrounded by an Army of Syrian soldiers and they were outnumbered. The text reads:

> *When the servant of the man of God got up and went out early the next morning, an army with horses and chariots had surrounded the city. "Oh no, my Lord! What shall we do?" the servant asked.*

But, upon second glance through the eyes of the spirit, it was quite the opposite. The numbers were in their favor. Elisha responded:

> *Don't be afraid, "Those who are with us are more than those who are with them." And Elisha prayed, "Open his eyes, Lord, so that he may see." Then the Lord opened the servant's eyes, and he looked and saw the hills full of horses and chariots of fire all around Elisha.*

The servant now saw what had already been revealed unto Elisha. They were never out numbered. The enemy never had the upper hand. They were never on the verge of defeat. The reality of the situation was they had the upper hand and it was only a matter of time before the Lord would give them the victory!

No Man Can

In Exodus 9-10, we read of Pharaoh's ill-fated and ill-advised plan to stop the children of Israel from leaving

Egypt. The Lord instructed Moses to tell Pharaoh "*Let my people go, so that they may worship me.*" *(Exodus 8:1)*

This was a non-negotiable, irrevocable, ironclad directive from the Lord. This was not a request to Pharaoh. It was a "time-sensitive" command.

Pharaoh did not have time to consider the command, to reflect on his response, or to look for an alternative. The only option he had was to obey. Not obeying would have significant consequences.

Granted, pharaoh had more horses, more chariots, more weapons, and more soldiers ready to fight. But, Israel had God. Pharaoh made the unwise decision to ignore God's command and now his time was up. As we see in the text, God took matters into His own hands.

Like the children of Israel, we all have Pharaohs in our lives. Pharaoh is any person, place or thing that is keeping you from doing the will of God. Pharaoh is any person who treats us unfairly, punishes us unmercifully or persecutes us unjustly. Pharaoh is anyone who hates and seeks to destroy you without reason (Psalms 69:4).

But for every Pharaoh there comes a moment when God will speak into our circumstances and say, *"let My people go!"* You see, when the time is right God will intervene to ensure His plan for your life comes to pass. No witch, warlock or wayward person can stop it from happening.

In his arrogance, Pharaoh ignored the Word of God and sought to maintain his control over their lives. If he could not control them, then he wanted to kill them. But he failed to realize:

- *No one can bind those whom God has set free.*

- *No one can destroy those whom God has restored*

- *No one can kill those whom God has given life*

So one of the first lessons your enemies can learn from what happened to Pharaoh is:

Never stand in the way of a worshipper on their way to worship. That's got problems written all over it!

When the Lord said to Moses *"Tell Pharaoh to let my people go"*, it did not matter what Pharaoh was thinking or what his plans were. Proverbs 19:21 declares, *"Many are the plans in a person's heart, but it is the Lord's purpose that prevails."* The reality is, when God says you are coming out, you are coming out. There are no if, ands, or buts about it.

I am reminded of the word of the Lord to the children of Israel in Genesis 15:14. He promised that if they endured, if they held on to the plan of God, afterward they would come out with great possessions. Amazingly, God spoke this promise that they would come out with great possessions before their suffering even began.

This was another lesson that Pharaoh had to learn the hard way. No man can stop God's plan. Job knew this when he said *I know You can do anything and no one can stop You* (Job 42:2).

To prove this point, God unleashed a series of unprecedented plagues upon the Land of Egypt so that the Egyptian's would know just how awesome God is. He used a swarm of locus, turned an entire river system into blood, allowed the land to be overrun with frogs and flies, blacked out the Sun, and allowed death to come to the first-born male in every Egyptian family (See Exodus 7-12).

I have said for years when God decides to raise someone up or set them free, I'd hate to be the one holding them down. In the end, Pharaoh had no choice. He had to let God's people go. Likewise, Israel had no choice. In spite of Pharaoh's plans to keep them broken and in bondage they were coming out of Egypt.

They were coming out victorious. They did not crawl out, limp out or barely make it out. The Bible says in Psalms 105:37 that:

God brought them out with silver and gold.

And, it happened just as the Lord had commanded in Exodus 3:21:

> *I will grant this people favor in the sight of the Egyptians; and it shall be that when you go, you will not go empty-handed.*

The Nevertheless Mentality

This dynamic of God's will being done regardless of the opposition gives rise to a phenomenon I call the *"Nevertheless Mentality"*. It's having the mentality that regardless of the obstacles we face we will keep pursuing the purposes, plans, promises and presence of God.

Pharaoh tried to keep Israel enslaved and shackled in Egypt. God said they were coming out. Pharaoh in his foolishness remained obstinate. Nevertheless, to Pharaoh's disdain, dismay and demise Moses and the children of Israel believed God's plan for their deliverance would came to pass just as He said it would.

Similarly, when Nehemiah was rebuilding the wall around Jerusalem he was confronted by his enemies. Instead of giving up, he responded *nevertheless we made our prayer unto our God, and set a watch against them day and night (Nehemiah 4:9).*

Rebuilding the wall was a monumental task that most believe could not be done. Their enemies said *if even a fox climbs on whatever they build their wall of stones will crumble.* But, Nehemiah was not fazed and he responded to his enemies:

> *The God of heaven will give us success; therefore we His servants will arise and build. (Nehemiah 2:20)*

With God on their side, they built the wall in 52 days (see Nehemiah 4:6) So, not only did they get it done, they got it done in record breaking time.

Nehemiah's enemies tried to stop the work they were doing. They attacked, ridiculed and mocked them.

Nevertheless, the children of Israel stood their ground, they refused to be stopped, and they kept pressing towards their goal.

Surrounded by nags, nonbelievers and naysayers they finish their assignment. In spite of the hostile working environment, the mocking of their enemies, and the enormity of their task, they finished their God given assignment. In the end, they did what others said could not be done.

For an even greater example, look no further than the life of Christ, as He completed His assignment on the cross. Beaten, brutalized and belittled He kept on fighting to complete His assignment.

In the Garden of Gethsemane, when the disciples had abandoned Him and Satan thought he had the upper hand, Jesus declared *nevertheless, not my will by thy will be done"* *(Luke 22:42)*. He fought through the pain and agony to ensure the right to eternal life for all just as God said it would be.

In the end, Jesus rose with all power in His hands. Faced with days of sheer cruelty, He refused to give up on the purpose and plan of God for His life. That's the *"Nevertheless Mentality"*.

Like Moses, Nehemiah and Jesus, what you and I need is a *"Nevertheless mentality"*. We must believe that even when we are in the midst of tragedy, trials and tribulation, it will not destroy, derail, detour or deny God's will for our lives.

Additionally, we must visualize our victory. This truth is critical because everyone has a picture of something in their mind and you will become what you visualize. If we don't visualize our victory, we'll spend our time mulling over the present pain or the pitiful parts of our past and we'll miss out on the promises of God.

Every day you must give your mind the opportunity to think about a brighter day, a new beginning, new mercies and a greater tomorrow (See Lamentations 3:22-23). You must make the conscious decision to forget the past, to look beyond the present, and to *"trust"* the Lord for a greater tomorrow. Then, as God births in you a vision of your victory and blessings, you must make bold decisions, take decisive actions, and you must trust God as you:

Vigorously defend the dream that God
has birthed inside of you.

The Power of Trust

Trust is from the Greek word *"Parathéké"* which means to deposit or to commit something to one's charge. For example, when you deposit money in the bank you are *"trusting"* the bank to secure it, to protect it, to increase it and most importantly to make sure it is available when you need to withdraw it.

It goes without saying God's bank is far greater. There is something supernatural that happens when we *"put"* or *"deposit"* our trust, our faith and our future with God.

Psalms 31:14 reads *but I trusted in you, O Lord: I said, "You are my God.* Psalms 56:3 reads *what time I am afraid, I will trust in you.* Psalms 84:12 gives this powerful promise. *Blessed is the man that trusts in you.*

Illustration – It'll Make You Jump

When I was in airborne school in the United States Army, the Jump Master taught us the key to conquering the fear of jumping from an airplane is *"trust"*. You must trust your instructions, your training and your equipment.

You must have confidence that the parachute will carry you safely to the ground. After all, jumping is not the hard part, its landing. But, once you have developed trust in your training and equipment, jumping from the airplane can be an enjoyable experience.

It's still scary, dangerous, and intimidating. Don't get me wrong the first jump almost made a brother embarrass himself. It almost made a grown man cry.

I'll never forget what the Jump Master told me, *"SGT Jordan, if you're standing in the door of the plane and you don't jump when the time comes, I'll kick your butt out the door!"* Now you and I both know he didn't use the word butt. But, this is a Christian book and I am a man of the cloth, so I had to modify his quote just a bit. Fortunately, when it was time for me to jump, I jumped.

Illustration Application

I admit, trust does not mean the danger has gone away. In fact, the danger and fear associated with jumping from an airplane with a parachute that *"looks"* flimsy are still present. However, trust conquers these fears and it frees you to move when the time is right.

Again, the issue was not the parachute. The issue was not the danger and fear. The issue was trust. At some point, if you say you have trust you have to put your trust where your mouth is and jump.

The same is true when it comes to trusting God. To trust God means you have a firm belief in His ability, availability, and reliability. This is imperative for unlocking the undefeatable spirit in our lives. This is important because you cannot *"grow"* beyond your level of trust. You cannot *"go"* beyond your level of trust.

To conquer your fears you must take God at His word. That is why Moses was emphatic when he wrote in the Pentateuch:

> God is not a man that he should lie. Neither the son of man that he has to repent. If He said he will do it, he will do it. If he spoke it, it will come to past *(Numbers 23:9)*.

In other words, once God said it that settled it. Trust it! King Solomon said you are to:

> Trust God from the bottom of your heart; don't try to figure out everything on your own. Listen for God's voice in everything you do, everywhere you go. He's the one who

will keep you on track. Don't assume that you know it all. Run to God! Run from evil! Your body will glow with health, your very bones will vibrate with life! (Proverbs 3:4-5, The Message Bible).

"Glowing with health" and *"Vibrating with life"* now that's absolutely awesome. That is the power of trusting in God's word. The Bible says in Psalms 13:5 *if you trust in God's mercy your heart shall rejoice"* and as King Solomon said, *"A joyful heart is good medicine" (Proverbs 17:22).*

The Dangers of Distrust

On the other hand, if you do not trust God you will repeatedly question, second guess and even ignore the prophecies, dreams, visions and other revelations He sends into your life. You will doubt the scriptures and end up doing things the hard way, the long way, or the wrong way.

Distrust is destructive, disruptive and disheartening. It is frequently the primary culprit in our failures and it can turn dreams into nightmares. If distrust continues unabated in our lives, it will:

- *Separate you from the love of God*

- *Increase fear and demonic strongholds in your life*

- *Weaken your resolve on the journey of life*

- *Foster a defeated mentality within you*

Again, I say to you – trust God. Trust is imperative. It is God's antivenin for the poisonous effects of distrust and the antitoxin for the contagion of fear. Unfortunately, too many Christians live defeated lives because they choose to trust in themselves, their feelings, their knowledge and their own understanding.

They have made the destiny damming decision to not trust in the Lord. They have opted for figuring things out and working things out on their own. Let me assure you that trying to do things on your own will have terrible consequences.

Illustration – It Can Kill You

I shudder to think what would have happen if I did not trust the Jump Master and attempted to figure out how to jump from an airplane with my own understanding. A relatively easy task and smooth landing would be dangerous, disastrous, and deadly in a matter of moments.

If you do not follow instructions, if you do not rely on your training and if you do not trust your equipment, things are bound to go horribly wrong. Make a wrong decision jumping from an airplane and it will be the end of the road, game over.

I have the same thoughts when I consider what my life would be today had I not trusted in the Lord. Tasks or challenges that were relatively easy to overcome would have been difficult, daunting, and deadly had I not trusted in God. Jeremiah the prophet said *cursed is the man who puts his trust in man (Jeremiah 17:5).*

Illustration Application

When we choose to trust people and ourselves more than we trust God, we are doomed. It is just that simple. Proverbs 28:26 says *he who leans on, trusts in, and is confident of his own mind and heart is a [self-confident] fool (Amplified Bible).* Psalms 146:3 states *do not put your trust in people because they cannot save.*

Conversely, when we put our trust in the Lord the plan that He has purposed for our lives is set in motion. Jeremiah 17:7 says, *"blessed is the man who trusts in the Lord, and whose hope the Lord is."* The Psalmist said, *"It is better to take refuge in God than to trust people" (Psalms 118:8).*

Like an Airborne soldier when he or she trusts their equipment, they jump from the plane without hesitation. The same must be true of the body of Christ. We must *"jump"* without hesitation when God speaks. This is a vital aspect of living with an unstoppable spirit.

Satan's Plan to Defeat You

Make no mistake about it, Satan wants you bound and broken in the hells of life. To accomplish this task he is restlessly, ruthlessly and relentlessly attacking you (See 2 Corinthians 4:4; 7-9). The Bible says in 2 Corinthians 4:4 Satan wants to *"blind you"* and 2 Corinthians 11:3 says he wants to *"deceive you"*.

He wants you sick spiritually, emotionally, socially and physically. He wants you completely subdued by the traps of life and convinced there is no hope for escape.

To accomplish this task he will use fear, pain and suffering (Job 1). He will use people that mean you no good (Matthew 13:38-39), ungodly leadership (2 Corinthians 11:3-5), lies and liars (Acts 5:3), deception, deceiving spirits and demonic doctrine (1 Timothy 4:1) as well as persecution (Revelations 2:10; Matthew 5:12).

Satan knows he has no authority over your life. In spite of this truth, he will continue his attacks to keep you from walking in your God given authority. Therefore, be prepared for Satan's outrageous lies. After all, *he is the father of lies (John 8:44).*

Consider this quote from Charles Stanley:

> *"One of Satan's most deceptive and powerful ways of defeating us is to get us to believe a lie."*

Satan will use liars to beguile and misguide you. He will use liars to stop you from trusting and walking with the Lord. He will use liars to intervene, interfere and invalidate your destiny.

He will use liars to pervert the truth, twist scripture and to spew out poisonous and destructive words. He will use liars to tell you who you cannot be, where you cannot go, and what you cannot do. He will use liars to keep you bound, chained and shackled.

He'll use chains of doubt, chains of confusion, chains of deception, chains of poverty, chains of the past, chains of sickness, chains of stress, chains of depression, chains of loneliness, chains of heartache, and chains of abuse. You name it and if it can hurt you, hinder you or hold you back from God's blessings, Satan will use lies to keep you bound to it.

He wants to undermine your trust in God. He will use anyone and anything, at any time and in any place to complete this task. Matthew 7:15 says he will use false prophets, who come to you in sheep's clothing, but inwardly are ravenous wolves.

Illustration –Family and Friends

Satan is masterful at using close relationships to launch his attacks against God's servants. From Satan's perspective, the closer the relationship and the more you trust that person, the more likely his attack will be successful.

Satan will even use your family and friends if they allow him. He will use a mother to tell her daughter you are a no body. He will use a father to tell his son you are a failure. He will use a boss to tell his employee you can't do anything right.

He will use a husband to tell his wife you are worthless. He will use a man to tell a woman you are no good. The bottom line is he will push people into your life, thoughts into your mind, and desires into your heart to weaken and wreck your walk with God.

After all, it was Joseph's *"brothers"* that attacked his dreams (See Genesis 37:5). It was Sampson's *"sweetheart"* that stole his power (See Judges 16). It was Paul's fellow *"church members"* that attempted to kill him (See Acts 26:21). It was Jesus' *"friends"* that wounded and crucified Him (See Zachariah 13:6).

Such demoralizing, degrading and demonic attacks and lies can destroy a person, leaving them shackled, chained and trapped in years of life crippling bondage. I am sure if you gave it some thought, you can think of a few people who have had a destructive influence in your life.

Illustration Application

When you allow Satan to use people to undermine what God is saying to you, you are in essence giving Satan permission to destroy your spiritual foundation. You are giving the people he is using too much control over your mind, your heart and your spirit.

You have literally become Satan's puppet on a string. Now, instead of trusting the Word of God, you are allowing the words of people who may be unfamiliar or uninterested in the will of God for your life to control you.

This is dangerous as African-American historian, author, journalist Carter G. Woodson said:

> *When you control a man's thinking you do not have to worry about his actions. You do not have to tell him not to stand here or go yonder. He will find his proper place and will stay in it.*

Now you can see why Satan wants to control your thinking. He knows if he controls your thinking, you are like a defenseless city. He can easily breakdown your walls and destroy your life (See Proverbs 25:28).

Satan knows he can come in and out of your life at any time. He knows he is free *to steal kill and destroy (John 10:10).* He knows there is very little you can do about it when you are not trusting in God. He knows he can lure you away from God and into the place that he has purposed for your life. It is a negative place, an ungodly place and a defeated place.

Dear reader this is why you need to love some folks from a distance. This is true regardless of the relationship and the sooner you recognize this powerful truth, the better off you will be. Their ungodly influence will slowly kill everything good and godly in your life if you let it.

Defeating Satan's Plan to Defeat You

Satan's intent is to drive you to your knees. What Satan does not realize is on our knees is where the Christian does his or her best work. What he does not realize is when we are on our knees we are in the perfect posture for prayer.

Two things are paramount for defeating Satan's plan to defeat you; they are the Word of God and prayer. In prayer, God's power is released, yokes are destroyed, burdens are lifted, and curses are broken. In the Word, we are strengthened and obstacles are removed.

In prayer, when we are troubled on every side, we rise above any distress. In prayer, when we are perplexed, God leads us through the despair. In prayer, when we are persecuted, God confirms He has not forsaken us. In prayer, when we feel cast down, we defeat those who are seeking to destroy us (See 2 Corinthians 4:8-9).

When you and I are walking in the truth of 2 Corinthians 4:8-9 our thinking is revolutionized. The storms of life are stepping-stones to higher places, deeper revelations and greater manifestations. Your hunger and thirst for the fulfillment of God's promises is intensified, the undefeatable spirit is unleashed and Satan's plan is defeated.

You see unlike the destructive lies of Satan, the Holy Spirit brings revelation, deliverance and truth (John 16:13-15). By the power of the Holy Spirit, the chains in your life are broken (Galatians 5:1). Satan's weapons are rendered powerless against you (Isaiah 54:17).

The devil knows this, your enemies know this, and you must know this. Until you do, you will remain bound by Satan's lies. Again I say, you must know the truth.

Illustration – It's Not Locked

The great escape artist Harry Houdini could effortlessly escape from any jail cell. The story is told of the one day he finally met his match. He entered a jail and once he was inside he began the task he had done so many times before of freeing himself.

For nearly an hour, he tried. He kept trying to no avail. Finally, after hours of trying to escape he collapsed in the heat of the day. When he fell to the ground, he bumped against the door of the jail cell and it opened.

You see the door of the jail cell had never been locked. But in Harry Houdini's mind, it was. He expected it to be locked. He acted as if it was locked. The truth was it was not. Had he known the truth, then all he had to do was push the door open and walk out.

Illustration Application

My friend open your eyes to Satan's schemes (See 2 Corinthians 2:11). If you are going to allow others to influence your thinking then you owe it to yourself to ensure they are speaking into your life those things that are edifying and in line with the promises of God. If it does not then you must recognize it, rebuke it and get rid of it before it can take root.

How do you do this? We do it with the Word of God. The Word of God strengthens our minds, burns up impure thoughts and it destroys the evil obstacles that stand in our way. Jeremiah the prophet said:

His word is like fire inside our bodies (Jeremiah 20:9)

He said it is like a:

Hammer that breaks rocks in pieces (Jeremiah 23:29)

As your mind is renewed and your faith increases, you will find it much easier to take dominion over Satan's evil ways. You will find it much easier to quickly push out of your mind any words and thoughts that undermine the knowledge of God and His plan for your life (See 2 Corinthians 10:4-5).

The bottom line is

You are fighting "against" a defeated enemy, and you are fighting "with" an undefeated God on your side, and as a result you are undefeatable. So fight back!

1 John 3:8 declares *"For this purpose the Son of God came into the world, that He might destroy the works of the devil."* The Apostle Paul tells us *"God disarmed the principalities and powers that were ranged against us and made a bold display* and *public example of them, in triumphing over them."* Jesus said *I saw Satan fall like lightening (Luke 10:10).* Can I hear you say "Beat Down"?

It may look as if you are locked in the jail cells of life. But, the truth is God has already freed you from the locks, the chains, and the shackles of life that are holding you. All you need to do is:

Make up in your mind to walk out of the bondage that has surrounded you.

The bondage cannot hold you. It never could hold you. It may look overwhelming, overpowering, or overly complicated. But the power of God at work in your life is too strong. Micah 2:13 says *the Breaker, the One who breaks open the way is standing on the head of your enemies.*

The truth is God has *rescued you and me from the domain of darkness, and transferred us to the kingdom of His beloved Son"* *(Colossians 1:13-14).* The truth is God has freed you from the tricks, traps, and trials Satan has set in your life. Will there be more? Certainly, but that does not matter. *Whom the Son has set free is free indeed! (John 8:36).*

Satan has taken so much from us. Our families, our joy, our peace of mind, you name it and he has tried to take or has taken it. However, those days are over.

It is time for you to get back into the fight. Take control of your life. Whatever Satan has taken, demand that he give it back.

"RIGHT NOW"
In the name of Jesus

Chapter 2

Never Giving Up Mentality

QUITTING IS NOT AN OPTION

*"Though a righteous man fall seven times,
he will get up"*
(Proverbs 24:16)

LIFE IS FULL of soul searching trials. These trials make you wander what to do, who can help you, or where you should go. The death of a love one, the agony of an abusive relationship, a diagnosis of a debilitating disease, losing your job, the roof over your head or your life savings can make you want to throw in the towel.

Some trials are so traumatic, so overwhelming, and so disruptive that they can take your will to live, your desire to fight, and the wind out of your sail. They can make you feel as if you have been pushed out of an airplane without a parachute or hope for a safe landing. Even after such trials are over, you are left with the arduous task of picking up the fragments of your life, your shatter dreams, and surviving on what is left.

On Broken Pieces

In Acts 27, the Apostle Paul was aboard a ship that was caught in a raging storm. The weather was so severe the Bible says that neither sun nor stars appeared for many days because of the raging wind and rain. They were in constant suspense and went without food for fourteen days (See Acts 27:33).

After days of sheer terror at sea, they gave up all hope of survival. Shortly thereafter, the ship struck a sandbar and was destroyed. That's what I call broken pieces.

Now, with their backs against the wall, it was time to make a choice. Their options were few. Sink or swim. Give up on life or fight for it.

They chose to swim. They chose to fight for life. The Bible says by holding onto broken pieces of the ship, the Apostle Paul and his fellow crewmembers all made it safely to land (See Acts 27:44).

A key factor in their survival was letting go of the crippling memories of their ill-fated voyage and the disappointment of the shipwreck. There was no sense wasting time dwelling on the past, feeling sorry for one another, or looking for sympathy. The ship was destroyed and it was not coming back.

Now they had to let go of *"what had happened"* and focused on *"what needed to be done"* to make it safely to land. It was now more important than ever for them to focus their energy and their faith on finding the broken pieces and making the most of what was left of the ship.

Like Paul's ship, we often find ourselves battered and bruised, tossed back and forth by the storms of life. Our finances are being blown asunder, our health is sinking, our relationships are up one day and down the next and we are frequently swept away in waves of repeatedly changing emotions.

However, there is no sense in crying the days away. It is not helpful to sit and sulk over the things you have lost along the way. Now is the time for you to swim and to fight for your life. It is time to keep moving forward. Now is the time:

We must make
the most of what we
have left.

Regardless of what we are going through, we must stick with God's plan. The Apostle Paul knew this when he told his fellow crewmembers *"Except we abide in the ship, ye cannot be saved" (Acts 27:31)*. For you and I that means we must stay on the path that God has us on.

Sure, we have lost some things in the storms of life. Certainly, it would be nice if we had more to work with. It would be great if we had a better job, extra money, or more friends. Nevertheless, it is what it is. Now, we must grab what we have left and *make the most of our time.* (Ephesians 5:16).

For my wife and me, it meant seeing beyond the damaging effects of a terrible car accident. We had to shake off the horrible memories we had experienced. We made the conscious decision to keep moving forward and we readied ourselves for the challenges that lie ahead.

ANOTHER TEST AND TESTIMONY
A Moment like This

On the day my wife was discharged from the hospital, we grabbed her belongings and made our way to the hospital exit. At the exit, we got our first real world test of life after the accident. We were told she could not use the wheelchair outside of the hospital. That meant we had no way of getting her to the car.

Upset, unaware and unprepared, we had to figure out what to do. Still recovering from her injuries, the amputation of her leg and portion of her hip, she was still too weak to stand on crutches. Furthermore, we had not arranged to have a wheelchair available when she left the hospital.

I did not see this coming, but God did and thankfully:

God is never
unaware or unprepared.

God has a masterful way of preparing us for those challenging moments in life and of using our gifts, talents and abilities to overcome them. 2 Corinthians 5:5 tells us *He who prepares us is God.*

For years, I had trained to be a professional football player. All through little league, high school and in college, I lifted weights, jogged, stretched, and exercised. You name it, I did it. I could bench press more than 450 pounds and squat more than 600 pounds. Strength and endurance were my specialty.

I spent my life training to play football; but God on the other hand was training me for something much different and far greater. Unbeknownst to me, God had already changed my plans. The Bible says *a person plans his course, but the Lord directs his steps (Proverbs 16:9).*

I trained to be a top-notch athlete. I trained so that I was ready to take advantage of the opportunities playing college football could bring. However, God had prepared me for a moment like this.

We did not have a wheelchair and she was unable to stand. However, that did not matter. Like Hercules rescuing a lovely lady, I carefully picked her up in my arms and carried her to our car.

Her body felt so fragile. She had endured so much over the past three months, so I held her in my arms like a porcelain doll and protected her like fine china until we made it to the car. Problem Solved.

If necessary, I was prepared to carry her for the rest of my life. I was born for this. God had anointed me for this. He kept me alive for this. This was my assignment, my purpose, my moment, and part of my destiny and it felt good.

Quitting is Not an Option

Quitting was not an option for my wife and I and I want to shake any notion of quitting out of your head as well. Do not quit because of the circumstances that you face or the enemies that are around you. Your enemies might hurt you and your circumstances may hinder you, but they should not halt you.

The point is tough times will come and people will try to stop you from reaching your destiny. Instead of focusing on the circumstance or the enemies' work and weapons, focus on God's word and His will. Colossians 3:2 says *set your minds on things that are above, not on things that are on earth.*

Let me tell you when you focus on the things of God it is like a breath of fresh air. It will revitalize you and it will position you so the blessings of God can flow into your life. The words written by Matthew say it best:

> *Seek first the Kingdom of God and His righteousness and these things will be given to you (Matthew 6:33).*

When Things Go Wrong

There are moments in everyone's life when we grow weary and feel defeated. There are moments when things just go wrong. It's inevitable.

But, just because we grow weary and feel defeated. Just because things may not go the way we want them to go, does not mean we give up. The Apostle Paul writes that *since God in his mercy has given us this new way, we never give up. (2 Corinthians 4:1, New Living Translation).* The message to you and I is – Don't Quit!

Arguably, the greatest basketball player off all times Michael Jordan said, *"If you quit once it becomes a habit. Never quit."* If you give up you will spend the rest of your life with deep regrets, life draining remorse, and musing over what could have been.

They Would Not Quit

The Bible provides so many examples of determination, courage and resolve. Life knocked them down, but they demonstrated great strength and perseverance. These people showed forth a pugnacious, ready to fight attitude in the face of defeat, disappointment and despair. Their lives epitomize the phrase *"Quitting is not an option"*.

The book of Job gives us nearly 21 chapters that recount the horrific events in Job's life. Yet he endured and in the end, God blessed him with more than he lost. The Apostle Paul in discussing the trials of his life said in 2 Corinthians 11:23-27:

I have worked harder, been put in jail more often, been whipped times without number, and faced death again and again and again. Five different times the Jews gave me their terrible thirty-nine lashes. Three times I was beaten with rods. Once I was stoned. Three times I was shipwrecked. Once I was in the open sea all night and the whole next day. I have traveled many weary miles and have been often in great danger from flooded rivers and from robbers and from my own people, the Jews, as well as from the hands of the Gentiles.

I have faced grave dangers from mobs in the cities and from death in the deserts and in the stormy seas and from men who claim to be brothers in Christ but are not. I have lived with weariness and pain and sleepless nights. Often I have been hungry and thirsty and have gone without food; often I have shivered with cold, without enough clothing to keep me warm.

In spite of all of this, the Apostle Paul declared:

None of these things move me, neither count I my life dear unto myself, so that I might finish my course with joy, and the ministry, which I have received of the Lord Jesus, to testify the gospel of the grace of God (See Acts 20:24).

Illustration - Get Back Up Again

On April 17, 1909, African American boxers Joe Jeanette and Sam McVey fought the longest boxing match in the history of professional boxing. The fight lasted 49 rounds. This is one of the greatest fights of all times and an extraordinary example of perseverance, endurance and never quitting.

During the fight, Jeanette's opponent knocked him down 27 times. In fact, in round 16 his opponent nearly knocked him out. However, Joe continued to fight until he finally won the fight in round 49 when his opponent, Sam McVey was unable to rejoin the fight when the bell rung.

Illustration Application

Life can seem like a never-ending boxing match. Like an endless array of energy draining body blows, repeated jabs to the gut, and dizzying punches to the head. Each new day brings with it new trials that are trying to knock the wind out of you, knock your head off, or knock you senseless.

Some days the trials knock us down and some days the trials knock us out. But I want you to heed this powerful word from the Lord found in Proverbs 24:16, *"For a righteous man falleth seven times, and riseth up again."* Micah the prophet said, *"For though I fall, I will rise again" (Micah 7:8).*

The principle of the scriptures is to anticipate that life will occasionally knock you down. But, the more powerful aspect is having the faith and determination to get back up again. Robert Schuller said:

"Most people who succeed in the face of seemingly impossible conditions are people who simply don't know how to quit."

Joe Jeanette was knockdown 27 times in one fight and he could have easily conceded he had lost. To the surprise of his opponent and to the on lookers, each time he got knockdown he got back up again until he finally won the fight!

Spirit of Determination

Victory in the fights of life requires determination. Determination means continuing to do something even when it is difficult. You see when the way gets hard having a spirit of determination keeps you moving in the right direction and along the path of God's blessings for your life (see Galatians 6:9).

The key as noted by an unknown author is:

Do not confuse your path with your destiny. Just because its storming right now does not mean you are not headed to sunshine.

I am sure you would agree that life is full of difficulties. Yet, it has been my experience when I wake up each morning with a sense of determination that my day is far more fulfilling. Furthermore, when I lay down at night I am even more satisfied. That's the power of determination.

The Determined Moabitess

After the sudden death of her husband, Ruth the Moabitess found herself widowed in a foreign land. Naomi, her mother-in-law, advised her to go back to her home in Moab, but Ruth would not. The Bible says Ruth *"clung"* to Naomi and committed herself to the God of Israel. Ruth said:

*Entreat me not to leave thee, or to return from following
after thee: for whither thou goest, I will go; and where
thou lodgest, I will lodge: thy people shall be my people,
and thy God my GOD: Where thou diest, will I die, and
there will I be buried: the Lord do so to me, and more
also, if ought but death part thee and me. (Ruth 1:16-
17).*

Her current situation looked bad, but that did not
matter. The outlook on her life looked bleak, but that did
not matter. Ruth made the decision to stay with Naomi
and the God of Israel. She refused to let the difficulties of
life stop her, turn her around or push her from God's path
for her life.

You and I must have the drive, determination and
spirit of Ruth. Operating in the spirit of Ruth means we
will not let bad circumstances, or bad counsel, bad storms,
or bad people stop us, push us off track or keep us from
succeeding. Just as Ruth would not leave Naomi, we must
with purpose of heart cleave unto the Lord (Acts 11:23).

The Determined Misfits

Imagine what would have happened if the woman
with the issue of blood for twelve long years had given up
(See Luke 8:43-48). If she did not push through the crowd
to touch the hem of Jesus garment, she would have missed
her healing. But, she kept on pressing and received her
blessing. That's determination.

What about the impotent folks in John 5:2-8 who were
waiting for the moving of the water? If this motley crew
walked away from the pool, they would have missed their
healing. Case in point, one man sat at the pool day after
day for thirty-eight long years. Yes, for thirty-eight years.

Second after second, minute after minute, hour after
hour, day after day, month after month, and year after
year, the impotent man stayed at the pool ready to receive
the healing he needed from the Lord. John 5:6-9 reads:

When Jesus saw him lying there and knew that he had already been there a long time, he said to him, "Do you want to be healed?" The sick man answered him, "Sir, I have no one to put me into the pool when the water is stirred up, and while I am going another steps down before me." Jesus said to him, "Get up, take up your bed, and walk." And at once the man was healed, and he took up his bed and walked.

Imagine what would have happened if the lame man in Acts 3 had given up on life. The Bible says on this day when Peter and John were on their way to the temple to have prayer they met the lame man. Yes, the lame man's situation was not the best. He was sitting outside the house of God begging for money. He, like many of us was a misfit and set apart from the others.

Sure, he had every reason to be a quitter. He was unable to walk. He was unable to make a living. The Bible does not mention any friends or family to assist him. His situation look bad and many in his situation would simply give up.

He could have relocated. When Peter reached out to help him to his feet he could have said, I have tried standing before and it did not work. He could have moved away from the house of God. He would not be the first person and he certainly would not have been the last to give up and walk away from the Lord.

Timothy 5:15 says, *"Some have already turned aside to follow Satan".* But bless God, many of us are still holding on to and refuse to walk away from the God of our salvation. Like the disciples' response to Jesus' question in John 6:67, *"Shall you also go away?"* The disciples responded *"to whom shall we go? You have the words of eternal life and we believe".*

Unbeknownst to the lame man in Acts 3 this was the day his life would be forever changed. This misfit was moments away from his miracle. Knowing he had faith to be healed, Peter and John said to him *"look at us"* and in faith, he did.

Peter and John then declared the life changing words to the lame man *"In the name of Jesus Christ rise up and walk" (Acts 3:6)*. Immediately he received the strength he needed and he leaped up onto his feet. *He then went into the temple walking and leaping and praising God.*

Because he was determined, because he did not quit, because he did not embrace a give up spirit, because he was in the right place, at the right time and in the right frame of mind, he received this mighty outpouring from God.

Some Tough Love

Even when you are operating with a spirit of determination, there will be moments when you have put forth your best effort, you have given your all, your time, and your money and have nothing or very little to show for it.

It is in these times that thoughts of giving up begin to haunt our minds. We see this in Luke 5, when Apostle Peter and his friends had finished a night of fishing. They had fished all night and caught nothing. They had the ability, experience, equipment and knowledge to catch fish. But on this occasion, they had nothing to show for their efforts.

Now, they were washing their nets and calling it quits. They were frustrated, they were tired, and they were beaten. Physically and spiritually, they were defeated. This is a dangerous state of mind to be in. Proverbs 18:14 says *the human spirit can endure a sick body, but who can bear a crushed spirit?*

Peter and his friends had given up. They were putting their nets away when Jesus appeared unto them. But notice Jesus did not enter into a pity party; neither did he feel sorry for the disciples. He simply gave them a word. In Luke 5:4, he said to them to get back into the boat, launch back out on the water, let the net back down, and you will catch some fish.

Jesus told them what they needed to hear, not what they wanted to hear. Jesus was challenging them to try again. Jesus mended their broken spirit, restored their bruised ego and healed their broken heart.

He told them the truth knowing they did not want to hear it. He could have pacified them. He could have said do not worry, it will be okay. He could have said go home and try again tomorrow.

Such words might have made them *"feel better"*, but it would not have *"stirred their faith"* or positioned them for the blessing. It would not have gotten them ready, improved their willingness, or provoked them to try again.

Jesus challenged them with some tough love. He told them the truth. It was the only way to position them for the opportunity that was waiting for them back out on the water.

The truth dared them to deal with their feelings of failure. The truth ignited their faith. The truth ridded them of the paralyzing effects of doubt, disappointment and despair.

A Real Friend

I pray that you have people in your life who will love you through the tough times. If you do, you are truly blessed. These are your real friends.

Real friends do not let their friends settle for less. Real friends do not let their friends give up when they miss the mark or fall short. Real friends do not let their friends quit when opportunities knock.

I believe even if it hurts, you should love someone enough to tell them the truth. After all:

Life is too short
and hell is too hot
for us to play
friends.

One of the greatest gifts you can have is a friend that loves you enough to tell you the truth. Someone who will tell you what you need to hear, not what you want to hear. Their words may hurt and in some instances, you may not want to hear it, but you need it. Your destiny needs it.

Jesus loved the disciples enough to tell them the truth. He loved them too much to let their disappointment stop them. The truth was they had given up and at the risk of

WORDS TO THE WISE

Find those people in your life who challenge you to make the most of your time and lose those people in your life that do not!

making them mad, He sent them a strong word to break the failure mentality that had taken hold of them. He told Peter:

> *Take the boat into deep water, and lower your nets to catch some fish." (Luke 5:4).*

As you can imagine Peter and his friends would have every reason to doubt. After all, they were experienced fishermen. Jesus was a carpenter. They had fished all night and caught nothing. They were now washing the nets and walking away with their heads hung down.

What the disciples did not realize was they were walking away from a magnificent blessing. An abundance of fish was waiting just beneath the surface of the water. The blessing the needed was underneath their boat.

Tragically, since they could not see it they no longer believed it. As a result, they could not receive it. It is in moments like these when we all need people in our lives that will encourage us when we cannot see the opportunity that God has sent our way.

Jesus would not let them give up. He challenged them to get up on their feet, to square their shoulders, focus on the task and keep moving forward. He challenged them to get back into their boat. He challenged them to do it again.

That's Just Insane

Overcoming failure starts with the decision to try again. Like the Apostle Paul, when he declared, *"none of these things move me"* we must refuse to let bad people, places or problems keep us down. This is true regardless of who, what or where the challenge comes from.

It could be a boss at the top of an organization, a disease with no cure, or a predicament with no apparent escape. We must not give up. We must keep trying. As W.E. Hickson, a British educational writer wrote:

If at first you don't succeed, try, try, try again!

In Luke 5 Jesus gave the disciples the opportunity to try again. He challenged them to get back into the same boat, to go back into the same area and do the same thing again.

Albert Einstein would call this the definition of insanity. Doing the same thing over again but expecting a different result. Some would say doing such a thing is madness, it is foolishness, and it is irrational. However, I beg to differ.

Peter and his friends trusted and

> **WORDS TO THE WISE**
> *When the Lord says "Do it again it" would be insane, foolish, and irrational not to do it again.*

obeyed the words they received from the Lord. They *"willingly"* got back into the boat and went back out on the water where they had previously failed. I am sure that many of his fellow fishermen must have thought they were out of their minds to get back into the boat after a night of catching nothing.

But Peter and his friends did it anyway. They were crazy enough to believe. The Bible says after they let down the net and they pulled in more fish than they could handle. At that moment, they went from catching nothing and walking in a give-up spirit, to catching more than enough and walking in divine victory and supernatural increase.

They trusted in Jesus' word and it resulted in a blessing that Luke would describe as *good measure, press down, shaken together, and running over (Luke 6:38)*. Malachi would call it *a blessing you do not have room enough to receive (Malachi 3:10)*.

You see, they were destined to be successful, not doom to fail. They were destined to catch a multitude of fish, not go home empty handed. They were destined to walk in God's goodness, not dwell in defeat.

They caught so many fish the boat began to sink. They had to call others to come help them pull in this great catch. The blessing was too much for one boat to handle. That's just crazy.

Illustration – That's How I Made It

When I consider all that God has done in my life and what He has brought me through, I am more motivated to keep moving forward. For example, when I was a little boy, I would ride my bike down to the lake a few miles from my house. It is a lake with plenty of alligators. For hours, I would play near the edge of the water.

One hot summer day I had been at the lake playing for about an hour. I had not seen any alligators. In a moment of juvenile stupidity, I sat with my feet hanging off the dock, just inches above the water. After fifteen minutes or so, I got back up onto the dock. It was getting late so I got on my bike and headed home.

As I rode away, I looked back at the dock and there was an alligator in the water. It was only a few yards from where I had been sitting with my feet just a few inches above the water. I am convinced the alligator had been there the entire time.

It would have had several opportunities to attack and potentially kill me. Only God knows why He spared my life that day. Someday I will have the opportunity to ask Him why I survived.

But Wait, There's More…

When I was a little boy a group of friends and I removed a manhole cover and climbed down into the large water drainage pipe. We then walked for several miles underground through a series of dark and wet corridors. We could have gotten lost and unable to find our way out, the drainage pipe could have filled with water and we all drown, or some other mishap could have occurred.

Looking back, even in our folly and childhood mischief, I am convinced the Lord was with us. I am convinced that we survived not by our own might or power, but by the Spirit of God (See Zechariah 4:6). The songwriter said, *"If it had not been for the Lord on my side, where would I be?"*

For me, if it were not for God, the alligator would have grab me and taken me under. If it were not for God, my friends and I would have drowned in a drainage pipe. Thankfully, God is an on-time God and He laughs at the foolishness of men (See Psalms 59:8; Psalm 2:4).

Not Done Yet…

While I was finishing this book, God spared my life once again. I was driving home in the rain after cutting the grass at my mother-in-law's house. She had gone home to be with the Lord, but it has remained a desire in my heart to help whenever I can.

As I drove across the crowded bridge at nearly 60 miles per hour with a huge tractor-trailer on my right, the railing on my left, and other cars in front and behind me, without warning my car hydroplaned.

Within seconds, my car went into a violent spin and the front of my car went underneath the 18-wheeler on my right. Seconds later, my car careened across the crowded highway and slammed into the retention wall. At the rate of speed I was traveling, I was sure I was going to go over the wall and into the deep water below.

Unexplainably, when I collided with the wall, the car stopped immediately. However, it was not from the impact of the wall, but by *"Something"* or *"Someone"* far greater. The Bible says *the angel of the Lord encamps about those that fear his name (Psalms 34:7)*.

I am convinced the truck did not crush me and I did not hit any other cars because God intervened. He prevented certain injury and death, and He kept me from flipping over the retention wall and into the water. Again, I ask the question, *"If it had not been for the Lord on my side where would I be?"*

When my car hit the wall, it felt as if I was going 6 miles per hour, not 60. Once my car came to a stop and I gathered my wits, I simply backed up from the wall, waved thankfully to the crowded highway of stunned drivers who had stopped in the middle of the road, and drove off down the highway.

Illustration Application

These are just a few examples from my life. I am sure you have some examples of your own. There are dangers seen and unseen that threaten our lives every day. The stray bullet that should have seriously injured me, the car that should have run the red light and killed me, the home invasion that should have happened.

You may be asking yourself why these events from my life are important to you. They are important because God is no respecter of persons. There is no secret what God can do. What He has done for others, He can do the same thing for you.

It Ain't Over

There are instances when something bad does happen and we are faced with situations that look to far gone for even Jesus. Case in point, in John 11, Lazarus the friend of Jesus has died. What is moving is verse 35 when the Bible tells us that *"Jesus Wept."*

Some of the onlookers asked the question *"Could not he who opened the eyes of the blind man have kept this man from dying?"* *(John 11:37)*. Unknown to all of them Jesus was getting ready to reveal a powerful truth. The truth is:

"It ain't over until
God says it's over!"

By this point, Lazarus has been dead for four days. Surely, any hope of him coming back to life must have been gone. But, with three words from Jesus, *"Lazarus come forth"* he did.

The Bible says in John 11:44:

The dead man came out, his hands and feet wrapped with strips of linen, and a cloth around his face.

Lazarus was alive. He rose from the dead with three words from the Lord. Like Lazarus, that is all it takes for you and I, a word from the Lord and like Lazarus we to can rise above the dead things that are around us. For this reason, it is easy to see why God's word is so important in our lives.

Jesus then declared:

Loose that man and let him go" *(John 11:44)*.

In other words, he was not simply alive, he was free from his tomb, healed of his aliment, and delivered from the expectations of men.

He was loosed from the dead reminders of his past. Lazarus had been dead for four days and everyone believed, *"by now he stinks."* But, Jesus' word brought total healing, total deliverance, and it bought him back to life.

When you talk about Lazarus, you must talk about his resurrection from the dead. In so doing, you must acknowledge the resurrection of his lifeless body. It was not by the wisdom of men, or power of people, but by the Spirit of the Lord (See Zechariah 4:6). It adds meaning to the song:

> *"Nobody but you Lord nobody but you. When I was in trouble, you brought me over. Nobody but you Lord nobody but you."*

When Lazarus rose from the dead, I am sure he was the talk of the town. Think about it. The brother was dead, the man was stinking and now he is standing there alive with Jesus and the disciples. Instead of talking about his premature demise and death, the people were flabbergasted by his new lease on life.

Similarly, I am sure there are people today who are watching, waiting and talking about you. Some are hoping you will quit, others are hoping you will turn and walk away, and some who want you and your dreams dead. Tell them to keep on looking.

> *You may be down today,*
> *but you want be down*
> *always!*

First That, Now This, What's Next

Remember, Lazarus had been dead for four days. Now by the power of God he is alive. John 12:9 says:

> *A large crowd of Jews found out that Jesus was there and came, not only because of him but also to see Lazarus, whom he had raised from the dead.*

Now you would think everyone would be rejoicing with Lazarus and his family. Indeed God had worked a notable miracle. However, the Bible says, *"the chief priests made plans to kill Lazarus."*

I mean, really! You have to be kidding me. After all Lazarus has been through, now he has to contend with their hatred. Lazarus must have been thinking, *"After all that I have been through, now I have to deal with this? What could be next?"*

Like Lazarus, people can see the miracle of your life and they can sense the presence of God all around you. Instead of celebrating what the Lord is doing, they are hell-bent on sabotaging God's work in your life, with making you quit, or hoping you will die.

The truth of the matter is everyone who is around you is not around to support you. Many are there to pull you down, to attack the newness of your

WORDS TO THE WISE

Don't give your enemies the luxury of laughing at you or the chance to say "I told you so."

life, to be there when you fall. They are patiently awaiting the death of your dreams.

Yes, you can cry and there will be days when you feel like throwing in the towel. But don't give up. If people are dumb enough to sit there and watch you, then give them something to talk about.

When it comes to God's destiny for your life, you have to be headstrong, pugnacious, and unwavering. Remember, that is what Jacob did in Genesis 32:22-30 when he wrestled with the angel of the Lord. He said:

I will not let you go unless you bless me.

Jacob could have easily let go of the angel. After all, the angel had already dislocated his hip. Yet, Jacob held on. Finally, after wrestling all night long, with the joint in his hip dislocated, in excruciating pain and extreme weariness, he got his blessing.

When people expect you to quit, stand up in the power of God's might. When people assume you will fail, try again in the blood of the Lamb. People may be gathering around to celebrate your demise, but they are being set up to witness your deliverance. God is preparing a table of blessings for you in the:

Presence of your enemies (Psalms 23:5)

My message to you is simple. Whatever you do, do not let go. Hold on to the promises of God for your life. Your blessings are on the way.

You Are Today's Lazarus

If you think your life is over you are wrong. If you think your dreams are dead, you are mistaken. If you think it will never get better, I am here to tell you nothing could be further from the truth.

God has not brought you through the storm and rain for nothing. In fact,

I don't believe
He brought you this far
to leave you.

You may have been counted out, left for dead, and in the eyes of many people your life is over and by now it *"stinketh"*. But, the Word of God being released unto you by way of this book is turning your life around and releasing you from the deadness of your past.

My friend, I say to you:

"Come forth by the power of God!
Be free of the dead things in your past
and the pain of your present."

As a child of God, you have been buried with Christ in baptism and just as Christ was raised from the dead, I declare to you today, you shall *walk in the newness of life (See Romans 6:4).* Paul said, *"In Him we live, we move and have our being" (Acts 17).* He said God *"has caused us to be born again to a living hope through the resurrection of Jesus Christ from the dead."*

We are alive. If people are going to talk about my life or your life, then we should give them something to talk about. Let them talk about our never quit mindset. Let them talk about our never say it is over, always getting back up again mentality. Let them talk about the walking miracles we are and how we are fearfully and wonderfully made by God (Psalms 139:14).

Our God took a handful of dirt, mold it into the shape of a man, then breathed life into it and man became a living soul (See Genesis 2:7). If God did it with Adam in the garden during creation, then why would anyone think God would not breathe the breath of life into our dead situations and bring us back to life?

You see, anyone can preach a sermon. Anyone can sing a song. Anyone can profess Christianity. However, it takes power to get up over and over again.

This is what your friends and enemies need to see. They need to see that you have risen above your circumstance. They need to see that you are alive. They need to see that in the storms of life you did not die. You are today's Lazarus. Let your enemies talk about that!

Let the church say
"AMEN!"

Chapter 3

Staying Steadfast In Faith

REFUSING TO LEAVE GOD'S PATH FOR YOUR LIFE

"Be ye steadfast, unmovable, always abounding
in the work of the Lord"
(1 Corinthians 15:58)

A FEW DAYS after the accident, my wife went into a coma. Her injuries were too severe and her body was calling it quits. The chances of her survival were slim and none. She had endured several surgeries and needed many more. She had survived a number of amputations and now we were running out of options.

Unfortunately, the prognosis remained bleak. Her internal organs were not working properly. Her kidneys were shutting down. Her heart was weakening. Her blood pressure was dropping. Infections were starting to set in. Once again, death seemed imminent.

A Talk with My Fathers

It was during this time while my wife was comatose, that my dad, my hero, asked me *"Son, what are you going to do?"* He knew it was time for me to return to college, he knew my aspirations to play college football, he knew I had a remote but realistic chance of making it to the NFL, and he knew I wanted to complete my degree and find a job in a lucrative career field.

Without hesitation, I replied:

*"I'm going to
stay by her side"*

My father looked at me and said *"Son, I was hoping you would say that."* I could tell by the look in his eyes and smile on his face that he was proud. He knew the years that he and my mother spent parenting, mentoring and training me in the way that I should go had prepared me for this moment.

Instantly I felt the presence of my *"Heavenly Father"* wash over me. This special moment was impossible to explain. You have to experience moments like this for yourself. The Bible calls them *times of refreshing which can only come from the presence of the Lord (See Acts 3:20).*

This time of refreshing in my life was confirmation that I had made the right choice. It was confirmation that I had made the God choice. My Heavenly Father had already spoken to my heart that my wife and I were destined to be a team, that we had work to complete together, that our souls had been knitted together like Jonathan and David (See 1 Samuel 18:1). A car accident was not going to tear this team apart.

Joshua Moments

Just as there are times of refreshing, there are times in life that I call *"Joshua Moments"*. Joshua, whose name in the Greek is *"Y'hoshua"* meaning Yahweh is salvation, was a mighty man of God. It is from the life of Joshua that I have drawn the phrase Joshua Moments.

There are moments in life that dare you to stand your ground, to step out in faith, and to trust in the Word of God. There are moments in life that challenge your mental makeup, your physical prowess, and your spiritual toughness. There are moments in life that test your will *to fight the good fight of faith (1 Timothy 6:12)* and your resolve to keep standing when *you have done all to stand (Ephesians 6:13)*. These are your Joshua Moments.

In the book of Joshua, God promised Joshua the land of Canaan. However to possess it, Joshua had to fight for it. He fought numerous battles from the Arnon Gorge to Mount Hermon and included Jericho in Chapter 6, Ai in chapter 7-8, and total more than thirty-one kings in all (Joshua 12:24).

Just like Joshua and the children of Israel, we all have a mighty *"Jericho"* to conquer (Joshua 6). These are battles that look too big, too strong, or too complex to handle. However, if you will follow God's instructions for your life you will defeat them.

We all have an *"Ai"* to defeat (Joshua 8). These are the small fights that look easy to overcome but you keep losing them. However, once you confess any sins that are holding you back, the next time you face your Ai you will win.

We all have *"Canaan lands"* to possess (Joshua 11; 14). These are the promises that appear too good or too awesome to be true. However, if you will trust God to bring them to pass, you will have them.

To be successful in these moments, you must be firm, unwavering, and determined. That is what Joshua showed us in response to his statement *choose this day whom you will serve? (Joshua 24:15)*. He declared *everyone in my house will serve the Lord. (Joshua 24:15)*.

It was as if Joshua was putting Satan and the whole world on notice that his family was committed to being steadfast in their faith. Joshua knew their salvation, deliverance, healing, breakthrough, guidance, and strength, all came from God. He knew their relationship with God gave them the ability to win the battles they faced and he was not willing to turn his back on the God of their salvation.

Just as it was with Joshua, so it is with you and I. Our lives are full of dialectical tension. There are conflicting choices, differing desires and opposing opportunities. This is particularly true in matters that affect your family, friendships, finances and faith. Like Joshua, we must remain steadfast in our faith.

In other words, each day we must commit to the path God has set before us. Regardless of what the day may bring, through its ups and downs, twists and turns, we must purpose in our hearts to serve the Lord and to keep His plans for our lives ever before us.

ANOTHER TEST AND TESTIMONY
My Joshua Moment

When my wife was in a coma, trapped in a tenuous battle between life and death, it was a *"Joshua Moment"* for me. Walking around her hospital bed day after day must have been a good example of how the children of Israel felt as they walked around Jericho.

There were moments when it felt like a waste of time. There were moments when it seemed all for nothing. There were moments when it looked as if keeping her alive with machines, medicine and other measures was simply delaying the inevitable.

She could not talk and I did not always know what to say. Like the first six days of Israel walking around Jericho, silence became my constant companion. In those quiet moments, I continued walking around her bed trusting God to bring down the walls of uncertainty, fear, and doubt that were surrounding our situation.

As strange as it felt, I kept on walking, praying and trusting God. I was determine to do everything I could to see her through this. The situation looked hopeless but I continued my journey around her bed, walking by faith and not by sight.

I just believed somehow or someway this wall was coming down. I knew God had the power to do it. After all, in Joshua 6 who do you think knocked down Jericho's wall? I will let you think about that...

Selah!

Shockingly, many Christians advised me to leave my wife and daughter and return to college. I was encouraged to go on with my life, to walk away, to leave her alone and lonely facing the greatest challenge of her life. That just proves Christians can say downright stupid things.

Even as a young Christian, I knew this was ungodly, unwise and unwanted counsel. Therefore, I ignored their counsel. Proverbs 17:17 says:

Families stick together
through all types of trouble
(The Message Bible).

You see when you know *"what"* your *"Heavenly Father"* has for you, and *"who"* He has for you, you cannot simply walk away from them. They are a part of your destiny. This is true of my life and it is true of yours.

The Power of Destiny

Destiny is more than reaching some milestone, accomplishing a particular task, or achieving a certain level of success. Destiny is more than moving into a new house, driving a new car and buying some new clothes. Destiny is about trusting God and moving forward on the path that He has for your life.

Destiny is being God focused, not goal or gold focused. It is fueled by the knowledge that with God each moment, each day, each season in life brings with it new opportunities and it keeps you aligned with God's objectives and goals for your life.

So now I ask you, what is your destiny? I will give you a few hints. Your destiny is greater than you could ever imagine and it may even look too good to be true. But that is consistent with God's word which says *No eye has seen, no ear has heard, and no mind has imagined what God has prepared for those who love him" (1 Corinthians 2:9).*

Granted, this scripture has as its primary focus the death, burial and resurrection of the Lord Jesus. However, it also reveals that God has plans for your life that you have not even imagined. Said differently, it means God has great things in store for you that He has not made known unto you. This thought alone should be enough to make you shout:

Glory, Glory!
Hallelujah!

The path to your destiny may not be easy. Nevertheless, it is God's path for your life. Therefore, come hell or high water, you must stay on the path that God is leading you. It's your destiny.

It's what God has predetermined you to do, to be and to become in His divine plan. Will there be some uncertainty, apprehension and nervousness? There most certainly will be. But as Corrie Ten Boom said:

"Never be afraid to trust an unknown future to a known God."

The Power of Promise

On the journey of life, you will have disappointments. Disappointments can happen at any time, in any place, and to anyone. Some disappointments are the result of your own missteps, others are the result of the people around us cause others, many are just a part of life and some are the will of God.

For example, an angel dislocated Jacob's hip (Genesis 32:25). Ruth unexpectedly lost her husband (Ruth 1:3). Job said that which I have feared has come upon me (Job 3:25). Jesus' friends wounded him (Zechariah 13:6). The Prodigal son was destitute after squandering his inheritance (Luke 15). My wife, my daughter and I were blindsided in a horrendous car crash.

However, in spite of her lost, Ruth stayed with the Lord. In spite of the sheer magnitude of his trials, Job trusted in God. In spite of his pain, Jacob kept wrestling. In spite of the suffering and sorrow, Jesus finished His assignment.

In spite of the accident and the pain my wife endured, God has raised her up. I can recall instances during my wife stay in the hospital the pain she endured when the doctors cleaned her skin grafts. The pain was so severe, even with high doses of pain reliever she would pass out from the intense pain.

I am not sure which hurt me more. Hearing her scream from the pain or the soul-piercing cry from within my heart, thinking she would not make it through the procedure. By the power of God, today she is a dynamic woman of God and a true champion for the cause of Christ. An article in the St. Petersburg Times newspaper called her *"The Remarkable Kisha Jordan"*.

How did they do it? Why did they do it? Simple, they held onto the promises of God. You see the answers to the disappointments of life are God's promises (See Deuteronomy 28:1-14).

Maybe this is why Corrie Ten Boom wrote:

"Let God's promises shine on your problems"

Maybe this is why D.L. Moody said:

"God never made a promise that was too good to be true."

The promises of God inspire us, strengthen us, and keep us moving in the right direction. God promised

Joshua, when he was still dealing with the death of Moses, if he meditated in His word day and night, and do what is written in it, his way would be prosperous (See Joshua 1:7-8). In other words, in spite of the disappointments he would face, the Lord assured Joshua he would enjoy good success if he stayed steadfast in faith.

That was God's promise to Joshua and Joshua had to walk in it. But God is no respecter of persons (See Acts 10:34). The promise from God to Joshua that he would have good success is available to you and me as well.

God's promise to Joshua and other promises throughout the Bible are for you and I to claim for our lives. However, to maximize and capitalize on the promises of God in your life you must embrace them as truth. Reading them is vital. Memorizing them is important. Hearing them over and over again is imperative. But, it's not enough.

Teaching them to others is commendable. Preaching them on Sunday morning is extremely valuable, and singing about them is uplifting. But, it's not enough.

You must believe
the Promises of God
for your life.

My wife and I believed God for healing in every area of our lives. In faith, we stood on God's promises. In return, God honored our faith in Him with blessings we do not have room enough to receive.

It Takes Real Faith

So then, what is faith? Faith comes from the Greek word *"Pistis"* and it is a fruit of the Holy Spirit. It is never something that we can create on our own. Thus, faith is decidedly different and far superior to positive thinking, positive confession, or having a positive outlook.

Real faith is not a feeling, emotion, knowledge, or intellect. Real faith is not probability, likelihood, or some other computation. Real faith isn't found in family, finance or friends.

Real faith is a divine persuasion by the Holy Spirit. It is a supernatural unlocking of your mind so that it agrees with God. Real faith fuels our confidence in God and it trumps all things.

In describing this type of faith, the Apostle Paul said it *is the substance of things hoped for, the evidence of things not seen. (Hebrews 11:1).*

Martin Luther King, Jr. said:

> *Faith is taking the first step even when you don't see the whole staircase.*

Hellen Keller said:

> *Faith is the strength by which a shattered world shall emerge into the light.*

Faith changes how you see God, the world around you, and the difficulties and disappointments. Faith changes how you deal with prosperity and the promises of God, open doors and it keeps you standing expectedly under the open windows of heaven.

In God's Hand

Faith takes the challenges of life out of our hands and puts them in the Hands of the Lord. I realize phrases such as *"Hand of the Lord"* are anthropomorphisms, meaning to describe God through humanlike characteristics.

There are more than 1,200 references to the Hand of God in the Bible (See examples in Psalms 18:35; Job 12:10; Psalms 138:7). Ecclesiastes 2:24 says *there is nothing better than to enjoy food and drink and to find satisfaction in work. These pleasures are from the hand of God.*

In 2 Kings 3:17 we are told of a large group of men and cattle that were on the verge of dying of thirst in a barren land. If they did not get something to drink soon they would surely die. The Bible says in verse 15 that while the harpist was playing, the hand of the LORD came on Elisha.

The instructions from God were to, *"Fill the valley with ditches"*. Now between you and me, what God said made absolutely no sense at all. They needed water, not more work. But, is not that just like our God to challenge our faith?

Furthermore, He didn't even tell them how He would do it. God simply said *you will see neither wind nor rain, yet this valley will be filled with water, and you, your cattle and your other animals will drink (2 Kings 3:17).*

By faith, the children of Israel dug the ditches as the Lord instructed them. I believe their commitment to fill the valley with ditches had a direct impact on the manifestation of the blessing they so desperately needed. I believe it set their miracle in motion.

The Bible says in Psalms 37 *"if you delight yourself in the Lord He will give you the desires of your heart.* However, it is not until we *"commit our ways to Him"* that *He will bring it to pass.* In other words, when we put our faith in action that is when God's plans begin to manifest in our lives.

The children of Israel dug the ditches. When they awoke the next morning, water filled the valley just as the Lord said it would. God rewarded their faith and their willingness to work, with the blessing they needed.

Here is the lesson for you and me. When God's ways are impossible for us to understand, we must trust the work of His hand. Isaiah 55:8-9 reads:

> *For my thoughts are not your thoughts, neither are your ways my ways," declares the Lord "As the heavens are higher than the earth, so are God's ways higher than your ways and His thoughts than your thoughts.*

Don't Wait, Move in Faith

When it comes to God's manifestations, I believe you must do something to get something. I believe you must give something to get something. Even salvation requires a person to *"confess"* with their mouth and *"believe"* in their heart (Romans 10:9).

Simply wanting salvation is not enough. Simply wanting a healing, deliverance or to be set free is not enough. You must do something to receive something. Matthew 7:7-8 says:

> *"Ask", and it will be given to you; "seek", and you will find; "knock", and it will be opened to you. For everyone who "asks" receives, and he who "seeks" finds, and to him who "knocks" it will be opened.*

Now let us apply the inverse to this scripture. That is to say, let us see what happens if you do not ask, seek and knock:

> *If you do not ask, then it will not be given to you; if you do not seek, then you will not find; if you do not knock, then it will not be opened to you. For everyone who does not ask will not receive, and he who does not seek will not find, and to him who does not knock it will not be opened."*

It is just that simple…! If you do not ask, seek, and knock, then you will not receive the good things God purposed for your life. You will not find the blessings that you need. You will not have the right doors opened in your life.

For the children of Israel, the blessing of God worked through their faith, and to operate in faith they took action. *"They dug the ditches"* and God provided the water. This is real faith in action.

ANOTHER TEST AND TESTIMONY
Faith is More Than a Feeling

So often, we find ourselves at the crossroad of fear and faith, sinking and swimming, fleeing and fighting, missing and hitting the target, losing and winning. The

stakes are often high, the pressure can be overwhelming, and typically, there are others who are depending on how we handle these situations. But, even the most faithful person has to admit sometimes moving in faith can *"feel"* wrong.

Now, hold up, wait a minute. Before you erupt into spiritual indignation, scream heresy from the rooftop, throw this book in the trashcan, drench the trashcan with gasoline, and set the trashcan on fire, allow me to explain by way of this life lesson.

When I was in the Army, my wife and I had to choose between paying our tithes and buying food for the family. We knew what keeping the tithe meant. According to Malachi 3:8-11, we would be robbing God, a curse could decent upon our family, God's blessing could be shut off and His protection removed.

Admittedly, we wrestled with the decision. Admittedly, it *"felt"* wrong. However, to make a long story short, we moved in faith and paid our tithes and God moved in a miraculous way. Friends of the family said the Lord had put it in their hearts to bless our family.

They brought bags and bags of food to the house. They brought enough food to last until my next paycheck. You had better believe we got our *"eat on"* and our *"praise on"* that day.

My point is there will be times in this life when doing what is spiritually right *"feels"* wrong. This is one reason why I caution believers about following their feelings. Following your feelings will:

- *Create conflict in your soul*

- *Build frustration in your spirit*

- *Undermine your faith*

Feelings are helpful in determining what you need to pray for or for understanding the enemies attack. However, when they are the primary determining factor in your decision-making they can be harmful. As Children of God, we must trust in the Lord and lean not on our feelings or understanding (See proverbs 3:4-5).

You see real faith, not feelings, moves the heart of God. Not pain, and neither will sorrow, money, phoniness, or drama move the heart of God. You can be a flamboyant speaker, a charismatic leader, an affluent pastor, or a world-renowned gospel singer with a knack for moving the heart of people. But just because you can move the heart of people and have the praise of men, does not mean you have moved the heart of God.

The Bible says *Esau sought repentance with many tears and could not find it (Hebrews 12:17)*. The brother cried a river of tears but it did not move God's heart. Only real, sincere faith moves the heart of God.

Undeniably, living by faith can be bewildering. Living by faith can be mentally, physically and spiritually exhausting and people who tell you otherwise are not telling the truth. But, being overwhelmed in faith doesn't mean you're not saved, it means you have feelings, it means you're human.

The Psalmist said *I am worn out from groaning; all night long I flood my bed with weeping and drench my couch with tears" (Psalms 6:6)*. David wrote in Psalms 42:3 *my tears have been my food day and night, while people say to me all day long, "Where is your God?"*

The Word of God tells us that sorrow and grief fills *"all our days"*. *Even when we lay down at night our minds cannot get any rest (See Ecclesiastes 2:23)*. Many nights I have worried myself to sleep. Like Job, I have tried to find God and:

> He is not there, and backward, but I cannot perceive Him; When He works on the left hand, I cannot behold Him; When He turns to the right hand, I cannot see Him (Job 23:8-9).

Like Job, we must believe that God *knows the way that we take and we shall come forth as gold (See Job 23:10)*. The

Amplified Bible reads we shall come forth *"pure and luminous"*. That's the benefit of having real faith.

Beware of Phony Faith

Simply being a church member does not make someone a person of faith. Simply acting like a Christian does not make someone a person of faith. Unfortunately, our world is full of people with Christian habits, talents and experiences that are often overshadowed by doubt, pride, greed and an ungodly life-style.

Phony faith can wrap itself in preacher's clothing. It can parade across the stage as a gospel singer. It can even shout, sing, and praise the Lord like other church members. These people are best described as wolves in sheep's clothing (See Matthew 7:15).

The bottom line is:

> *Phony faith is no more than*
> *a powerless form of godliness.*

How do you know when faith is phony? If Jesus is not the head of your life and you are not trusting in Him, then your faith is phony. If you are trusting in your own ability and not the power of the Holy Spirit, then your faith is phony. If you are leaning on your own understanding and not acknowledging God, then your faith is phony.

Said differently, if you trust in things such as your money, friends, doctors, medications, possessions, jobs, coworkers, boss, your church and fellow church members your faith is phony. It may look real, but the evidence of its phoniness is obvious.

When compared to real faith the difference is greater than night and day, sunshine and rain, east and west. Where real faith opens the windows of heaven, phony faith will lead you to the doorway of hell. In fact, phony faith is having no faith at all. Phony faith is powerless, godless and worthless.

Phony faith is all smoke and mirrors. It is no different from a magician's bag of tricks. Its religious hocus pocus and sleight of hand. It is a devilish scheme to

WORDS TO THE WISE

Phony faith is like a mirage. The closer you get to it you realize it's just an illusion.

manipulate people, to distort people's perceptions, and to make them believe or perceive things that are not true. Unfortunately, phony faith is everywhere. Even in the Church.

Instead of operating in real faith, there are apostles who are actors, bishops who are beguilers, pastors who are pretenders, evangelist who are equivocators, teachers who are tricksters, prophets who are pseudo seers and lay members who are liars, and church members who are charlatans.

Thus, the church has a lot of people who are parading around passing off phony faith as if it is the real deal. Phony faith might fool the people; but, it will not work with Satan and it certainly will not work with God. Sadly, phony faith is everywhere like phony money.

Illustration – Its Counterfeit

The United States Department of Treasury estimates there are nearly 70 million counterfeit bills in circulation. That is a lot of phony money being passed around as if it is the real thing. Any person whose job it is to accept money must be on the lookout for counterfeit money.

Counterfeit money feels different, it does not have the same thickness, and it lacks important details and characteristics. When you hold it up to the light, there are certain features such as security threads and watermarks that must be present. If they are not, then you know immediately you are holding counterfeit money.

Illustration Application

Likewise, many people use counterfeit faith as if it is the real McCoy. People may be shouting, dancing, and speaking in tongues but are just as phony as a three-dollar bill. People hand out counterfeit faith in church, exchange it in people's homes, and dole it out in the community.

When you look at this type of faith through the light of God's word there is very little *evidence the person has been with Jesus (Acts 4:13)*. If you don't see the markings of Jesus or the Holy Spirit, it's not real.

Don't Fake It

We all face situations that look impossible. We all face moments when it seems like God will not come through or the situation is too bad for even God to restore. For me, believing God could heal my wife from the horrible life threatening injuries she sustained in the car accident seemed ridiculous.

It is in times like these that we realize just how much we need God. It is in seasons like these when we must pray to the Father to help us as we struggle with our faith. It is in seasons like these we must cry out *"God, I need more faith."*

In Mark 9:14-29, a man on the verge of losing his son to demon possession cries out for help. Yet, he is struggling to believe Jesus could deliver his son from his tormentors. In that moment, He prayed one of the shortest but most powerful prayers in the Bible *"Lord, help my unbelief."*

Similarly, we all face situations in which we must answer the question, *"Do you believe God will bring you through?"* But, before you answer the question, again I encourage you take a moment to get your feelings in check. Remember, feelings are misleading and following your feelings can be detrimental.

You see deliverance and dominion over demonic strongholds in your life is an act of faith. Thus, it is imperative that you pray for God's help in moments of unbelief. The reality is:

You can't fake it
'til you make it

The father in Mark 9 recognized the shortcoming in his faith and he immediately asked Jesus for help. This simple, yet powerful prayer to help his unbelief resulted in a mighty move of God. Instantly, Jesus healed the father's wounded faith and freed his son from his tormentors.

If the father had faked his faith, it would not have brought about the deliverance his son needed. Yet, confessing his unbelief and asking for the Lord's help did. Now, that's a powerful, practical truth worth remembering.

Somebody's Watching You

God is watching you and He knows the type of faith at work in your life. Likewise, Satan and his imps are also watching you and they have a knack for determining the type of faith operating in your life as well. Reminds me of the 1980's song by Kenney "Rockwell" Gordy:

I always feel like somebody's watching me and I have no privacy, I always feel like somebody's watching me, tell me is it just a dream?

When it comes to operating in faith, it is not a dream. You are not hallucinating, nor are you living in a fairy-tale. Forces for good and evil have their eyes on you.

When Satan sees real faith, he knows his plans will be defeated. On the other hand, when he sees phony faith he knows doubt has taken root and ungodly habits will manifest. He knows his plans have a greater chance of success.

Satan can recognize these doors of opportunity from miles away. When he does, he will use it as an opportunity to slip into the person's life. Once inside he will amplify and exploit any weaknesses he discovers.

The Ananias and Sapphira Syndrome

In the chilling account of Ananias and Sapphira his wife in Acts 5, Satan seized the opportunity to enter their hearts. Satan had been watching them. What was he watching for? He was watching for phony faith.

Once he recognized the signs and symptoms of doubt, he quickly moved on it. Once inside it did not take long for his evil debauchery to manifest. With their hearts filled with Satan's evil influence, Ananias and Sapphira lied to the Holy Spirit and operated in a phony faith.

Just that quick Satan exploited Ananias and Sapphira's weaknesses and destroyed their destiny. Instead of giving in faith, they acted with deceit, disgrace and disregard for the Holy Spirit. In so doing, Satan foiled their opportunity for a bountiful blessing.

I call it the Ananias and Sapphira Syndrome. It manifests itself when godly people are actively involved in ungodly things. I repeat it manifests when godly people are actively involved in ungodly things. Its consequences are deadly. The Bible says when the evil in their hearts was exposed they *fell down and died (Acts 5:5; 10).*

Just that quick they went from reaping a blessing to inheriting a deadly curse and destroying their destiny. This is why you must trust in the Lord with all your heart, not on your own understanding, and let God direct your path.

Exposing Phony Faith

To expose phony faith the Apostle Paul wrote in 1 Corinthians 5:5 *some people should be delivered to Satan.* The New Living Translation says they should be thrown out and handed over to Satan to destroy their sinful nature.

As we see in Acts 19:13-16 when the sons of Sceva attempted to rebuke evil spirits:

> *They said to the evil spirits, "I command you in the name of Jesus, whom Paul preaches." But the evil spirit said to them, "I know Jesus, and I know about Paul; but you— who are you?" The man who had the evil spirit in him attacked them with such violence that he overpowered them all. They ran away from his house, wounded and with their clothes torn off.*

Like so many Christians today, they were trying to use a phony, imitation, powerless faith. This type of phony faith:

- *Is quickly recognized by evil spirits*

- *Crumbles quickly underneath demonic attacks*

- *Falls quickly to demonic trickery*

- *Withers quickly in the storms of life*

As you can see in Acts 19, the evil spirit effortlessly overpowered the sons of Sceva. They were *"acting"* spiritual, playing church games, and not *"operating in"* real faith.

Jekyll and Hyde Faith

So often, we miss our blessings because we are not steadfast in faith. One minute we trust God to work it out and the next minute we doubt Him. One minute were are hearing and obeying His voice. The next minute we are listening to and obeying our own words, or the words of someone else.

One might call it schizophrenic or a Jekyll and Hyde faith. Our thoughts are disorganized and distorted. The Bible calls such people double minded.

Double minded comes from the Greek word *"Dipsuchos"* which means to have two minds. It is as if two people are living in the same body. One person that trusts God and one person that does not.

A double-minded person has wishy-washy faith. In other words, they have a faith that is weak, whimsical, and wavering. This double mindedness is a spiritually lethal condition that plagues so many in the body of Christ.

The New Living Translation says the loyalty of a person that is double minded *is divided between God and the world and they are unstable in everything they do (James 1:7).* Such people should not expect to receive anything from God.

Illustration – Make Up Your Mind

A husband and wife went out to dinner at an upscale restaurant. The restaurant had an extensive menu, just about anything a person wanted to order, was on the menu. The wife knew just what she wanted and quickly placed her order. After reading the menu, the husband finally called the waiter and said, *"I'll have the steak medium well".*

The waiter quickly scurried to the kitchen to place the order with the chef. But, the husband continued looking at the menu. After a few more minutes, he called for the waiter. *"Instead of the steak, I'll have the fish".* *"Yes sir",* the waiter replied. *"Let me hurry up and tell the chef who had begun preparing your steak".*

The husband continued looking at the menu. Once again, he called for the waiter. *"I really hate to do this. Can I cancel the fish order and have soup and salad instead?"*

With some reluctance, the waiter replied, *"Yes sir. Are you sure you do not want the fish, it is just about ready?"* The man replied, *"I'm sure".* The waiter quickly ran back to the kitchen to tell the chef to cancel the fish order.

A few moments later, the waiter arrived with his wife's meal. It was right on time. Seeing his wife's meal, the man said, *"I'll have the steak medium well after all".* The waiter and the chef were furious. The wife had ordered and received her meal. Her husband on the other hand was still waiting.

Illustration Application

I am sure you can see the spiritual application. When you are indecisive and frequently changing your mind, you will have to wait longer for God's promises to manifest in your life. There are people today who are still waiting for blessings from God that would have manifested years ago had they stayed in faith. Don't let this be you.

On the other hand, there are people who are enjoying the blessings of God today because they moved in faith, stayed in faith, and reaped the benefits of their faithfulness. This should be you.

Illustrations - I Can Only Imagine

Real faith is about visualizing what God has revealed in your spirit. Then with each passing moment, your imagination and anticipation of its manifestation should become greater and greater. Even if it takes longer than you anticipated, you must *"stay on course"* and keep the vision that God has birthed in your spirit alive.

Road Trip

Imagine going on a road trip with no destination. You could simply drive aimlessly around the country never knowing if you had completed the trip. You would have spent time, money, gas, and resources for absolutely nothing. Even worse imagine yourself on a road trip and you keep changing the destination during the trip.

One moment you are heading to Alabama, the next hour you are heading to Louisiana, three hours later you are heading to New York, the next morning you are heading to Las Vegas. You are just about to Las Vegas and you change your mind again.

Initially the trip might be fun and exciting. However, at some point the constant changing of the destination is going to become extremely exhausting, frustrating, costly and wasteful.

Now imagine a road trip when you knew where you were going. The longer you drive the closer you are to your destination and the greater the expectation. This is how your faith should be operating.

Rod in Hand

Imagine what would have happened at the Red Sea when the Lord commanded Moses to stretch out the rod in his hand, if after Moses stretched out the rod for a few moments, he changed his mind. Then after a while he stretched the rod back out again. Over and over, he kept stretching out the rod, then changing his mind and pulling it back

One moment the water is divided and the people are walking on dry land. The next moment the water is crashing in on them and they are drowning. They would have drowned because Moses changed his mind.

Now imagine the frustration and the calamity upon the people who are following Moses. Thus, doubt and indecision will have serious negative consequences in your life and in the life of those that are following you.

Fortunately, Moses moved in faith. He stretched out the rod in his hand as directed and the Bible says in Exodus 14:21-22, the Lord divided the Red Sea and Israel walked across on dry land.

Raging River

Imagine when the Prophet Elisha instructed Naaman the leper to dip in the Jordan River seven times. When he did as the prophet instructed him, God healed him of his leprosy. Ironically, his blessing was almost lost.

The Bible tells us in 2 Kings 5:10-14 that:

> *Elisha sent a messenger unto Naaman, saying, Go and wash in Jordan seven times, and thy flesh shall come again to thee, and thou shalt be clean. 11 But Naaman was wroth, and went away, and said, Behold, I thought, He will surely come out to me, and stand, and call on the*

name of the Lord his God, and strike his hand over the place, and recover the leper. 12 Are not Abana and Pharpar, rivers of Damascus, better than all the waters of Israel? May I not wash in them, and be clean? So he turned and went away in a rage.

Naaman, in his anger and arrogance refused to dip in the river as instructed. The raging river of rage and pride flowing in his life nearly ruined his miracle. He wanted the blessing on his own terms. However, it does not work that way with God. It is God's way or no way at all.

When Naaman finally moved in faith and dipped in the Jordan River seven times as he was commanded his skin was restored and became clean like that of a young boy (See 2 Kings 5:14).

Illustration Application

Like a family on a road trip, you must know where you are going in God and you must stick to the path that God has for your life. As the manifestation of God's word gets closer and closer, your sense of expectation should soar higher and higher.

Like Moses, who moved in faith at the Red Sea, this is how you must move in faith. The things you see or how you feel should not stop you from moving in the will of God. Crossing the Red Sea looked impossible. However, God's children were steadfast in faith and God worked a miracle.

Like Naaman, you must heed the voice of God in your life. If you move in faith and do as God has instructed, the miracle working power of God will be set in motion in your life.

Receiving, believing, visualizing, and acting upon the Word of God for your life is critical to living with an unstoppable spirit. This is what it means to remain steadfast in your faith. If you do, I can only imagine the level of blessings that are going to manifest in your life.

Luke would describe it as being *"good measure, press down, shaken together and running over!" (Luke 6:38)*

ANOTHER TEST AND TESTIMONY
Against All Odds

The day came when every attempt to save my wife's life had been exhausted. The doctor presented us with one final surgical procedure known as a Hemipelvectomy. It is the rarest and most dangerous of the amputations. Given the survival rate of the procedure, this was not good news.

The first Hemipelvectomy ever performed was by Dr. Billroth. The patient survived only a few hours. A doctor by the name of Jabulay operated on a patient who died immediately after the procedure. The first successful Hemipelvectomy was performed by Dr. Girard (Wedemeyer and Kauther, 2011, para 1).

According to a case report released in June 2014 Hemipelvectomy, which is a very rare and catastrophic procedure that usually results in death (Traumatic Hemipelvectomy: It is amputation of a person's leg and the hip on that side: A Rare and Catastrophic Injury, 2014, para 1).

Given my wife's condition doctors feared she would die during the procedure. History suggested she would. The science suggested she would. The struggle we faced was remaining steadfast in our faith (2 Corinthians 15:58).

But, are we always steadfast and unmovable in our faith? No way. Are we always abounding in the work of the Lord? Absolutely not!

Nevertheless, God's goodness is revealed because even when our faith is failing, He remains faithful. 2 Timothy 2:13 says:

> *If we are unfaithful, He remains faithful, for he cannot deny who He is".*

During the surgery, against all odds we held to the belief that God is able. We trusted He would bring her through. To God be the glory, she survived the procedure and after the surgery, she awoke from the Coma.

Can I get an
AMEN!

Get in Position

As a result of the injuries sustained by my wife, doctors believed she could not have any more children. She no longer had the bone structure to support a baby in the womb through the full term of the pregnancy. In fact, if she got pregnant both she and the baby could die during the pregnancy.

So whose report should we believe? The report of the doctors founded upon sound factual evidence or the report of the Lord founded upon faith.

God's report in Jeremiah 32:17 says *nothing is too difficult for God.* In Matthew 19:26, Jesus said *with God all things are possible.* Knowing the word of God, my wife and I believed the report of the Lord (See Isaiah 53:1).

We knew the blessings God had promised us and we were unwilling to walk away from them. I must admit we did not understand it. We did not know how God would do it. Nevertheless, we got in the position for God's favor and blessings to manifest in our lives.

- *We meditated on scriptures about God's great power*

- *We dedicated ourselves to living by God's word*

- *We waited for God's perfect timing*

- *We rested in God's unfailing love*

- *We studied God's promises*

As children of God we are challenged to *"Walk by Faith"* and *not by sight (2 Corinthians 5:7)*. God honors steadfast faith with real results. This we need!

By faith, we know that God has healed our bodies when we are still hurting. By faith, we know that God has delivered when we are still in bondage. By faith, we know that God has given us more than enough in seasons of lack.

This type of faith is uplifting, edifying, strengthening and it ushers you into the overflow. This type of faith surrounds us with God's favor, inundates us with His presence, showers us with His love and prepares us for His blessings.

Christians who walk in this type of faith do more, give more, hope for more and receive more. We enjoy blessings that are good measure, press down, shaken together, running over (See Luke 6:38). We live in the overflow and are equipped to cope with the storms of life. But we don't just cope with trials, or barely make it through them.

We conquer them!

Chapter 4

Triggering the Triumphant Mindset

THINKING AND ACTING LIKE A CHAMPION

"All God's people clap your hands.
Shout unto God with a voice of triumph"
(Psalms 47:1)

YOU MUST KNOW that you are victorious. This is important because as a man thinks in *"his"* heart so is he (Proverbs 23:7). Notice, it does not say what someone else thinks in their heart, it says what a man thinks in *"his"* heart, determines who he is. *"I thank God for that!"*

The principle of scripture is *"your thinking"* is one of the most important factors in the success of *"your life"*. It should not matter how others see your life. Living your life through the eyes and opinions of others can be difficult and distracting. Your time on earth is limited, so there is no sense wasting it by living your days through someone else's eyes or their expectations.

Regardless of the attitudes, perceptions, beliefs and expectations of others you must allow the Holy Spirit to unlock your mind so you can see yourself as victorious and triumphant in Christ Jesus. This must be your mindset as you face the challenges of life. You must have the unshakable belief that *"God always leads us in triumph" (2 Corinthians 2:14)* and it must be your mantra for every trial that comes your way.

ANOTHER TEST AND TESTIMONY
God Is Able

After the accident, the medical community agreed my wife would die. Nevertheless, I believed God was able. If she survived most believed she would live the remainder of her life in a persistent vegetative state. I just believed that God was able.

If she did regain consciousness, many surmised she would never stand or walk again. However, I believed that God was able. The doctors believed she would not be able to bear children. Through it all, I still believed that God was able.

If she made it through all of that, many people said there was no way our family could remain intact. Most believed that such turmoil at such a young age would destroy us. In spite of their opinion, I believed that God was able.

Ironically, even in those moments when we experienced a setback my faith in God was still blossoming. This is a vital aspect of being unstoppable because everyone, even God's faithful, will experience failures and setbacks in life. But, even in these moments, we must believe that God is able.

For my wife and I God was doing a new thing in us and we knew we had the victory through Christ Jesus.

Notice, we did not believe victory was on the way. We believed we already had the victory and we purposed in our hearts to walk in it.

We soon discovered that our setbacks or any bit of bad news were simply setups for something even greater. However, to receive the greater things God had in store for us we knew we had to put all of our faith in God. That is exactly what we did and God honored our faith with victory, after victory, after victory. With each victory, our faith was sky rocketing to new levels.

Yes, there were enemies and we still have them to this day. Yes, there were dark days and we still have them to this day. Yes, there were haters and we still have them to this day. However, I say:

> *Don't get caught up in the hate. Let the haters hate, while we celebrate our victories in Jesus!*

Faced with insurmountable odds we celebrated the goodness of God. We did not deny the facts. We chose to stand in faith. Like Abraham in Romans 4:17, who was called the father of many nations *"before"* he even had children, we had to believe against all odds. The facts said Abraham and his wife Sarah were past the age of child bearing. Yet, Abraham believed that God was able to do what he said:

> *Without becoming weak in faith he contemplated his own body, now as good as dead since he was about a hundred years old, and the deadness of Sarah's womb; yet, with respect to the promise of God, he did not waver in unbelief but grew strong in faith (Romans 4:19-20).*

Initially, Sarah laughed when God said she would have a son and like Sarah, today many of God's people laugh at the promises of God. Abraham did not. He believed God and as a result, Sarah gave birth to a son, Isaac.

The name Isaac is from the Hebrew word *"Yitzchaq"*. It means to laugh or rejoice. The revelation in Isaac's name is God's word will come to pass and those who trust it will have the last laugh.

Think and Act Like a Champion

To think and act like a champion you must forget those things that are behind you and reach forward to what is before you. Even when the trials before you look insurmountable, you must keep pressing toward God and the goals He has given you (See Philippians 3:13-14).

Will it be easy? Certainly not! Will it always make sense? No way! But, I can assure you it will be worth it. After all, God rewards those who seek Him (See Hebrews 11:6).

Illustration - David's Mighty Men

We are told of David's mighty men in 2 Samuel 23:8-39. The Bible says Josheb-Basshebeth, fought eight hundred men by himself with a spear and won. Eleazar fought against an army of Philistines by himself and came out with the victory. He fought so hard that his sword was stuck to his hand. The Bible says, *"The Lord brought about a great victory that day."*

Shammah fought by himself and successfully defended a field against a Philistine army. Abishai fought against three hundred men, whom he killed. Then there was Benaiah who struck down two of the Moabities best fighters, he then crawled down into a pit on a snowy day and killed a lion.

Using just a club he struck down a huge Egyptian armed with a spear. Finally, there was Shamgarah in Judges 3:31, he was not one of David's mighty men but he single handedly killed 600 Philistines using a cattle prod.

Illustration Application

A true champion is not a champion because of what he or she has accomplished. You can win the Lottery, the Super Bowl, Lord Stanley's Cup, and the World Series, a hand full of Olympic Gold Medals, the FIFA World Cup and the Presidential Election and still live a defeated life. You see I am convinced that a true champion is a champion because of what he or she thinks and believes.

Muhammed Ali said:

> *Champions aren't made in the gyms. Champions are made from something they have deep inside them – a desire, a dream, a vision.*

David's Mighty Men were champions *"before"* the fight began. They were champions *"before"* they won their battles. In the face of seemingly insurmountable odds, they believed that victory was guaranteed with God on their side.

Now, you and I may not face the challenges these men faced. However, we will face our own unique set of trials. In these moments we must think like and act like a champion. No, not when the battle is over and you have the victory. We must think and act like a champion before the battle even begins.

It Starts in Your Mind

Thinking and acting like a champion is a mindset. It is a divinely inspired mindset that flows from the knowledge of God in your heart and the revelation of the Holy Ghost living in your spirit.

What is so awesome is the moment you believe it, embrace it, and walk in it; a divine transformation takes place in your life. Instantly, you are transformed into a champion! Instantly, you are a winner and nothing can stop you.

You see, I am convinced that *"believing precedes manifestation"*. As minister and author, Norman Vincent Peale said:

> *People become really quite remarkable when they start believing they can do things.*

Charles Kettering said we must *"believe and act as if it were impossible to fail".* 19th Century poet Walter D. Winkle writes:

If you think you are beaten, you are
If you think you dare not, you don't,
If you like to win, but you think you can't
It is almost certain you won't.

If you think you'll lose, you're lost
For out of the world we find,
Success begins with a fellow's will
It's all in the state of mind.

If you think you are outclassed, you are
You've got to think high to rise,
You've got to be sure of yourself before
You can ever win a prize.

Life's battles don't always go
To the stronger or faster man,
But soon or later the man who wins
Is the man who thinks he can!

This is what the woman with the issue of blood did in Luke 8. She had a victorious mindset and she believed that if she just touched the hem of Jesus' garment, she would be healed (See Luke 8:43-48). Her victorious mindset moved her into action.

She steadily reinforced her faith by saying *"if I touch his garment I will be made whole."* Faced with years of bleeding, belittlement, and being left behind she still had a victorious mindset. That's powerful.

As she reinforced her faith, it began to build in her cognitive mind. Out of the cognitive, the physiological was set in motion. Said differently, her statements gave her motivation and it got her moving towards her miracle.

Crowds of people were standing in her way. She was weak and exhausted from the years of bleeding. Yet, the knowledge in her cognitive increasingly stimulated her physiological and she kept pushing through the crowd. When she finally touched Jesus' garment, instantly she received the blessing she so desperately needed from the Lord.

Mark 5:29-30 reads:

> *Her bleeding stopped at once; and she had the feeling inside herself that she was healed of her trouble. At once Jesus knew that power had gone out of him.*

Jesus then said to her in verse 34 *"My daughter, your faith has made you well. Go in peace, and be healed."* The blessing that she received started with her thinking and the powerful truth being revealed in her story is *"Believing precedes manifestation."*

Change Your Mindset

For me and my wife, thinking like a champion was the beginning of a life altering mental makeover and it felt good. This is important because changing your mindset is one of the *"greatest things"* you will ever do. As minister and author, Norman Vincent Peale wrote:

> *Change your thoughts and you change your world*

However, as we see in the account of the children of Israel's deliverance from the land of Egypt, change is not easy (See Joshua 3). They had spent the previous 400 plus years learning the ways of slavery, bondage, harsh treatment and the Egyptian life style and religion. Now they were free and heading into a land of new opportunities and promises.

Yet, they were still holding onto the enslaved and defeated mindset developed during their slavery (See Exodus 16:3). As a result, the blessings they were heading into were being sabotage by their past. It is this struggle to live free of one's bondage that draws attention to a truth that I want you to be cognizant of:

*One of the hardest
things for a person to change is their
"Mindset"*

Some people can change their spouse easier than they can change their way of thinking. Some people can change their address easier than they can change their mentality. Some people can change their church easier than they can change their state of mind.

Overcoming this difficulty is critical because you cannot live in the fullness of your freedom in Christ with an enslaved and defeated mentality. You cannot govern your life like a prince with the mindset of a minion. You cannot rule your life like a king if you think you will never be more than a peasant.

If you are living with an enslaved and defeated mindset, than I challenge you to look in the mirror of God's word and challenge yourself to change!

WORDS TO THE WISE
Living in the fullness of your freedom happens when Christ liberates your mind

You are blessed not cursed so change your mindset. You are living not dying so change your mindset. You have more than enough, you're not living in lack, so change your mindset. You are on your way to greatness, not doomed for destruction so change your mindset.

The blessings of living with a triumphant mindset was manifesting in our lives. Now my wife and I could see God working things out. He was answering our prayers and doing amazing things.

But this change in our thinking was not based on God *"doing"* everything we asked. It was much deeper and profound than that. It was based on the knowledge that *"He could do, if He chose to"* everything we asked.

Like the three Hebrew boys just before they were thrown into the fiery furnace. In the face of death, they proclaimed:

Our God is able to deliver us. "But if He chooses not to" we will not serve other Gods (Daniel 3:17-18).

They trusted in God to see them through the ordeal. If they had to go into the fire, then they were going in confident that God's will would be done and they would be victorious. They refused to walk in a *"woe-is-me"* victim mentality.

Instead, they took the limits off their thinking and embraced the limitlessness of God. They believed God could save them even if they went into the fire. That is the triumphant mindset. That is the mentality of a champion.

Champions see victory in situations in which others see defeat. Champions do not cower in the storms of life. Champions are always moving forward in the power of God's might

Champions are not worried about the deepness of the valley, the height of the mountain, or the strength of the enemy. Champions focus on the blessings God is releasing, not the mess that Satan is creating. Champions know that every attack is just another opportunity to triumph over evil.

For the three Hebrew Boys having the triumphant mindset meant believing they would:

*Survive, thrive
and come out of the fire
alive!*

When you embrace this type of radical, life altering thinking a divine transformation takes place in your life. A fundamental shift in your attitude happens. You will radiate the nature and character of God. You will begin to walk like, talk like, and show forth a God-like persona.

Biblically speaking:

Your light will shine before men, they'll see the work you are doing, and it will glorify your Father in heaven (See Matthew 5:16).

Now consider this. If this transformation were the only thing God did for you and me, it would still be enough to praise Him for the rest of our lives. Such a total mind, body and soul makeover is worth its weight in gold and for that, we must give God the praise.

Check Your Attitude

Everyone has a set way of doing things. We call this your attitude. It is your way of thinking about someone or something. It shows in your behavior.

Thus, your attitude is a window into your mind. Your attitude is a reflection of the inner you, the real you. It allows others to see unfiltered what is in your heart, in your mind, and in your spirit.

Make no mistake about it. Your attitude will have a significant impact on your life. Maybe this is why the psalmist declared *"This is the day which the Lord has made; we will rejoice and be glad in it"* (Psalms 118:24).

Like the psalmist I believe:

Your day is what you make of it! So you should awake each morning with the attitude that you will make it a great day?

Thomas Jefferson said:

Nothing can stop the man with the right mental attitude. Nothing on earth can help the man with the wrong mental attitude.

I totally agree! Your attitude is that powerful. As someone once said:

A bad attitude is like a car with a flat tire. Until you change it, you will go nowhere and everyone else will pass you by.

Wade Boggs, famous baseball player who played 18 years in the major league rightfully said:

A positive attitude causes a chain reaction of positive thoughts, events and outcomes. It is a catalyst and it sparks extraordinary results.

James Kisner writes in the poem, "Victorious Attitude:

You cannot win the race,
unless you follow through.
You cannot blame the others,
for it all depends on you.
You cannot win the battle,
if you do not raise your sword.
You cannot claim a victory,
if there is no reward.
You cannot shape the future,
if you wait until it's here.
The future has no purpose,
if you live today in fear.
Your future lies within your hand,
to do with what you may.
For tomorrow brings results,
of what you've done today.
The choices that you make today
reflect the life you seek.
But first of all, the seeds are sown,
before the gardener reaps.
The future's like a lump of clay,
you hold within your hand.
As time goes by, the clay gets hard,
so mould it while you can.
Failure is an attitude that haunts the mind of man.
But, results will be successful,
for the one who knows
he can!

Make no mistake about it. Your attitude will affect your day, your direction in life and therefore your destiny.

Inevitably, you will end up where your attitude is taking you.

You may be dreaming of heavenly places and have powerful prophecies spoken over your life. But your attitude may have you hell bound. The questions you must ask yourself are *"Where is your attitude taking you"* and *"Is that where you want to go?"*

The truth of the matter is you are who your attitude says you are. If you trust God, your attitude will show it. If you believe in divine healing, your attitude will show it.

If you know you are blessed, your attitude will show it. If you are studying God's word, you are full of the Spirit of God, and you are on your way to heaven with a mighty shout your attitude will show it.

My questions for you to consider are *"How do you respond when things don't go your way, when the cards are stacked against you, when life hurts you?"* Do you complain obsessively, pitch a fit and open the door for Satan to come in? Or, do you hold your peace and trust in God to bring you through the storm.

Your answers to these questions are important because your attitude will affect your success. You should not act like a belligerent buffoon and expect bountiful blessings. It just doesn't work that way. If you don't like the direction your life is heading, change your attitude.

Muhammad Ali said:

> *When I said I am the greatest. I said it before I knew I was.*

He knew who he was and was not afraid to let the world know. More importantly, Ali did not wait for someone else to define him or to tell him he was great, he told himself.

The right attitude can take you from defeat to victory, from falling down to rising up, from dreadful days that feel like hell on earth to a life that is happy, heavenly and Holy Ghost filled.

Really, Really

As I have taught for years, if I really want to know someone I only have to watch them. Do not get me wrong, talking is important. However, words can be misleading. A person can purposefully say one thing and mean another (See Psalms 12:2; Psalms 28:3; Psalms 55:21).

However, you can only fake your actions for so long. Inevitably, the real you will show up in your attitude. The real you will show up in your actions. You can hide it for a while, but unescapably the events of life will pull the covers back on you.

I have used this approach in every facet of my life. At work, at home, at church, you name it. I may not talk as much as most people, but I am an excellent listener and I am very observant. You see a person's mannerisms, behaviors, and proclivities reveal who they really are, what they truly believe and what they really want.

Again I say,
if you really want to know someone,
just watch them.

If you watch a person over time, they will do outwardly, what they are thinking inwardly. People will show by their actions, what they may be too afraid or embarrassed to say or are trying to hide on the inside.

If a person is sneaky, their actions will tell. If a person is a liar, their actions will tell. If a person is deceptive, their actions will tell. If a person dislikes someone, their actions will tell. If a person has favorites, their actions will tell.

If a person is racist, their actions will tell. If a person is perverted, their actions will tell. If a person is a hypocrite, their actions will tell. If a person is ungodly, their actions will tell. If a person is afraid, their actions will tell.

Similarly, if a person is filled with the Holy Spirit, their actions will tell. If a person is reading their Bible, their actions will tell. If a person is walking by faith, their actions will tell. If a person is hungry for righteousness, their actions will tell. Make some sense?

Noted Christian author John Maxwell said:

People may hear your words, but they feel your attitude.

In other words, people will remember what you do more than what you say. You may be saying all the right things, while sending a very different message with your body language. Thus, your body language is a *"big billboard"* telling the whole world who you really are.

Here is one last point regarding attitude. I believe you cannot go through life pessimistic and with a mad at the world attitude. What benefit is there in walking around with a grimacing look on your face as if you have been sucking on lemons all day.

There comes a point when you have to turn your own frown upside down. When you must make up in your mind to *count it all joy (James 1:2), to rejoice and be glad (Matthew 5:12) and to be strong and courageous (Joshua 1:9).*

Like Job you have to forget your complaining, put away your sad face and be cheerful (See Job 9:27). If you are still mad today over something that happened years ago, it is time to *"get over it"* and move on. Easier said than done I know. However, to overcome the challenges set before you it is an approach to life you must live by. It is paramount for living a triumphant life!

Tragedy to Triumph

The Bible gives so many accounts of men and women who faced extremely difficult trials and tribulation, but they triumphed by the power of God. In 1 Kings 17:7-16, the widow of Zarephath and her son faced certain death through starvation. David, the soon to be king, walked into a fight with the Philistine giant Goliath that he could not win (1 Samuel 17).

Moses, the great deliverer was trapped between the Red Sea and Egypt's mighty army (Exodus 14). Joseph's brother tossed him into a pit. He was sold into slavery, accused of rape and thrown in prison (Genesis 37-50). Job, the wealthiest and righteous man of his day, lost everything in a matter of moments. To make matters worse, those who knew him best accused him of unrighteousness (Job 1).

Shadrach, Meshach, and Abednego, were tossed into a fiery furnace (Daniel 3:23). King Darius threw Daniel into a lion's den (Daniels 6). Jesus Christ was beaten unmercifully and hung on a cross (Luke 23:32-43). The Apostle Paul was stoned and left for dead (Acts 14:19), rejected (Acts 18) and shipwrecked (Acts 27).

These are just a few examples of tragedy from the Bible. I am sure you and I can think of hundreds more from the Bible and from our lives. I think it is safe to stipulate that trials and tribulation are a part of everyone's life and they are everywhere.

Job rightfully stated:

> *Man, born of a woman, are of a few days and they are filled with trouble (Job 14:1).*

David said:

> *Many are the afflictions of the righteous (Psalms 34:19).*

Jesus said in John 16:33:

> *In this world you will have tribulation.*

The bottom line is we must deal with trials and tragedy. But God's power and presence in our lives helps us overcome them. The key is seeing your victory in Christ Jesus *"before"* it manifest. When we can see, believe and speak our victories in God, then trials and tribulation cannot stop us. In fact, God turns our trials and tribulation into stepping-stones to our destiny.

This is what happened for the widow of Zarephath. She trusted the Word of God given to her and God blessed her with enough oil to pay her debt and live the remainder of her life off the rest. This is what happened when David defeated Goliath by the power of God and went on to become the king of Israel.

This is what happened to Moses when he obeyed the voice of God at the Red Sea. With God on his side, he delivered more than two million people from the hellacious slavery of the Egyptians. As discussed in Chapter 1 of this book, Moses knew the power of God and boldly declared to Pharaoh "*Let my people go.*

They had been in bondage for more than 400 years. They had endured centuries of bondage, beatings, and belittling. Nevertheless, he acted on the word God had given him. As a result, God moved in a miraculous way.

Like Moses, you need to declare to your enemies, let me and my family go! You need to Tell Satan to take his hands off your stuff, right now in the name of Jesus!

Don't be shy, don't be nervous, and don't second-guess the power of God. You see the moment you declare God's promises the enemy's dominion over your life is gone. It is just the benefits for being one of God's children.

This is what happened to Joseph who survived a series of trials and God promoted him to a top leadership position in Egypt. This is what happened to Job. Job trusted God through his trials and God blessed him with more than he lost. The Bible says:

> *The Lord blessed the latter days of Job more than his beginning. (Job 42:12).*

This is what happened to the three Hebrew boys. They survived the fiery furnace and felt no harm (Daniel 3). This is what happened to Daniel. He escaped the lion's den because an angel of the Lord closed the mouths of the lions (Daniel 6). This is what happened when Jesus rose from the dead with all power in His hand (Mark 16; Matthew 28:18).

Victory in Your Valleys

The world will tell you that you must see the blessings of God before you should believe them. But I beg to differ, Jesus said in John 20:29 *"blessed are those who have not seen and yet they believe."* In other words, you should not have to see God's power to believe it. In fact, if you are waiting to see it, before you believe it, you may never receive it.

Case in point, surrounded by thousands of enemy soldiers the Lord told King Jehoshaphat *you do not need to fight in this battle (2 Chronicles 20)*. The challenge for the children of Israel was to believe they had the victory when defeat seemed inevitable.

They were challenged to believe the battle was already won before the fight begun. They were challenged to see God bringing them out of combat before the war had even started. They were challenged to believe God's promise before they could see its manifestation.

So what did they do? They stopped worrying, complaining and crying and *"They began to sing and praise"* the Lord. That is having the right attitude. That's triggering the triumphant mindset.

The children of Israel focused on God and what God had showed them. Even though they could not see their victory in the natural, they could see it in the spirit and they believed God's word would come to pass.

This is important because:

> *What you focus your attention on has a direct impact on your attitude and the manifestations in your life.*

The children of Israel received the Word of God, they focused their attention on God with their praise, and God worked a miracle. The Bible says:

The Lord set ambushes against the men of Ammon and Moab and Mount Seir who were invading Judah, and they were defeated." (2 Chronicles 20:22).

After the battle was over:

They assembled in the Valley of Berakah, where they praised the Lord (2 Chronicles 20: 26)

The word *Berakah* is from the Hebrew word meaning *"Blessing"*. Thus, this valley once considered a place of certain defeat was now a *"Valley of Blessings"* for God's people. But, a critical point that I want you to glean from these scriptures is when you are in the battles of life and you can't see your victory you have to...

Keep Looking, It's Coming

That is what the children of Israel did. They kept their eyes on the Lord. They said:

We are powerless against this mighty army that is about to attack us. We do not know what to do, but we are looking to you for help." (2 Chronicles 20:12)

The King James Version reads:

...but our eyes are upon thee.

In another example in 1 Kings 18:41 Elijah the prophet told his servant to look toward the sea. Elijah heard the sound of a heavy rain coming. When the servant went and looked, he saw nothing.

Over and over again the servant looked. Each time the servant looked, he saw no evidence that it was about to rain. But, Elijah new the revelation he had from God. He knew what God had showed him.

Therefore, he told the servant to keep looking. That's a word for your life. Keep looking! Keep looking for the promises of God to manifest. Regardless of how it looks, keep looking. If you cannot find a job, keep looking. If you cannot find a true friend, keep looking. If you cannot find a way out of no way, keep looking.

Whatever it is that you cannot find that God has revealed will be yours, do not quit. Do not give up. Do not get discouraged. Keep looking!

Elijah refused to give up on the revelation he received from God. He told his servant repeatedly, to look again. On the seventh time the servant reported, *"I see a cloud as small as a man's hand is rising from the sea."* In other words, the servant finally saw in the natural what Elijah had already seen through divine revelation.

This is the revelation that God is stirring in your spirit. You see there will be times in your life when others will not see what God has shown you. When this happens, do not get upset or discouraged.

"Keep Looking"

The truth of the matter is God did not show them, He showed you. Their lack of excitement or support does not mean they do not believe you. It could mean they have not seen what God has shown you.

Regardless of what they may or may not have seen, you cannot let their lack of support affect your attitude and focus on God. The good news is the manifestations of God's promises for your life are not contingent upon what others see or believe. *"Thank God for that!"* He showed you and now He expects you to:

- *Hold onto the promises He's shown you*

- *Talk about the promises as if you already have them*

- *Act like you know the promises will come to pass*

For these reasons, I do not spend much time focusing on things that are happening in the natural. These are the troubles, the issues, the mountains, the valleys, and the giants of life. Focusing on these things will negatively affect my attitude.

The truth of the matter is you have seen too much spiritually to let what is happening to you in the natural stop you. Deuteronomy 10:20-21 tells us we must:

> *Worship him and cling to him, and take oaths by his name alone. He is your praise and he is your God, the one who has done mighty miracles you yourselves have seen.*

Choose Your Words Wisely

I believe words have power, and when we use them to declare and decree the promises of God, they set the atmosphere for their manifestation. Therefore, my advice to you is:

> *Keep speaking the promises of God over your life. But don't just speak them; speak them in faith and with authority!*

When you are living with a triumphant mindset, you will want to tell others about it. You are not bragging for personal gain, but boasting in the goodness and greatness of God.

Proclaim God's riches over your life even in times of lack. Declare your joy even in times of pain. Speak your brand new morning and profess a sun shiny day even when it is starting to rain.

The people around you may not always understand the words coming out of your mouth and they may not always agree with what you are saying. But, that doesn't matter. Keep declaring your victory because there is power in your words.

Illustration – Watch What You Say

In Acts 16, locked in jail Paul and Silas prayed and sang praises to God. The Bible said the other prisoners heard their praise (Acts 16). More importantly, God heard their praise.

As they were singing and praying, the power of God opened the prison doors and loosed everyone's bands. Thus, their words activated the power of God in their lives. As a result, not only was Paul and Silas' delivered, but freedom and salvation were released to all of the prisoners.

Using these scriptures as an example, I give these words of advice to you my friend. Do not underestimate the relationship between the words you speak and the release of God's power in your life. Maybe this is why the Prophet Jeremiah could not help but talk *"about"* God. He said:

> *If I say I'll never mention the Lord or speak in his name, his word burns in my heart like a fire. It's like a fire in my bones! I am worn out trying to hold it in! I can't do it! (Jeremiah 20:9)*

In Acts 4:19-20 Peter and John said:

> *Whether it is right in the sight of God to listen to you rather than to God, you be the judge. We must talk about what we have seen and heard.*

In another example in the valley of dry bones, the power of God is released as Ezekiel spoke the Word of God (See Ezekiel 37). The Lord asked Ezekiel can these bones live again. Ezekiel responded Lord only you know if these bones can live again.

The Lord then commanded Ezekiel to speak to the dry bones and tell them to live. Ezekiel immediately began to speak the words of God. In other words, he started talking like God and he started calling those things that are not as thou they were.

As the words came out of his mouth, the Bible says in verse 7-10:

> *7 there was a noise, and behold a shaking, and the bones came together, bone to his bone. 8 And when I beheld, lo, the sinews and the flesh came up upon them, and the skin*

*covered them above: but there was no breath in them.
9 Then said he unto me, Prophesy unto the wind,
prophesy, son of man, and say to the wind, Thus saith the
Lord God; Come from the four winds, O breath, and
breathe upon these slain, that they may live.10 So I
prophesied as he commanded me, and the breath came
into them, and they lived, and stood up upon their feet, an
exceeding great army.*

What Ezekiel is seeing is in the spirit. But, what it
reveals is the power that is manifested in our lives when
we talk like God talks and when we say what His word
says.

Illustration Application

Anthropologist Edward Sapir and linguist Benjamin
Whorf suggested our words shape our reality. Said
differently, the words we speak ultimately shape our day,
our direction in life and therefore they affect our destiny.
They call this phenomenon the *"Sapir-Whorf Hypothesis".*

What researchers call the *"Sapir-Whorf Hypothesis",* the
Bible describes as having a tongue [that] can bring death
or life (Proverbs 18:21). Furthermore, when it comes to
watching our words the Bible says *the one who guards his
mouth preserves his life; The one who opens wide his lips comes to
ruin. (Proverbs 13:3)* and *he who guards his mouth and his tongue,
Guards his soul from troubles (Proverbs 21:23).*

The psalmist knowing the impact of his words asked
God to set a guard over his mouth and keep watch over
the door of his lips (See Psalms 141:3). He didn't want to
speak foolishly or try to dazzle God with big words. He
simply wanted to speak God's words with authority and by
so doing get the expected result!

The key is to speak the word of God confidently,
knowing God's word will come to pass. The key is
speaking in the *"prophetic tense".* The key is to speak of the
revelation of God as if it has already happened, before it
has happened

That's what the Prophet Isaiah did when he said Jesus would be wounded for our transgressions and bruised for our iniquities and that by His stripes we are healed (See Isaiah 53:5). Isaiah spoke those words more than 2,000 years *"before"* the manifestation on the Cross.

ANOTHER TEST AND TESTIMONY
Talk About It

When my wife's heart stopped twice after the car accident and each time the Lord brought her back that was enough for me to talk about the greatness of God for a lifetime. When she recovered with no brain damage, I knew it was nobody but God. When she made a full recovery from the accident, I was convinced beyond any doubt that God is real.

When God blessed us with two more children after the doctors said both her and the baby could die during the pregnancy, I was totally amazed. I could not help but give him the praise. You see when you have seen what I have seen and experienced what I have experienced; it increases your belief that nothing is too hard for our God.

Our confidence in Him soared to new heights and we believed He could do anything but fail. My wife and I began speaking as if the blessings we needed had already been received, as if the miracle we wanted had already manifested, as if the opportunities we desired had already been revealed.

In essence, we were talking like God talks. The Bible says *God calls those things that are not as if they already exist (See Romans 4:17)*. Thus, to talk like God you must speak about the promises of God as if you already have them.

You must say, *"I am healed while you are still hurting"*. You must declare, *"I am blessed while you are still struggling"*. You must proclaim your deliverance while you are still in bondage, and profess your victory in the face of defeat. That's talking like God talks. Make some sense?

You do not have to make words up as you go or try to find some mystical, magical, or magnificent set of words in hopes of impressing God. Read His word, listen for His voice, and then speak it over your life. That is what Ezekiel did when he spoke just as the Lord told him.

For my wife and I that meant no longer waiting for God to bless us, bring us out, or to be good to us, to talk about what He was doing in our lives. Even when we find ourselves in the valleys of life this is how you and I must talk as well. When we say what God's word says we'll get the results He has purposed for our lives.

Illustration – Speaking With Authority

When I was a little boy, my older brother took a ball from me. I demanded that he give me the ball back, but he refused. Like any little brother, I immediately told our father what had happened.

I returned a few moments later, faced my brother and said *"Dad said Give me the ball back!"* Instantly, he handed the ball over. I was like *"Dang. That was easy!"*

Now, I was in no position to stick my chest out and say, *"Look what I did."* I was wise enough to know he did not give me the ball because of who I was. He did not give me the ball back because of fear of what I would do, which at that age and my size would not have been much.

Although my brother had the strength, size and power to beat me down, without hesitation he gave me the ball back. My brother gave me the ball back because I spoke in the authority granted to me by our father. Make some sense?

Illustration Application

As Satan tries to take things from you, it is up to you to walk in your God given authority. Do not be intimidated by Satan's attacks. *Stand fast in the liberty in which Christ has made us free (See Galatians 5:1).*

This is a deliberate act on your part to claim your freedom over Satan. If you do not then you will continue living like a fugitive. You may have run away from Satan and sin. However, until you start operating in your Father's authority, you are no more than a powerless runaway slave futilely attempting to escape the hells of life.

"You" must tell the devil that *"you"* are free in Jesus name. This is important because Satan knows that we have the right to be free. He knows that God has set us free and he cannot bind what God has loosed.

The Bible says *the Lord brought them out of darkness, the utter darkness, and broke away their chains (Psalms 107:14).* Nahum the prophet said, *the Lord is good, a stronghold in the day of trouble (Nahum 1:7).* The psalmist declared *the Lord protects defenseless people. When I was weak, he saved me (Psalms 116:6)*

Satan knows *"The Lord himself watches over you!" (Psalms 121:5)* He knows the blood of the Lamb has freed you. He knows the power of God has broken every chain in your life. He also knows when we demand our freedom he has no choice but to hand it over. Now you need to open your mouth and let him know that you know it to.

Just as my brother handed the ball back when I told him what our father said, Satan must hand back everything he has stolen from you when you speak in the authority of Jesus Christ. Remember, *devils believe and tremble (James 2:19).* They know there is power in Jesus name. Now that you know it, use it!

Act Like You Know

Now is the time for you to push beyond Satan's deception. Break down the walls of doubt. Walk past the doors of defeat. It is time for you to live free of the restrictive chains of dissolution, disappointment and despair. You are a child of God, you have the victory and you are destined for greatness.

Jesus said *"And you shall know the truth, and the truth shall set you free"* (John 8:34). The key words for you and I are, *"you shall know".*

WORDS TO THE WISE

It is not "the truth" that sets you free. It's the truth that "you know" that sets you free!

I know I have repeated the phrase *"You Are Free!"* I have repeated it because I want to get this into your spirit, into your thinking, into your psyche. Now that you are free, you must stand fast in your freedom. You must walk in your authority; its freedom and authority that God has already given you.

Jesus said in Luke 10:19 *I have given you authority over all the power of the enemy.* The Bible says in 2 Chronicles 13:12 *God is with us so do not fight against the Lord God of your fathers, for you will not succeed.* Now that's a word for your enemies.

God is showing us in His word that it makes no difference what your enemies are trying to do to you behind the scene, it cannot stop the plan He has for your life. Jeremiah 29:11 gives us this powerful promise of victory from the Lord:

> For I know the thoughts that I think toward you, saith the Lord, thoughts of peace, and not of evil, to give you an expected end."

"Now, let the church say
AMEN!"

Chapter 5

Opportunistic and On-the-Move

BEING READY, WILLING AND ABLE

"Move from your place and go after it"
(Joshua 3:3)

TO MAXIMIZE GOD'S blessings in your life you must be *ready, willing and able* to move when God's opportunities are manifesting. Being *"ready"* means you are prepared to take action. To be *"willing"* means you are agreeable to do as the Lord has commanded. Finally, being *"able"* means you are flowing in your God given power, skill, and abilities so you can do what must be done for the Lord.

That was the message from God to the children of Israel in Joshua 3:3. They were told when *"you see"* the ark of the covenant of the Lord your *"God move"* from its place, you must move from your place and *"go after it."* In other words, when God moves, when He opens a door or a window in heaven, we must be on the move with Him.

This is critical because to walk in the great things that God has for us, the onus is on us to move when God's opportunities are manifesting. As the Apostle Paul said *a door of great opportunity stands wide open for us (See 1 Corinthians 16:9).* I am convinced that God is still opening doors today. My message to you my friend is do not miss your open doors.

ANOTHER TEST AND TESTIMONY

The Escape (Attempt)

One day my wife attempted to sign herself out of the hospital. I remember it like it was yesterday. She was still under a doctor's care. She was still receiving vital medical treatment. She had not regained all of her strength and mobility. Nevertheless, the sister was ready to go.

She mustered up enough strength to get out of the bed, into her wheelchair, roll down the hall, get in the elevator and make her way down the hall to the main exit of the hospital. Girlfriend was on her way out of the hospital. At least that was her plan.

Much to her dismay, hospital security foiled her plan. She was only a few feet away from the steep car ramp at the main exit when they stopped her. Considering her condition and physical limitations, she would have severely injured herself had she made it to the ramp. But, God intervened and stopped her before she put herself in harm's way.

We laughed when she told me about her failed escape attempt. You got that right, we laughed. I mean one of those head tossed back, mouth wide open, tears in your eyes, holding your belly, stomping one foot, while falling out of your chair kind of laughs. Like Sarah,

God made us laugh and everyone who hears will laugh as well (See Genesis 21:6).

You see laughter is a good thing. Proverbs 15:13 says *a merry heart makes a cheerful countenance*. In our laughter, God was healing the hurts and restoring our joy. He was doing a work in us and the happiness filled our mouths with laughter and our tongues with shouts of joy, the Lord was doing great things (See Psalms 126:2).

Now I do not recommend signing yourself out of the hospital prematurely. Nor do I recommend trying to use a wheelchair to go down a steep hospital exit ramp with limited strength and mobility. Both are bad ideas on so many levels. But, this escape attempt signaled something much greater and far more profound than getting out of the hospital.

My wife's escape attempt signaled that it was time for a change. It signaled she had become frustrated with her current situation. It was a signal that her current situation was no longer right for her. It was a signal that it was time to move to a new location, into the next phase of her recovery, to go to the next level and into a new season.

The Three Deadly C's

Change is not easy. If change were easy, everyone would do it. For this reason, change often requires motivation. For my wife, being angry, annoyed, and agitated with the confinements she now faced in the hospital motivated her to take action for the change she desperately desired in her life.

Motivated to change her place in life she refused to be complacent, get comfortable or to accept these confinements. Likewise, such motivation can keep you and I from becoming complacent, getting too comfortable or lulled into accepting situations that confine us. This is important because complacency, comfort and confinements will leave you unprepared, unwilling and unable to move when God makes away for your escape.

Illustration – Don't Die

Complacency, comfort and confinement are like carbon monoxide. They are silent and deadly killers. They will keep you distracted, disinterested and discombobulated when God opens a door of opportunity. They will lull your desire and passion to sleep until your dreams are dead, your vision is voided, and your destiny is destroyed.

My friend do not allow yourself to die in a situation that God has purposed for you to survive. Thus, when these destiny destroying tendencies are looming in your life they must be conquered; there are no if, ands, or buts about it. Your destiny depends on it.

I can tell you from my own experiences there have been instances in which frustration pushed me to reach for God's best for my life. Furthermore, let me tell you, I would rather deal with someone who is frustrated with their situation, then someone who has gotten satisfied with less.

Settling for less is a demonically inspired mentality that will sabotage your destiny. Settling for less is a trick of the enemy that will keep you trapped in defeated places. I rebuked this type of thinking in our lives right now.

Illustration – Enough Is Enough

In 1 Samuel 1, the writer introduces us to a man by the name of Elkanah, and his two wives Penninah and Hannah. Yep, that is correct. He had two wives. But let's save that discussion for another day.

The Bible says Hannah's *rival Penninah provoked her bitterly, to irritate and embarrass her, because the* LORD *had left her childless (1 Samuel 1:6)*. However, it was this mistreatment, agitation and frustration that motivated Penninah and it pushed her into prayer, praise and her promise.

In Luke 15, we are introduced to the Prodigal Son. The term Prodigal is from the Latin word *"Prodigo"* which means wasteful. True to his name, he had wasted his inheritance and now he was poor, wretched and homeless.

Yet, in the midst of his frustration he declared, *"I will arise." (Luke 15:18)*. He had finally grown tired of kicking it with the pigs. He was now ready for the palace.

While sitting in a pigpen fighting pigs for food the Prodigal son finally came to his senses and said, 'How many of my father's hired servants have plenty of food? But here I am, starving to death! I will get up and go back to my father. (Luke 15:17-18).

Please note he did not make this statement when all was well. Ironically, he made it when he was at his lowest point in life. At this crucial moment in his life, he finally had the impetus to do something about his situation. Maybe this is why the writer of Ecclesiastes 7:3 stated, *"Frustration is better than laughter."*

To his credit, he did not just give lip service. He did not wait for someone to encourage him, to pick him up, or tell him he could do better. He did not wait for a motivational speech or a *"you-can-make it"* message.

He got up. He walked out of the pigpen, back to his father's house and into a better situation. For the Prodigal Son he had reached the point when enough was enough and he took action to change his situation for the better.

Illustration Application

Some things in life should upset you, frustrate you, make you uncomfortable and get under your skin. Maybe you have searched and searched but you cannot seem to find a job. Maybe you have gone to doctor after doctor with no cure for a persistent health issue. May be you are lonely, lost, or lacking something in an area of your life.

Maybe you are dealing with an insidious and incestuous family matter. Maybe there is a pervasive generational curse smothering your household. Maybe your ministry has not blossomed as you had foreseen it.

When the dream birthed in your spirit does not match the life you are living, you should be annoyed and agitated. The pain of seeing one thing from God, but living another should shake you. These discrepancies between the revelation in your spirit and the reality of your life should motivate you to change.

Let me assure you God does not intend for your life to be a perpetual storm, a never-ending trial, or a continual string of unfortunate events. But, He will use these seasons in life that hurt, harass or hunt you to help you. God knows if you get comfortable in the pigpen, you will never make it to the palace.

Hitting Rock Bottom

The Prodigal Son, when he had money he was running around town living it up, breaking it down and dropping it like it was hot. Until his money ran out. Because of his *"undisciplined and dissipated living, he wasted everything he had.* Luke 15:30 says he *"squandered his money on prostitutes."*

If that was not bad enough *"there was a bad famine throughout the land" (Luke 15:14)*. So now, he is penniless, friendless, homeless, and foodless. In fact, he was *so hungry he would have eaten the corncobs in the pigpen, but no one would give him any (Luke 15:16)*. So, once his money was gone, instead of kicking it with people, he was sleeping with their pigs.

The lesson being when your ability or willingness to give is no more some people will quickly walk out of your life. If you are not careful, you may find yourself in need of assistance and everyone has left you down and out.

That is what happened to the Prodigal Son. When he had money, he was partying with his friends. Now that his money is gone, there are no friends to be found.

Moment of Clarity

Penniless, friendless, homeless, and hungry and now the Prodigal Son finally had hit rock bottom. He had reached the lowest possible point in his life. He had reached the point when things could not possibly get worse for him.

But, hitting rock bottom did not mean that his life, or anyone's life for that matter, is over. Hitting rock bottom does not mean you have to stay there. In this instance, hitting rock bottom *"Brought him to his senses"*.

Hitting rock bottom gave him the platform he needed to rebuild his life. Hitting rock bottom gave him the jolt he needed to gain some much-needed clarity. When he hit rock bottom he finally saw the need for change and had the impetus to do something about it.

When I was a teenager and getting into things, I remember my mother saying to me on numerous occasions *"Come here boy so I can knock some sense into your head"*. Between mom's tough love, my father's steady but stern hand, and the occasional beat down in the School of Hard Knocks, I came to my senses and changed my life.

But, some people have to hit rock bottom before they recognize the need for change. In fact, for some people, hitting rock bottom is the only way to dust off their dreams, awaken their desire, to reignite their passion, and to reopen their heart to the promises of God.

An unknown author wrote:

> *Sometime you have to get knocked down lower than you have ever been, to stand taller than you ever have.*

After many years of his life spiraling out of control and now at his lowest point the Prodigal Son said, *'All those farmhands working for my father sit down to three meals a day, and here I am starving to death. I'm going back to my father's house"* (Verse 17-20). In the midst of his filthiness, frustration and misfortune he finally had a much needed moment of clarity.

Don't Get It Twisted

The Prodigal Son dreamed of the palace, but lived a deplorable life in a pigpen. He dreamed of the fatted calf, nice clothes, signet ring and the comforts of home. But, now he lived each day fighting pigs for scraps, dressed as a destitute, and covered in dirt, grime and filth, and who knows what else.

Sadly, the Prodigal Son had adjusted to life in the pigpen and was surviving on pig leftovers. One could even argue for a while he had become content. However, it is one thing to be content with where you are in life. The Apostle Paul said *I have learned to be content (Philippians 4:12)*.

But don't get it twisted. It is one thing to be content with where you are in life. But it is something totally different and ungodly to accept failure, underachieving or less than what God has purposed for your life. That type of thinking is from the devil.

Reading Philippians 4:12-13 we see the Apostle Paul was not settling for less. In times of poverty and persecution, He was still believing God for more.

> *I know how to get along with humble means, and I also know how to live in prosperity; in any and every circumstance I have learned the secret of being filled and going hungry, both of having abundance and suffering need. 13. I can do all things through Him who strengthens me. (New American Standard Bible)*

Never, Never, Never, Never

However, in Luke 15, the pain of the Prodigal Son's predicament gave him the motivation he needed to break free of his deplorable life. The lessons from the Prodigal Son for you and I are:

- *Never think your situations are inevitable, inescapable or invincible. They are not.*

- *Never accept, adapt to or approve of any situation that denies your blessings. They shall not.*

- *Never trust that people will always be with you, bring you out, or bear your burdens. They cannot.*

- *Never say God has forgotten, forsaken or forfeited His word to you. He will not.*

If you have adjusted to someone, something, somewhere or to some situation that is less than the word that God has spoken over your life, it is time for you to break free of its grip on you. I declare to you that it's time to arise. Your new day and your new life, starts right now!

Finally...

Finally, the need to make a change became clear to the Prodigal Son. Finally, he acknowledged that it was time for him to do something about his situation. He was finally ready, willing and able to break free from his deplorable position in life.

When you come to such moments in life, you have a few choices. You can let it either:

- *Define you*

- *Defeat you*

- *Develop you*

The Prodigal Son did not let his deplorable situation define him. He reminded himself of who he was and who his father was. He did not let it defeat him. He got up and changed his life for the better. He did however let it develop him. He developed a renewed outlook, a renewed identity, and renewed purpose.

Like the Prodigal Son, we all experience moments when we become tired of settling for less than what God has purposed for your life. Tired of seeing your dreams, but not living them. Tired of your job, tired of the neighborhood you live in, tired of the company you keep, or even tired of the direction your life is heading.

Being tired of something does not always mean that the situation is sinful. In could mean the situation is no longer right for you. It could mean one season of your life is over and the next is waiting to begin. It could be the Holy Spirit's signal to you that it is time to make a change.

For these reasons, we all need divine moments of clarity. We will all have moments when we need our outlook restored, our identity in Christ reestablished or our resolve to rise rekindled.

When these divine moments finally come, when the blinders are finally lifted from our eyes and the bondage is finally broken over our lives we cannot afford to be complacent. When we reach that point in life when we become sick and tired of a particular situation, when we come to the realization that we can do better than this, we cannot stand there and do nothing. We must be bold enough to *"bust a move"*.

I know that's old school 1980's rap lingo, but it fits so well into my message to you my friend. The bottom line is you cannot wait around for a hand out, helpful hand or house full of friends. You must rise and take your rightful place in God.

When these divine moments happen, when the blinders are finally lifted from your eyes and the bondage is finally broken over your life, you must:

> *Discipline yourself so that you are ready to take advantage of every divine opportunity that comes your way (Ephesians 5:16, NET Bible).*

Now, there's a word that is critical to you being unstoppable. The word is discipline. Discipline is doing what is required of you to accomplish a particular task. Spiritually speaking it is as the Apostle Paul says in 1 Timothy 4:7 to *"train yourself to be godly."*

You see discipline will keep you growing and developing in your walk with God. It will keep you focused on the prize (see Philippians 3:13). It will move you beyond the immobilizing effects of complacency, comfort and confinement.

Discipline ensures you get things done, when they should be done. It ensures you are ready, willing and able to change when the opportunity finally presents itself. This we all need!

Are You Ready

Change happens for a variety of reasons. Jobs change, relationships change, finances change, and people, places and things change. Sometimes change is caused by something that is in us. Sometimes change is caused by something that is happening around us. Sometimes change is cause by something happening to us.

Sometimes change is caused by something the Holy Spirit is doing on the inside. As the Holy Spirit completes His work in us we are transformed into the same image from glory to glory (2 Corinthians 3:18). Sometimes change happens as God moves and changes things around us. When He does we must move and change with God.

God told Joshua and the children of Israel:

> *When you see the Ark of the LORD, and the priest and the Levites bearing it up, then you shall remove from your place and go after it (See Joshua 3:3).*

In other words, God was telling the children of Israel when I cause things to change you must change. When I move, you must be on the move. The same is true for us, as God changes things, we must be so in tune with the Spirit of God that we readily, willingly and ably move with the leading of the Holy Spirit.

In fact, the quicker you change, the sooner God can get down to the business of blessing you. Knowing this Job looked forward to change when he said *all the days of my appointed time I will wait for my change to come (Job 14:14).* Knowing this the Apostle Paul said:

> *When I was a child, I spoke like a child, I thought like a child, I reasoned like a child; but when I became a man, I stop doing childish things (1 Corinthians 13:11).*

The point is in the ever changing world we live in we must be *"Ready, Willing and Able"* to change. Don't stop, change. Don't delay, change. Don't get discouraged, change. Don't fight what God is doing in your life, change.

President Barack Obama said:

> *Change will not come if we wait for some other person or some other time. We are the ones we've been waiting for. We are the change that we seek.*

Famed poet and activist Maya Angelou said:

> *If you don't like something, change it. If you can't change it, change your attitude.*

Actor Gillian Anderson said:

> *I hope everyone that is reading this is having a really good day. And if you are not, just know that in every new minute that passes you have an opportunity to change that.*

Like a caterpillar, longing to be a butterfly, today you may find yourself living a life of unfulfilled dreams, crawling over broken promises, yet dreaming of the day

WORDS TO THE WISE

Read God's Word and you'll emerge stronger, wiser, greater, and with renewed passion, purpose and promise. If you don't you won't.

when you spread your wings and fly away. I challenge you to embrace the changes God is speaking into your life. I challenge you today to wrap yourself in the cocoon of God's word.

You see as the Word of God takes root in your life, a transformation takes place. The Word of God renews, restores, reprograms, and revitalizes us. These changes validate the old cliché, *"Something on the inside, is working on the outside, O' what a change in my life."*

It is Holy Spirit inspired change that keeps us aligned with God's destiny for our lives. It does not have to be some huge mega change. It could be a simple change such as praying more often, developing a regular Bible study habit, or eating healthier, exercising more, or spending more time with love ones.

Again, the point is to be *"Ready, Willing and Able"* to change as God speaks into your life. By so doing, you will be ready…

When Your Opportunity Knocks

Jesus said, *"Here I am! I stand at the door and knock"* and at this very moment, He is knocking on the door of our hearts. His promise to us is *"If anyone hears my voice and opens the door, I will come in and eat with that person, and they with me" (Revelations 3:20)."*

Unfortunately, for thousands of people and for a variety of reasons they are oblivious to the knocking of God in the lives. Their ears are clogged so they cannot hear and their eyes are blinded so they see what the Spirit of God is revealing unto them (Matthew 11:15). I am reminded of Doubting Thomas in John 20 when the disciples told him, *"We have seen the Lord!"*

Thomas responded:

> *Unless I see the nail marks in his hands and put my finger where the nails were, and put my hand into his side, I will not believe. (John 20:25).*

Standing in the presence of the greatest blessing in human history, Thomas could not see the opportunity knocking on the door of his heart. It took a strong rebuke from Jesus, *"Stop doubting and believe"* (John 20:27) to open Thomas' eyes.

Doubting Thomas Spirit

We have all had moments when we question a revelation from God like Doubting Thomas. I call it the

"Doubting Thomas Spirit". When people are infected with the Doubting Thomas spirit, they need more than a word from God to believe.

They need to see, touch, or receive the manifestation promised by God before they will believe it. These are folks who walk by sight and not faith. Instead of moving in faith, people infected by the Doubting Thomas spirit rely on natural eyesight, worldly wisdom, head knowledge, science, feeling, and logic to make decisions.

Jesus says these are people who have *eyes but cannot see (Mark 8:18)*. I believe such people are spiritually blind. They are in essence spiritually handicapped. They are unable to *"Walk"* in faith because they are living by sight. They are unable to *"Stand"* on the Word of God because they are trusting in their own power and might.

Such people are unable to *"Hear"* what the Spirit is saying to the church because they are listening to the wrong things. The cannot *"Run"* for the Lord without getting weary or walk without fainting because they are doing it in their own strength. Don't let this be you.

Fortunately, for Doubting Thomas, and for you and me, Jesus is the God of the second chance. The Bible says:

> *Eight days later Jesus appeared to Thomas and said "Reach your finger here, and look at My hands; and reach your finger here, and put it into My side. Do not be unbelieving, but believing: (John 20:27).*

Seize the Moment

In contrast to Doubting Thomas, in John 5 the Bible says *a large number of sick people were lying—blind, lame, or paralyzed—waiting for the movement of the water (3)*. To their credit, they could sense a spiritual opportunity was going to manifest at any moment. That is more than I can say for so many Christians today whose faith is waning, whose spiritual eyes are blurred, and their spiritual ears are dull.

In John 5, every day these people waited patiently and eagerly for the opportunity to be healed. They understood miracles can come at any moment and they needed to be ready.

They believed in the supernatural. They believed it would happen at any moment and every person believed it would happen for them. That is what I call living with an unstoppable spirit.

Then one day, Jesus appeared and:

> *He said to a man waiting at the pool, "Get up! Pick up your mat and walk." At once the man was cured (John 5:8-9).*

Immediately he obeyed the instructions from Jesus and as a result, he received the blessing God had for him. Because he was ready for his opportunity and he obeyed the voice of God, he received the miracle that had been purposed for his life that day.

I am reminded of the Centurion soldier in Matthew 8 whose servant was lying at the point of death. He saw an opportunity to receive a blessing from the Lord and he pounced on it. He said to Jesus:

> *You do not have to come to my house. But if you will say that my servant is healed I believe that it will be done (See Matthew 8:5-13).*

The Centurion saw a divine opportunity. Without hesitating, he capitalized on the blessings and grabbed it. Because of his faith and his actions, God healed his servant.

The same thing is true for blind Bartimaeus in Luke 18. The Bible says that blind Bartimaeus heard that Jesus would be walking through his neighborhood. Blind Bartimaeus took hold of the opportunity.

The Bible records when *Jesus was passing by blind Bartimaeus screamed out son of David have mercy on me (Luke 18:38).* When the disciples told blind Bartimaeus to quiet down the Bible says *He screamed out all the more (Luke 18:39).*

That is because a person who sees a divine opportunity for a blessing cannot be stopped by those who do not. They know God's blessings are going to be released. Numbers 23:20 confirms this truth as it reads, *"God has blessed, and I cannot reverse it!"*

Blind Bartimaeus had the mindset that somebody is going to be blessed, so it might as well be me. He refused to be denied. He saw an opportunity to change his life and he seized it. When the time was right, he moved. In Mark 10:52 Jesus said to him *"You may go. Your eyes are healed."*

Sadly, in Luke 18 only Blind Bartimaeus was healed. But, I am convinced that there were other people in the area that needed a blessing and the opportunity for a blessing was knocking on their door. Only blind Bartimaeus seized the opportunity.

Blind Bartimaeus heard that Jesus would be passing by, he responded when Jesus called for him, and as a result, he received the blessing he needed. I am convinced that something absolutely awesome happens in your life when you hear, believe and respond to the voice of God.

This is God's word to you as you are reading this book. God's word to you today is opportunities are coming your way. Are you ready? If not, then get ready, get ready, get ready! Do not let these opportunities pass by you.

When you can *"hear"* what God is *"saying"* and you *"believe"* He will do it, it will literally prepare you for your opportunities. It will literally position you in the right place for their manifestations. It will literally propel you into your blessings from God in the moment they are manifesting.

Do You Believe This

We all have *"do you believe this"* moments. These are moments in life when the Word of God will challenge you to believe something that seems impossible or illogical. A good example is after the death of Lazarus in John 11, when Jesus said to Mary and Martha, *I am the resurrection and the life he that believes in me even if he were dead he shall live (John 11:25).*

He then asked the question *"Do you believe this?"* A few verses later, Jesus said to Mary and Martha *"If you can believe you will see the glory of God" (John 11:40).* Jesus was speaking an opportunity into their lives. He was drawing attention to their ability to see in the spirit what was not yet manifesting in the natural.

This is important because the ability to see in the spirit is critical for conquering the storms of life and for capitalizing on God's divine opportunities. This is important because what you see in the natural can be discouraging, demoralizing, and demeaning.

This is what makes the faith of the centurion in Matthew 8 all the more impressive. His servant was dying. Nevertheless, he said to Jesus in Matthew 8:8 *"Just say the word, and my servant will be healed".*

The centurion only needed a word from the Lord and he knew that his servant would recover. In other words, the *"Word of God"* was the only evidence he needed. He believed once Jesus spoke the word it would come to pass just has He said it would.

Similarly, Blind Bartimaeus heard that Jesus would be passing by and he believed that in Christ he would be healed. In other words, Bartimaeus saw his healing before it was manifested. When the opportunity presented itself he was ready to move and he, *"shouted out Son of David have mercy on me".*

He refused to be stopped. He refused to allow his blindness, the mistreatment and obstruction of others, or the failures of life to stop him. He did not let his blessing pass him by and the rest as they say is history!

The lesson for you and I is we must keep our spiritual eyes and ears open to God's opportunities. We need them to conqueror the storms of life and we can't afford to miss them because we didn't see or hear them. In the face of trials, tragedy and tribulation we must *walk by faith and not by sight (2 Corinthians 5:7)*. Figuratively speaking, we must close our natural eyes so we can see things more clearly in the realm of the spirit. I heard a friend say one day:

> *When you can't see what God has said,*
> *close your eyes.*

Look, Listen and Live

God is always speaking revelations and opportunities into our lives. Hebrews 1:1-2 tells us that throughout history, God has spoken *in many different ways to our fathers through the prophets, in visions, dreams, and even face to face, telling them little by little about his plans. But now in these days he has spoken to us through his Son (Living Bible)*.

The issue isn't God speaking. The issue is we are not always listening. Not listening when God is speaking into your life is a recipe for disaster. Thus, we are encouraged in Proverbs 3 to *listen for God's voice in everything you do and everywhere we go. (Proverbs 3:6, the Message Bible)*. Matthew 11:15 declares *anyone with ears to hear should listen and understand! (New Living Translation)*

Unfortunately, for so many people when God speaks His words go in one ear and out the other. Many people are operating with a *"pseudo listening"* spirit and are pretending to listen. Even worst, some have a *"Rebuttal Spirit"*. They argue with God, they reject His word, they quench the Spirit, and then they make their own decisions. The dangers in such behaviors are obvious.

Illustration – Warning, Warning

A pastor shared a story of a man who was driving along a narrow, winding road. When all of a sudden a woman driving a large Rolls Royce came speeding around the corner, nearly driving him off the road.

As she drove by the man, he heard her shout, *"Pig!"* Immediately, the man retaliated by yelling back, *"Fat old cow!"* Then he drove around the bend himself and crashed head on into the biggest pig he had ever seen.

You see instead of listening, the man was too busy fussing and rebutting, and he missed the warning. His failure to listen resulted in him crashing into the pig. This was a crash that could have been avoided had he just listened to the lady's warning.

Illustration Application

The Bible is filled with scriptures that validate the importance of listening to God. In Psalms 81:8, God says to you and me:

> *Hear me, my people, and I will warn you-- if you would only listen to me."*

The truth of the matter is you and I have not always listened to and obeyed the voice of God. We have not always made the right decisions or moved at the right time. We have all ignored His voice, overlooked His warning, and made mistakes in serving the Lord.

I am by no means making excuses, or encouraging you to purposefully make mistakes, or to ignore the voice of God. Both would be very bad ideas with dire consequences. Listening to and obeying God is always in our best interest. It boils down to doing things the hard way or God's way, to missing God's opportunities or receiving them.

Hard Way or God's Way

Remember what happened to the Prophet Jonah when he ignored and disobeyed God. He made the dreadful decision to board a ship bound for Tarshish instead of Nineveh as he had vowed to the Lord (See Jonah 1:3; Jonah 2:10).

The Bible says he *"went in the opposite direction to get away from the Lord"* (New Living Translation). Once Jonah boarded the ship and they set sail, immediately a violent storm arose. Realizing Jonah's disobedience caused the storm, the crew through him overboard.

When I first read the story of Jonah, I was like *"Dang, that's cold".* Then, if being thrown overboard by the crew was not bad enough, he was swallowed by a fish,

> ## WORDS TO THE WISE
> *Any action that takes you away from God will have terrible consequences and result in increased calamities and missed opportunities.*

taken to the bottom of the sea for three days until the fish vomited him out on the shore three days later (See Jonah 1-3).

That's what you call a situation going from bad to worst. It started because Jonah did not listen. Yet, the truth of the matter is we all make mistakes, bad decisions, and disobey God. The Apostle Paul wrote, *"All have sinned and come short of the glory of God." (Romans 3:23)*

The key is when you make a mistake, fall short, or disobey God, don't hide it. Confess it. Don't lie about it. Tell the truth.

If you hide it, if you lie about it, there will be consequences. To make matters worse, Satan will use it as an opportunity to bring condemnation, criticism, and to coerce you into doing what he wants. Who needs that?

Furthermore, it is not like hiding it or lying about it will keep God from knowing what happened. Hebrews 4:13 says *nothing in all creation is hidden from God's sight. Everything is uncovered and laid bare before the eyes of him to whom we must give account.*

The truth of the matter is God knows our faults and He is simply waiting for us to acknowledge our shortcomings before Him and to ask for forgiveness. *God is just and will forgive us of our sins and cleanse us from all unrighteousness (1 John 1:9).*

Micah 7:19 tells us *God will have* compassion on us and He will tread our sins underfoot and hurl all our iniquities into the depths of the sea. Psalms 103:12 says as far as the east is from the west, so far has He removed our transgressions from us.

Thankfully, our God is the God of a second chance. After Jonah's act of disobedience, the Bible says *the word of the Lord came unto Jonah the second time, saying, Arise, go unto Nineveh, that great city, and preach unto it the preaching that I bid thee".* And, this time *"Jonah arose, and went unto Nineveh, according to the word of the Lord (Jonah 3:1-3).*

After all of this, Jonah still ended up doing what the Lord asks him to do. When he did what the Lord said there were no storms, he was not tossed overboard or swallowed by a fish. He did not spend three days trapped in another vile situation, nor was he violently hurled out of the mouth of the fish like food poisoning from an upset stomach.

Jonah went to Nineveh and preached as he had promised. The Bible says the whole city repented when they heard the preaching of Jonah (Matthew 12:41). The revelation for you and I is, it would have been better for Jonan had he did it *"God's Way"* and not *"his own way"* the first time.

Selah!

ANOTHER TEST AND TESTIMONY
Obeying His Voice

When I was in school in Atlanta, Georgia completing my doctorate the Lord spoke to me. I had just finished a grueling day of class and was heading back to the hotel for the evening. It was one of those days when I just wanted to get a bite to eat, take a shower, and go to bed.

On the way, I stopped by McDonald's to get something for dinner before heading to the hotel. After ordering my food, I found a table in the lobby to enjoy my meal. Admittedly, I was starving after a long day in class. A brother was hungry.

Before I could take the first bite, the Lord spoke to me and said, *"Pack up your food and leave right now. You need to eat this meal in your hotel room."* Talk about God's timing. I was hungry and it was cold outside. I really did not feel like waiting to eat and those hot McDonald's fries were looking so good. I was like *"Lord, do I have to go now."*

All jokes aside, I got up just as the Lord said. As I exited the McDonald's to go to my car, the Lord showed me two men that were waiting outside. He said to me *those two men were preparing to rob you.*

Thus, the Lord thwarted their plan when I harkened to His voice. By moving in the moment God said that I should, God rescued me before the robbers could put their plan in motion.

The lesson in my testimony is we must listen and obey God. No, not sometimes, not when we feel like it, not when it is convenient. We must listen and obey the voice of God in our lives at all times.

The songwriter reminds us that:

> *God's voice makes the difference. When He speaks He relieves my troubled mind. It's the only voice I hear that makes the difference. And I will follow Him one day at a time.*

In John 10:27–29, Jesus said:

> *My followers listen to my voice; I know them, and they follow me. I give them eternal life, and they shall never perish; no one will snatch them out of my hand. My Father, who has given them to me, is greater than all.*

When God spoke to me, it was not in a loud bellowing voice. It was not like Saul's divine light experience on Damascus Road (Acts 26:13-15). God did not knock me down or surround me with a bright light. Surprisingly, His voice did not sound like thunder (Job 37:5) or a mighty river (Revelation 1:15). He spoke to me in a still small voice that was unexplainable, but easily recognizable (See 1 Kings 19:12).

I knew it was God and I could have easily ignored His voice. He was not demanding, domineering or dictatorial. He did not threaten to punish me, put me in a headlock, or push me off a bridge if I did not move.

But all jokes aside, I knew it was God. I know His voice (See John 10:27) and I knew it would be unwise to disobey it because *whoever listens to God will live safely and be at ease with no fear (Proverbs 1:33)*.

Spiritually Opportunistic

Opportunity is from the ancient Greek word *"Kairos"* meaning the right, well-timed or supreme moment. It is a predetermined moment in time when something is to happen. For the child of God, it is that moment in life when the conditions are right for the inevitable, supernatural, intervention of God to occur.

Thus, being spiritually opportunistic is capitalizing on the moves of God in your life. This is important because I am convinced that God's blessings are multiplied to those who are *"Spiritually Opportunistic"*.

Spiritually opportunistic people are people who are ready for a blessing. These are people who, in spite of their past failures, keep getting back into the boat. They keep launching out onto the water. They keep casting their nets and they keep pulling God's blessings into their lives (See Luke 5).

James 1:17 tells us *"Every good and perfect gift is from above, coming down from the Father of the heavenly lights"*. Today God is throwing open the floodgates of heaven and pouring out blessing (See Malachi 3:10). The key is you must *"be ready"* when the floodgates of heaven open and the gifts from above are falling down. Every moment of every day, you should be living your life *"spring-loaded"* to move when God says move.

You cannot afford to spend your days crying over the fish you did not catch, or the ones that got away. You cannot afford to spend your days pouting over the blessings you did not

WORDS TO THE WISE

If you are waiting to see your blessing to believe your blessing, by the time you see your blessing, it will be in someone else's hand.

grab hold of or daydreaming about the ones you did not see.

If you are focus on what you have lost or what you are missing, you will fail to see the bountiful blessings God is now sending your way. If you focus on what you have lost or what you are missing, you will fail to see the abundant school of fish God has prepared to jump into your net.

You see those who are unprepared or unwilling to move will simply miss out on the opportunities He has prepared for them. If Peter and his friends did not get back into the boat, launch out into the deep, and lower their nets as commanded, in the moment it was commanded, the fish would have simply swam away and would have been caught by someone else.

This is why Satan wants you unprepared, unwilling and unable to move. Instead of being on the lookout for God's opportunities, Satan wants you distracted, doubting, and discouraged. He knows it will lead to missed opportunities and you will remain stuck in the defeated places of life.

As we see in the life of the Prodigal Son in Luke 15, Satan wants to hold you captive in the pigpens of life. He wants you unable to reach the doorsteps of the palace you are dreaming about. He wants you trapped in the past, stuck in the moment, living in fear and afraid of the future.

This was one of the many lessons Jesus taught the disciples in Luke 5. He taught them the importance of getting over the failures of the past and of being ready for the new opportunities that will arise. It is the same lesson He's teaching you and I today.

You never know *"when"* God will open a door of opportunity for you or *"when"* He will speak a blessing into your life. But, you must know He *"will"* open doors and He *"will"* speak blessings into your life. If you are ready, willing and able when He does, that's when you can claim the blessings of God for your life and Satan can't do anything about it.

Just Walk It Out

When you know, that you know, that you know, that you know, that God is working things out, the only thing left for you to do is *"Walk it out"*. In Genesis 12, the LORD said to Abram *Go from your country, your people and your father's household to the land I will show you. I will make you into a great nation, and I will bless you; I will make your name great, and you will be a blessing. I will bless those who bless you, and whoever curses you I will curse; and all peoples on earth will be blessed through you.*

God said to Abraham, here is your opportunity for an unprecedented blessing. To receive it you must leave your home and leave your country. Furthermore, I am not telling you where you are going. Without hesitation, *Abram went, as the Lord had told him.*

Talk about *"Walking it Out"*. Talk about having an *"Opportunistic Attitude"*. Talk about *"Not wasting an opportunity"*. With only a word from God, Abraham moved in faith. He walked away from his wealth and a good life and obeyed the voice of God.

In Abraham, we see that a person who is spiritually opportunistic is not preoccupied with the ups and downs of the past, the good and bad of the present, or the uncertainty of the future. They forget what has happened (See Philippians 3:13) and they keep moving forward, getting stronger and stronger (See Job 17:9, New Living Translation).

Spiritually opportunistic people approach each day with a sense of Holy Ghost inspired purpose. Regardless of what they are heading into, going through, or just came out of, they are always on the move for God.

Abraham heard the voice of God and refused to let his position in life stop him. That's confidence, that's assurance, that's faith, that's being ready, willing and able, that's being spiritually opportunistic. As Children of God, this is how you and I must live. With each new opportunity from God:

> *We must*
> *Move from where we are*
> *and go after it*
> *(Joshua 3:3).*

Chapter 6

Pressing Your Way Through

UNYIELDING IN YOUR PURSUIT OF GOD

"Forget the past, reach forward"
(Philippians 3:13)

SUCCESS DOES NOT come easy. It requires focus, optimism and an indomitable spirit. It requires a mindset that believes in spite of the hell I have gone through, I am going through, or will go through, the blessings God have purposed for my life *"will be mine!"*

Success requires an outlook that says regardless of what has happened in my life, *"the best is yet to come!"* It requires an attitude that says no matter how high the mountain, *"I'm heading to the top and I'm never looking down!"*

When it comes to success, and by success I mean the fulfillment of God's plans for your life, you must be persistent in your pursuit of it. You must be spiritually tenacious in fulfilling God's will because Satan will do everything he can to hinder, harass and halt you.

Every day you must be actively pursuing the plan and purpose of God for your life. Therefore, the question I have for you is *"What are you doing right now?"* Not, what will you do? That's in the future. Not, what have you done? That's in the past. The question is *"what are you doing right now?"*

Get Your Head Out of Your...

God spends very little time dealing with your past. The past is what it is, *"in the past"*. Good or bad, it is over and we must turn our attention to what is happening now with an eye toward the future. This is important because holding on to yesterday, while trying to press forward in God is a recipe for disaster.

Learn from your past. Grow from your experiences, then put them in God's hands and leave them there. After all, God's favor is for those focused on today, not those who are stuck in the past. You can be forgiven of your past and healed from those experiences, but God will not invest much time dwelling over what has happened.

My message to you is *"Stop dwelling on the past."* It's time to release yourself from the life draining vice of your yesterday. It is time to forget those things that are behind you and to reach for what is before you.

There is no need to worry about yesterday. The Bible says, *the former troubles are forgotten and hidden out of sight (Isaiah 65:16).* As the songwriter said:

> *Yesterday is gone,*
> *today I'm in need."*

So, I say to you my friend

Forget the past.

That was God's message to Joshua after the death of Moses. He said to Joshua *"Moses My servant is dead; now therefore arise, cross this Jordan, you and all this people, to the land which I am giving to them." (Joshua 1:2).*

As great as Moses was, his accomplishments were in the past. God was telling Joshua, stop dwelling on what has happened. You have work to do. In other words, Joshua needed to get his head out of the past so that he could move forward.

Granted, we all need time to mourn, to grieve, but God's message to us through Joshua is:

You cannot mourn
for a life time.

There are people who are still crying today over things that happened five, ten, fifteen years ago. I am not trying to minimize the heartache and pain of their experiences. However, holding on to the pains of yesterday keeps you tied to your past and it sabotages your future. At some point, you must let it go.

Jennifer Hudson sang, *"You've got 10 minutes to cry"*. Now, that may not always be enough time to get over all of the issues that we face in life. But, what the lyrics imply is we have to get over the hurts of the past so we can heal.

Admittedly, it is easier said than done. But the rewards of letting go of the past and being healed of its hurts are phenomenal. Then and only then, can you truly press forward without being stymied by things that are in the past.

Illustration – Turn Yourself Around

Pressing forward in God while holding on to the pain and problems of the past, is no different than driving a car while staring in the rear view mirror. It goes without saying that a person doing such a thing is bound to crash. They can have good intentions and know their destination.

But, as you might expect they are going to crash and the results will be catastrophic.

A person doing such a thing will inevitably make the wrong decision or take the wrong actions because they are looking in the wrong direction. Their focus is off, their perceptions are distorted and they will inevitably collide with something or someone they could have easily avoided had they been looking in the right direction.

You see I am convinced that success isn't a dime-a-dozen commodity that is handed out like candy. To the contrary, success is invaluable and it is achieved by those who are willing to keep trying and are always reaching forward.

Illustration Application

The point is you must keep your attention on what God is doing in your life right now and what He has revealed about your tomorrow. You should not waste your anointing looking back at what did or did not happen yesterday. The danger in keeping your head in the past is you will miss the new opportunities that God has given you the power to possess.

For example, a woman who is still angry and holding onto the pain of her ex-husband walking out years ago, may not see the Boaz that is now standing in front of her. The man, who is still wallowing in self-pity and anger because he did not get the job or promotion, may not be prepared when the next opportunity comes his way.

From my perspective, you should only look back in the past to learn from your experiences. You should only look back to reflect on the goodness of God and all the things He has brought you through. However, you should not look back to dwell on your experiences, or to relive them over and over again in your mind.

Now it's time to turn yourself around, focus on what lies ahead, and trust that God will cause the things in the past to *"work together for your good"* (See *Romans 8:28*).

This mentality is vital for living with an unstoppable spirit. After all, God's favor is released upon those who are pressing forward, not those who are fixated on the past. God's anointing fills those who are standing in the liberty in which Christ has made them free, not those who are anchored to the bondage and brokenness of yesterday.

The truth of the matter is you don't need God's favor and anointing for what has already happened. You need them for what is happening now and for the challenges and opportunities that are ahead. You need them as you leave the past behind and put your hope in the new opportunities God is bringing your way.

Higher Hope

Hope is an inspiring sense of success. It is from the Greek word *"Elpizó"* which refers to anticipation, excitement and desire for a certain thing to happen. But, hope isn't just wishful thinking or looking at the world through rose colored classes.

Hope is the persistent push of the Holy Spirit that we need to wipe off the dust, square our shoulders, lift up our chin, stick out our chest, and do it again. Hope is God's answer to the naysayers and haters in our lives and it is birthed in us through the Holy Spirit. Romans 15:13 reads:

> *Now may the God of hope fill you with all joy and peace as you believe in Him, so that you may overflow with hope by the power of the Holy Spirit. (Berean Study Bible)*

Hope is the Holy Spirit inspired belief that we will *see the goodness of the Lord in the land of the living (Psalms 27:13)*. Hope is being confident that *all things are working together for the good of them that love God"* (See Romans 8:28). Hope is heavens reminder that tomorrow will be a brighter day and it is the key to overcoming the storms of life and to breaking free of the chains of your past.

Hope is fearless, it is daring, it is courageous, and it is bold. Hope is so powerful that in the face of certain defeat, repeated failures, and glaring mistakes, it will not let you quit. That's the power of Hope

Hope helps you recover quickly when you are feeling down and it will pull you out of the doldrums of life. Anglican Bishop Desmond Tutu said:

> *Hope is being able to see that there is light despite all of the darkness.*

As Pastor Robert Shuller said, you must:

> *Let your hope, not your hurts, shape your future.*

When you have hope, you can dance in the rain. When you have hope, you can sing while you are in pain. When you have hope, the sun always shines again. When life looks like it is going to hell in a hand basket, hope reminds you that things are going to get better.

Thus, hope is the unshakable belief that it isn't over until God says it's over. Therefore, I encourage you *to rejoice in hope (Romans 5:2)* because God can use the smallest of opportunities to release the greatest blessings in your life.

Illustration – Fight For It

Consider the attitude of the four men in 2 Kings 7. They were faced with certain death by leprosy, starvation or by the sword. The choices were simple. Do nothing and die, or do something and have a chance to live.

> *They said to each other, "Why stay here until we die? 4 If we say, 'We'll go into the city'—the famine is there, and we will die. And if we stay here, we will die. So let's go over to the camp of the Arameans and surrender. If they spare us, we live; if they kill us, then we die.*

Talk about having bad choices. Yet, they said if we do nothing we most certainly will die. But, if we take our chances, we have an opportunity to live. They could have stayed where they were and died of starvation, or they could fight for their survival. They could go find some food and *"the chance"* to keep on living.

These men said *let's take our chances (2 Kings 7:3-4)*. They realized some opportunities only come along once in a lifetime, so they purposed in their hearts to take advantage of this one. They were not going down without a fight. That's the attitude of people living with an unstoppable spirit.

Illustration Application

Sometimes there is no other way to get your breakthrough other than facing your challenges head on. That might mean making the most of a bad situation, shaking off disappointment, getting up after you've been defeated, trying again after you have failed, or asking again after you have been rejected.

Like these men with leprosy, you have to make bold decisions and take decisive actions when your back is against the wall. Their situation was bad, but they found a glimmer of hope. It was a glimmer of hope worth fighting for.

Was it an easy decision, probably not? Did they have some reservations and uncertainty, I am sure they did. However, they made the bold and daring decision to face their trial.

They epitomized the power of hope. Their attitude said, *"We can do this"*. Their attitude said *"We're not dead yet, and we have a chance to change our situation for the better"*.

That is the lesson from these men with leprosy. Don't just sit there and die. Do not agree or accept doom, death or defeat. This is your life, your ministry, your family, your finances, your well-being and peace of mind, so fight for it.

Like the men with leprosy, today is your day to make a bold decision. This is your moment for decisive action. This is your season to get what God has said is yours. My friend, do not give up without a fight. This is your life. Again I say to you, fight for it.

Go Hard or Go Home

Only God should decide how far you can go and what you can accomplish. When others tell you what you cannot do, don't lower your expectations, or abandon your dreams or forsake your destiny. That's not the will of God for your life.

Christians who lower their expectations, abandon their dreams, or forsake their destiny are signaling to Satan that his attacks are working. They are also signaling to God that they do not trust Him to bring it to pass. That's not good.

Researches call this phenomenon of lowering your expectations, abandoning your dreams, and forsaking your destiny, *"downward goal revision"*. I call it a lack of faith. It is inspired by Satan himself. I rebuke this type of thinking in your life and my life right now in the name of Jesus.

Faith is not about lowering our expectations. Faith is about pressing forward. Faith is to know that every round with God goes higher and higher. Faith is being bodacious enough to prove others wrong.

Faith is about raising our expectations. Faith is about following hard after God. Faith is about expecting overwhelming victories, complete healing, and total deliverance.

For example, when the Lord delivered Israel from Egypt, he did not bring them half way across the Red Sea; He brought them all the way. When the Lord had the five-thousand people sit down to eat, He did not feed most of them; He fed all of them. When the Lord touched the blind man in Mark 8:24, he did not restore some of his eyesight; He completely restored it.

The lesson for you and I in Mark 8 is Jesus did not allow the blind man to settle for less. Nor will He allow you and me to settle for less than His best for our lives. Until we have the complete promises of God manifested in our lives, we must keep on praying, believing and pressing forward until we have them.

No matter how big your problem or how high the mountain you must climb, they will never be too big or too high for God. In fact, God will use your challenges to stretch the limits of your faith, to help you dream bigger, to encourage you to believe for more, and to inspire you to aim higher. Then He will still *do exceedingly and abundantly above all that we may ask or think (Ephesians 3:20).*

Partner With Positive People

Trials and tribulation can come from the most unlikely source and at the most inopportune time. Thus, keeping a positive mindset and staying focused takes effort. The last thing we need is people surrounding us who are negative, whose words are ill advised and ungodly.

An important aspect of pressing your way through the storms of life is surrounding yourself with the *"right people"* and having the right people speaking the *"right message"* into your life.

We need people around us who can encourage us when we are feeling down. We need people around us who can stir up the gifts in us when we need the Holy Spirit's power. We need people around us who can remind us that our best days are ahead of us.

Proverbs 11:14 reads *where no counsel is, the people fall: but in the multitude of counselors, there is safety.* Proverbs 15:22 reads *without counsel purposes are disappointed: but in the multitude of counselors, they are established.*

The truth is everyone will experience moments in life when we need a pat on the back, a word of encouragement, comfort or wisdom. When we have people around us who can speak these things into our lives, our lives are so much more rewarding.

We are as Isaiah the prophet said:

> *Brightened as the noon day and the dark clouds looming around us are dissipated. We are strengthened and we are*

like well-watered gardens, and like ever-flowing springs (See Isaiah 58:11).

I cannot count the number of times I have spoken a timely word into someone's life, and I could see God's glory manifesting in them right before my very eyes. With a timely word from the Lord, the sparkle in their eye returned, the confidence in their voice was back, and the strut in their step was renewed.

Again, the point is we need the *"right people"* speaking into our lives. I encourage you to surround yourself with godly people who will challenge you to do more, reach for more, and dream for more. People who will mentor, coach and tutor you in the things of God and help you deal with the negative situations we all deal with

No More Negativity

Negativity is the tendency of thinking things are harmful or bad. It is focusing on the bad qualities of someone or something. It describes a person who is pessimistic, pouting, and likes pity-parties.

If anyone had a right to be negative it was Job. Consider Job's plight. He had lost his entire family, his wealth was gone, and he was in extremely poor health. Covered in painful sores from the top of his head to the bottom of his feet, his situation looked helpless, hopeless and horrible.

But, instead of giving into the negativity, Job did three things. First, Job recognized the negativity around him. Second, he stopped those who were being negative. Lastly, he conquered their negativity. It is these three deliberate actions that aided in Job's rise from his dreadful situation.

Recognize the Negativity

Consider Job's terrible support group. His wife said to him, *"....Are you still holding firmly? Curse God, and die!" (Job 2:9 NET Bible)*. His friends suggested the calamity and affliction was his fault.

They said he was living a sinful life and that God was punishing him for his evil ways. But, nothing could be further from the truth. God declared that Job was *blameless and upright (Job 1:1; Job 1:8).*

The counsel of Job's wife and friends could have been catastrophic. Their counsel could have crushed his character, his heart, his spirit

> ## WORDS TO THE WISE
> *All friendships are not good friendships. All counsel is not good counsel.*

and a *crushed spirit dries up the bones (Proverbs 17:22).* The New Living Translation reads *a broken spirit saps a person's strength.*

But Job recognized his wife's foolishness and his friend's miserable efforts to comfort him (See Job 16:2). With friends like these, he did not need enemies.

Stop the Negativity

Satan wanted Job to be negative. Negative toward God, negative in his faith, negative in his situation, negative about his life. Satan knows that negativity can cancel the word of faith. Even a right now, rhema word for your life can be rendered powerless if you receive it with a negative mindset.

Negative thinking keeps you focused on the bad experiences, failures, and disappointments of your past. It keeps you focused on the height of the mountains, the deepness and darkness of the valleys and the strength of the giants in your life. The result is a lack of enthusiasm, your faith is diminished, and fear takes root in your life.

When this happens, the storms in your life will feel like they never cease. Even when the storms are over, negative thinking keeps you reliving these bad experiences over and over again in your mind so it feels like your storms are never-ending.

Satan knows that negativity blinds the mind of God's children. He knows that negativity restricts the flow of the anointing. He knows that overtime negativity builds distrust, disregard, and disdain for the things of God.

He also knows that negativity is like shooting yourself in the foot or poking yourself in the eye. It results in self-inflected wounds that hinder your progress and limit your effectiveness. He knows a negative mindset will make your journey in life that much harder and his goal of stopping you from reaching your destiny that much easier. This is not the will of God for your life.

Job was not deterred by the negativity of his wife. He stopped her ill-advised counsel when he said, *"you are speaking like a foolish woman."* That my friend is how you stop the negativity of others from having a negative influence upon your life!

Conquer the Negativity

To Job's credit, he did not let the horrific events of the past, his current situation, or the negative words of others affect him. In the midst of his pain he said, *"I shall come forth as gold." (Job 23:10)*. The Amplified Bible reads *"...I shall come forth as gold pure and luminous"*.

In other words, Job declared, *"I shall"* come out of these trials better then I went into them. Like Job, every morning you should wake up with the mindset that something good, wonderful and amazing will happen in your life today.

I am convinced that if you live each day with this mindset, more often than not you will be right. On one of the darkest days of his life, Job declared, *"the Lord giveth and the Lord taketh away. But, blessed be the name of the Lord" (Job 1:21)*. That my friend is how you conquer negativity!

Personal Pep Talk

To defeat the negativity in your life there will be times that you have to minister to yourself. You cannot wait around for someone else to lift you up, encourage you, or inspire you. It's a wonderful thing when it happens and you should give God the praise when it does.

Unfortunately, those moments can be few and far between. In many instances people will tear you down, not build you up. For this reason, it is vital that you take time out to *"build yourself up on your most holy faith"* (Jude 1:20). That's what Job did.

At one of the lowest points in his life, Job said, *"I shall come forth as gold."* He did not let the negativity of his wife and so-called friends change the message that he preached to himself.

This is important because negative people, speak negative words and breed negativity. Listening to them continually will have you seeing yourself as a victim, living like a vandal, with no hope of victory. Their words will have you going through life seeing yourself as a no body, a nincompoop, or namby-pamby with nothing to lose.

This is why you should refuse to hang out with people who are negative, or have a defeatist mentality, low expectations or are always talking about what's wrong. Negativity will affect how you see yourself and foster within you a poor self-image.

Make no mistake about it. A poor self-image will undermine your faith and rob you of your Kingdom membership benefits. It will keep you from pushing through the obstacles you face in life. It will stop you from believing in what God is doing through you.

The truth of the matter is what your detractors think about you should be of little importance to you. American author and psychotherapist Virginia Satir said:

> *We must not allow other people's limited perceptions to define us."*

I know it is not scripture, but

> *Can I get an*
> *AMEN!*

Stronger Than You Think

Every morning you must define who you are. Yes, you have been hurt. Yes, you have been knocked down. Yes, you have made some missteps along the way. I will agree with you that some of the experiences in your life were not fair. But at some point, you have to stop living your life as a looser and letting the hells of this life label you.

You are too anointed to live like that. I'm reminded of King David in 1 Samuel 30:6. He was greatly distressed because the people talked about stoning him. Now, he could allowed their hateful words and evil intentions to tear him down. But, David gave himself a personal pep talk.

The Bible says he *encouraged himself in the Lord his God (1 Samual 30:6)*. In speaking of encouraging yourself, my daughter, Keona Jordan, said it best in her song, *"Stronger than You Think!"*

> *The battle is tough, but I won't back down. The Lord is on my side so I won't quit now. I'm more than a conqueror. I'm stronger than you think!*

In another stanza she writes:

> *I'll keep moving through the pain. Through the storm and the rain. This is not the last of me. I'm stronger than you think!*

She concludes with these powerful words:

> *Thank God I found a Savior. He's the reason I can take it My strength comes from the Lord. In Him I carry on.*
>
> *I might fall, but I'll never break. I'll stand strong, through all the pain. I'm not a loser, I'm not a quitter. I'm a dreamer. With my strength, I will accomplish my dreams!*

This type of powerful personal pep talk is absolutely awesome and it should not be underestimated. The bottom line is you must believe in you and in what God is doing through you. Consider this, even Jesus' own brothers did not believe in him (John 7:5). But that did not matter. Jesus believed in himself and in the Father. He knew who He was and He boldly declared to his doubters *"If you have seen me you have seen the Father" (John 14:9).*

Even though people disagreed with who He said he was, it did not matter. Jesus knew who He was. He did not allow people problems, persecution or pain to stop the work God had ordained for His life. He did not let their opinions, perceptions or way of thinking negatively affect His determination, His desire or His destiny.

Illustration – Diamonds in the Rough

Many years ago, I was preparing a sermon series on the blessings of pressing through trying times. One message was titled *"Diamonds in the Rough"*. The message focused on how God uses people problems, pressures and the pains of life to prepare and position us for more of His presence, promotions and prosperity.

During my time of preparation, the Lord pressed upon my heart to learn how a diamond is formed. I am by no means a geologist, trained in the science of how solid and liquid matters are shaped in the earth over thousands of years. Nevertheless, here is what I learned.

A diamond is formed from materials that have been repeatedly crushed, subjected to extreme pressure and seared in temperatures in excess of 2000 degrees deep below the surface of the earth. This process can last for thousands of years.

Ironically, it is this violent crushing, continuous pressure and extreme heat second after second, minute by minute, hour by hour, day after day, that transforms these materials into priceless diamonds. Without it, the transformation cannot take place.

What the earth does in the natural, God does in our lives both in the natural and in our spirits. As the Apostle Paul put it in 2 Corinthians 4:8-9, God allows trouble on every side, perplexing problems and persecution, and the events of life to knock us down, around and upside down.

Illustration Application

Today, many people are facing hard, challenging, and tough times. I have faced them, you have faced them, and we will continue to face them. It is just an unpleasant fact of life. Life is stacked against us.

If we are not careful, these challenges can alter our self-perception, self-worth, and self-esteem. We may start believing we are meant to be outcasts, worthless, and destined to die losers. We may start believing life will never get better.

This type of thinking is demonic, demoralizing and detrimental and it will lead you to a defeated place. Researcher Dr. Carter G. Woodson said:

> *If you make a man feel that he is inferior, you do not have to compel him to accept an inferior status, for he will seek it himself.*

Spiritually speaking, Instead of pursuing the prophecies, dreams and visions that God has birthed in your spirit, you will become discouraged, dejected, and disillusioned.

If this is you, please listen closely. This is not the will of God for your life. Don't let your difficulties get you down. You are not defeated or destined to be a looser. You are just a diamond in the rough.

Illustration – The Aladdin Analogy

Allow me to illuminate this point using the animated movie *"Aladdin"*. Aladdin lived his days as a poor boy in the fictional Arabian city of Agrabah. Society considered him just another nobody, an outcast, a derelict.

He was labeled a *"Street Rat"*. He was told, *"You are a worthless street rat. You were born a street rat. You will die a street rat. And only your fleas will morn you."*

He suffered, faced lack, and ridicule. Aladdin had every reason to be bitter and angry. He had every reason to lash out at society. He had every reason to give up.

But, Aladdin met each day and each trial with a since of purpose. He faced each trial with a positive outlook. He did not allow his circumstances to determine his approach to life. He did not allow the words of people to change the way he saw himself.

He dreamed for more. He worked for more. The trials of his life molded him, drove him, and pushed him to keep moving forward. That is the message of God to you in a nutshell. God is saying to you press your way through.

Illustration Application

The story of Aladdin gives us a picturesque view of how we should respond to the storms of life. The pains of Aladdin's day served as motivation to his success. Unbeknownst to Aladdin he was destined to be great and his pain, plight and predicament were the catalyst that propelled him into it.

Although this is a fictional story, it speaks to a reality in which many people today can relate. Maybe you have been counted out and rejected. But, here's a lesson we can glean from Aladdin that adds some perspective to the scriptures. The suffering you are enduring is not worthy to be compared to the greatness to be revealed in you.

As a pastor, I am routinely mentoring and encouraging people facing hard, challenging, and tough times. For so many, their self-perception, their self-worth, and their self-esteem have been distorted by the hell they have endured.

They see themselves as outcast, worthless, destined to die losers. They are not. They are diamonds in the rough. Diamonds in the rough are people who may be facing dark days and sleepless nights, who may be suffering financially, socially, and emotionally. Yet there is a God ordained dream in them that will not die.

Diamonds in the rough are people whom society has deemed are no bodies and have written them off. These are

people who are facing seemingly impossible trials, tragedies and tribulations in life. If this is you, let me assure you God is using the difficulties and darkness of your days to mold you into a dazzling example of His glory. Do you believe this?

Dear reader you are a member of God's royal priesthood (1 Peter 2:9), you are the apple of God's eye (Zechariah 2:8; Psalms 17:8), and part of His holy nation (See Exodus 19:6). I can assure you that membership in the Kingdom of God has its privileges.

As children of God, we are God's masterpiece. *He has created us anew in Christ Jesus, so we can do the good things He planned for us long ago. (Ephesians 2:10, NLT).* The key is you must believe it. If you do, it will radically change your thinking, your attitude, your behavior and ultimately your destiny. I pray that you receive this word, in Jesus name!

Your Haters Can't Hold You

Greatness is an inherent quality of your life. It is what it is. Just accept it and anyone who says otherwise doesn't know the Word of God. They are just *"haters"* who are *"hating"* on you.

Unfortunately, the world is full of haters. Everywhere you go there may be haters. There may be haters in your house, haters at work and haters in the hood. There may even be haters in the house of God.

Haters come in all shapes, sizes and colors. There are haters from all walks of life. There are haters who are rich, poor, saved, lost, black, white, fat, tall, big and small, and on and on.

Joseph and His Haters

Consider what happened to Joseph. The Bible says Joseph had a dream. Excited about the revelation from God he told his brothers. To Joseph surprise instead of rejoicing and showing him some love, it kindled a bitter hatred in their hearts towards him (See Genesis 37:8).

Satan used their deep-rooted hatred to launch his attack against Joseph. He sought to destroy God's favor on Joseph's life and to prevent Joseph's dreams from coming to fruition. But it did not work as Joseph confirmed, *thou they meant it for evil, God meant it for my good (Genesis 50:20).*

To put it another way, his haters could not stop him from reaching his divine destiny. Joseph was too blessed to be bound by their feeble attack to hold him back. Instead of stressing, he kept pressing forward, and received his blessing.

Nehemiah and His Haters

Nehemiah faced similar hatred. As he and the children of Israel were rebuilding the wall around Jerusalem as the Lord instructed, Satan launched his attack. Working through Sanballat the governor of Samaria, he sought to put an end to the work they were doing for the Lord (see Nehemiah 4).

The Bible says Sanballat and others were furious, indignant, and they openly mocked the work Nehemiah was overseeing (Nehemiah 4:1-3). But to God be the glory Nehemiah kept pressing ahead and he responded to his enemies *"Why should the work cease?"*

Said differently, Nehemiah asked why the work of God should be put on hold for people who mean them no good. Nehemiah recognized his enemy was attacking the assignment that God placed in his hands. He recognized his enemy wanted them to think their efforts were a waste of time.

You and Your Haters

If given the chance Satan will use anyone he can to distract, delay, derail and destroy your destiny. He wants you to think your efforts are in vain and that the prophecies, dreams and visions God has given you are untrue, unobtainable and unlikely to come to pass.

He knows if you start thinking that your prophecies, dreams and visions are beyond your reach, you will become dejected, disappointed and dismayed. Feelings such as these will foster a negative outlook and they will undermine the work that God is doing in your life.

If you believe the assignments, prophecies, dreams, visions, and goals birthed in your spirit from God are not attainable, your effort level to reach them will decline. You are likely to pray less, study less, and serve God with less effort. This is exactly what Satan wants.

Conversely, if you believe the revelation and the Word from God given to you will come to past, your drive to possess them will increase. You will serve God with more passion and zeal. Satan fears this happening in your life.

This is why Satan will assign haters to haunt, harass, hinder and halt you. If you haters knew better they would *"rid themselves of every kind of evil and deception, hypocrisy, jealousy, and every kind of slander" (1 Peter 2:1)*. They are only hurting themselves. Proverbs 14:30 says such envious behavior *"rots the bones."*

Illustration – Blessing In Pressing

In Joshua 1, Joshua was now in charge after the death of Moses. The children of Israel were leaving the dark days of Egypt and moving into the brighter days that awaited them in the Promise Land. This was to be a swift transition out of bondage and into freedom. But like lots of transitions, it was not going to be easy.

The challenges for Joshua and the children of Israel as they transitioned out of Egypt and into the promise land were many and they were huge beginning with the city of Jericho. Jericho was a mighty and well-fortified metropolis. Victory looked impossible and no doubt, there were some traveling with him that thought it was foolish to keep moving forward.

They could have easily turned around and given up on the promise of God. But the only way to the promise land was going *"through"* Jericho. The children of Israel believed God and continued marching around Jericho. You see God assured them:

> *Every place that the sole of your foot shall trod I will give it to you. No man shall be able to stand before you all the days of thy life. As I was with Moses, so I will be with thee. I will not fail thee, nor forsake thee. Do not be afraid. Do not be dismayed. I will be with you everywhere you go (Joshua 1).*

As they quietly marched around the city of Jericho, I am sure it seemed foolish. But, they did it anyway. I am sure some of them questioned why they were doing what they were doing. But, they did it anyway. I'm sure the people of Jericho laughed at them. But, day after day for seven days, they did it anyway.

When the time finally came for them to let out a shout they shouted and the walls of Jericho came crumbling down (See Joshua 6:20). By faith they faced the trial, they kept pressing forward, they trusted in the promises of God and Jericho's wall came crumbling down.

Illustration Application

For you and I Jericho is any trial that looks too big, too strong, and too tough for you to overcome. In these moments, we may be tempted to turn around, to give up, and to walk away. But, if we follow the instructions God has laid out for our lives, we will see the walls of Jericho in our lives come crumbling down.

For the children of Israel, their faith in God made them bigger, stronger and mightier than Jericho's wall. Their willingness to keep pressing forward conquered the ridicule and uncertainty. Their obedience kept them focused on the task at hand and in the end, Jericho was defeated.

Here's a powerful hidden truth for you and me. *If you obey, you will truly see the glory of God, you will reap his blessings and you will have plenty (Isaiah 1:19).* But, the question you must answer is *"are you willing to press your way through your Jericho?"* I hope that you are because it's standing between you and the promises of God for your life.

Like Joshua, don't be deterred by your trials and let nothing stand in your way. Easier said than done I know. But in the end, it was just that easy for the children of Israel at Jericho. They purposed in their mind to do what God had said, they kept pressing forward and God gave them the victory.

Finally, after all of their efforts, the Bible says the Lord gave them rest on every side. (Joshua 21:44)

Illustration - No Excuses, Just Do It

Reflecting on my first jump in Air Borne School, I remember the Jump Master saying to me:

> *One way or another you are leaving this aircraft while it is in flight. Voluntarily or involuntarily, the easy way or the hard way, you are going out the door. There are no excuses.*

Was I afraid? Bet your bottom dollar I was. Did I have excuses for why I should not have to jump from the plane? You best believe I did.

I had an endless stream of thoughts and excuses for not jumping from the plane running through my mind.

> *What was I thinking when I decided to do this?" "Why should I jump from a perfectly good aircraft?" "Soldiers*

have gotten hurt, severely injured, and even killed doing this."

In that moment, fear had a hold of me and I was hoping the Jump Master would change his mind. But I knew he would not be moved by my excuses. Weeks of training, practice and instruction and now we were moments away from my first jump. We had come too far to turn around now.

Suddenly, I heard the door of the plane open and I could see the ground thousands of feet below. Undeterred by my fear or that of my fellow soldiers, the Jump Master shouted, *"Drop zone coming up stand in the door!"* With my parachute strapped to my back, and my knees knocking like a nervous snotty-nosed kid on the first day in school, I stood ready to go.

Then with one final shout the jumpmaster said, *"Go!"* and out the door I went. Seconds later, my parachute opened and the fear was gone. At that moment, I saw the world and everything around me from a whole new perspective. I did it and it felt great!

Illustration Application

Like the Jump Master in airborne school, God is shouting, *"Go".* Go get your life back. Go get your dreams. Go get your ministry. Go get your family. Go, go, go!

I am sure you can think of lots of excuses for not trying. But, as I have learned over the years, excuses are for people who are not willing to try hard enough, don't want it bad enough or believe they are not good enough.

Those who are flowing in the blessings of God, who see the promises of God manifesting in their lives are the

WORDS TO THE WISE

Don't make excuses. Losers make excuses. Christians make things happen.

ones who do not make excuses. If something is broken, damaged or out of place, through the gifting of the Spirit they pray for restoration. And, it is so! If something is wrong or out of whack, as the Holy Spirit moves in them they work to make it right.

The only thing you should do when God releases His word in your life is *"Just do it!"* No more putting off for tomorrow, things you should be doing today. No more waiting for someone else to do for you what you can do for yourself. Once a word from God is released in your life, there are no excuses. You've got to *"Get-er-done".*

The Best is Yet to Come

God *is a "rewarder" of those who diligently seek Him (Hebrews 11:6).* This truth speaks to the goodness of God that is bestowed on us when we pursue His will for our lives. It speaks to the miracles that manifest when we make up in our minds to press toward *"the high calling of God."* It adds credence to the old adage *"There is a blessing in the pressing."*

I cannot tell you *"when"* God's rewards are going to manifest. But what I can tell you is they *"will"* manifest. The key is to *"Keep Pressing Forward"* because the best is yet to come. My friend I do not want you to miss your reward.

Job, as he endured his affliction, believed it was simply a matter of time before the good times would return. He remained optimistic. He remained hopeful. He kept looking forward. He kept pressing forward.

God told Joshua if you obey My word *your way will be prosperous and you will have good success (Joshua 1).* With so much at stake, Joshua could not afford to listen to his doubters.

The Apostle Paul had this mindset:

*I am bringing all my energies to bear on this one thing:
I'm forgetting the past and looking forward to what lies
ahead. (Philippians 3:13, Living Bible)*

Like Job, Joshua and the Apostle Paul, you and I have
too much at stake to have our hopes dashed to pieces by
others. We must forget the past and we must keep
pressing forward. It's vital for living with an unstoppable
spirit.

Chapter 7

Persistent In Praising God

GIVING GLORY AND RECEIVING STRENGTH

*"I will hope continually and
will praise you yet more and more"*
(Psalms 71:14)

L ATER THAT NIGHT after the accident everything changed with one phone call. *"Mr. Jordan you need to make it to the hospital right now! Kisha is dying. How soon can you be here? She may not last much longer. She could go at any moment."*

To hear the nurse in the intensive care unit say she was in the final hours of her life was heart wrenching. Nothing prepares you for a moment like this. We quickly got into the car and headed to the hospital.

What an emotional roller coaster ride. I went from singing Christmas songs in the early morning to contemplating what I would say in a eulogy before the sun went down on Christmas night. Instead of singing dashing through the snow on a one-horse open slay, over the fields we go, laughing all the way; we were speeding down the highway, crying and praying that God would save the day.

Upon arrival, the news was not good. The doctors, nurses and hospital staff agreed her death was imminent. Sorrow filled the air like smog. A sinister like darkness was casting its gloomy shadow over the room and the Grim Reaper was closing in.

In those moments, it felt like my entire world was in the hand of the evil one (See 1 John 5:19, NASB). My fire for life was fading fast. Given the facts, it seemed all hope was lost.

Ignited By His Word

I know you are probably thinking *"What an odd way to start a chapter on praise."* I encourage you to keep on reading. I have learned over the years that God will often release the greatest proclamations, manifestations, revelations and impartations when we praise Him in the storms.

It is in these experiences, we really get to know the comfort, compassion and concern the Lord has for us. It is in these times that our admiration and adoration for God moves to a new level. It is in these encounters that genuine, powerful, heartfelt praise is ignited.

You see, just as I heard the life shattering words that my wife was dying, I also heard the heart healing voice of the Lord when He said to me:

> *These injuries are not unto death. I have allowed this to happen that I might be glorified and so others might believe. Be strong and courageous, not dismayed. If you will believe then you will see My glory.*
>
> *I AM with you wherever you go. My peace I give unto you. Live holy and let your light shine so others will see*

the work of God being done in your life and give glory to your Father in heaven.

God knew just what I needed. I needed His word and the hope, help, and healing that it brings. In that moment, *He sent His word and healed me (See Psalms 107:20).* For this, I give Him the praise.

Some people wait a lifetime for a moment like this. This powerful word from the Lord to me is what a theologian calls a *"Rhema"* word. These are words spoken by God into our lives.

When my passion for life was fizzling out fast, His words rekindled a much-needed fire within me. At that moment, not only could I hear His words, but I could feel His words like a warm fire on a cold winter's night. I could sense the Holy Spirit's *"electricity"* being activated in me.

Now my praise was more than just singing and dancing. My praise transformed into a tailor made expression of my admiration and adoration to God. My praise had morphed into an authentic reflection of the joy in my heart for what God had done for me. My friend, I am still praising Him today.

Foundation of Praise

God's word became the substratum, the foundation, the bedrock of my praise. It ignited an unquenchable fire in my bones (See Jeremiah 20:9). As His word continued to take root in me, more and more songs of praise began resonating from within my spirit (See Psalms 108:1).

Now consider for just a moment, what the Lord had done for us. From the moment the stolen car slammed into ours, we were shackled and burdened by a mountain of devastation and doom. We found ourselves buried beneath a load of depression, despair, disillusionment and discouragement.

However, in one of the darkest moments in my life:

God spoke directly to me and I believed that He could do just what He said. Out of this experience my praise was born.

At that moment I:

Experienced the Breath of God
that Giveth Life

So, paradoxically the near fatal car accident had changed my life in ways that I would have never envisioned. It seems absurd, that something so horrific could turn out so magnificent. My praise had been ignited, illuminated, and invigorated by the powerful promise that she would live. Again I say for this, I give him praise.

An Exposé on Praise

According to Baker's Evangelical Dictionary of Biblical Theology, praise is a theme that pervades the whole of Scripture. It is an act of our will. It is an expression of the joy that flows out of our awe and reverence for God.

Praise calls to God's greatness and glorifies Him for His magnificence. Words that are often used as synonyms or in parallel with *"praise"* and so help point to its meaning, are *"bless, " "exalt, " "extol, " "glorify, " "magnify, " "thank, "* *and "confess."*

Praise builds a conduit to the world of the divine and it ushers us into the realm of the Spirit as we:

Enter his gates with thanksgiving and his courts with praise. Be thankful unto Him and bless His name (See Psalms 100).

Praise is so powerful that it establishes a supernatural meeting place with God and in it:

God is leaning back on the cushions of our praise. God is resting in our praise and we are blessed in His presence." *(Psalms 22:3, the Message Bible)*

When I read scriptures like these, I am more encouraged to *rejoice always, praying continually, giving thanks in all circumstances (1 Thessalonians 5:16-18).*

That is the spirit of praise. That is the heart of a *"Praiser".* That is having a *"Praise Mentality".* That's *"Praising Your Way Through."*

It's a Praise Party

Praise is not just a solo. Even when you are alone, you are not praising God by yourself. In fact, when you know the Word of God you quickly discover real praise is never a solo. You are never praising on your own. It is impossible.

David knew this when he said *magnify the Lord with me, let us exalt His name together" (Psalms 34:3).* The children of Israel knew this in Exodus 15 when God delivered them from Egypt and brought them through the Red Sea. The Bible says:

> *Then Miriam the prophet, Aaron's sister, took a timbrel in her hand, and all the women followed her, with timbrels and dancing".*

In another example of corporate praise, Nehemiah 8:6 reads, *"Ezra blessed the Lord the great God. And all the people answered, "Amen, Amen!" while lifting up their hands; then they bowed low and worshiped the Lord with their faces to the ground."*

Then, when you include the angels and the host of heaven, praise is more than a duet, it is the largest mass choir in the universe. Revelation 4:8-11 gives this amazing account of praise in Heaven:

> *They rest not day and night, saying, Holy, holy, holy, Lord God Almighty, which was, and is, and is to come. 9 And when those beasts give glory and honour and thanks to him that sat on the throne, who liveth for ever and ever, 10 The four and twenty elders fall down before him that sat on the throne, and worship him that liveth for ever and ever, and cast their crowns before the throne,*

> saying, *11 Thou art worthy, O Lord, to receive glory and honour and power: for thou hast created all things, and for thy pleasure they are and were created.*

Isaiah 6 records this magnificent account of praise in Heaven:

> *I saw also the Lord sitting upon a throne, high and lifted up, and his train filled the temple. Above it stood the seraphims: each one had six wings; with twain he covered his face, and with twain he covered his feet, and with twain he did fly. And one cried unto another, and said, Holy, holy, holy, is the Lord of hosts: the whole earth is full of his glory. (Isaiah 6:1-3).*

But Wait There's More

All of creation praises the Lord. Psalms 145:10 proclaims *"All your works praise you, Lord; your faithful people extol you."* Psalms 98:8 says, *"Let the rivers clap their hands, Let the mountains sing together for joy."* Isaiah 55:12 reads, *"The mountains and the hills will break forth into shouts of joy before you, And all the trees of the field will clap their hands."* Moses wrote *"The heavens declare the glory of God; the skies proclaim the work of his hands." (Psalms 19:1)*

I told you, *"It's a praise party".* In Psalms 150 we read:

> *Hallelujah! Praise God in his holy house of worship, praise him under the open skies; Praise him for his acts of power, praise him for his magnificent greatness; Praise with a blast on the trumpet, praise by strumming soft strings; Praise him with castanets and dance, praise him with banjo and flute; Praise him with cymbals and a big bass drum, praise him with fiddles and mandolin. Let "every living, breathing creature" praise God! Hallelujah!*

Mindboggling Praise

Then there are those special moments when God's *"Shekinah Glory"* fills the room. In 2 Chronicles 7 as the children of Israel were rebuilding the temple, they entered into a time of prayer and praise. During the dedication service, the *Bible* reads:

> *When Solomon had made an end of praying, the fire came down from heaven, and consumed the burnt offering and the sacrifices; and the glory of the Lord filled the house.*

If that is not enough, in Zephaniah 3:17 the prophet writes *the Lord thy God in the midst of us is mighty and He will joy over us with singing.* Yes, God rejoices over you with singing. According to John Gills Exposition of the Bible:

> *He rejoices with joy, and joys with singing; which shows how delighted he is with his people, as they are his chosen, redeemed, and called ones (para 1).*

This one scripture totally changed my view of praise. It reveals a powerful truth that while you and I are praising God, God is singing over us. Yes, let that sink in.

I repeat, while we are praising God, God is singing over us. That's right. Take another moment to let that marinate, to sink into your subconscious, into your spirit.

The Power of Praise

Praise is like the engine in a plane. The engine is the source of the planes power and when it is engaged, it makes things happen. As the power supplied by the engine increases, the plane takes flight and it moves higher and higher.

Praise is like the engine on a train. The power from the engine pulls the train along its tracks, up mountains and through valleys until it reaches its destination. As the engine provides more power the train can pull more stuff.

Similarly, praise is like the engine in a racecar. The power supplied by the engine moves the racecar around the track. As the driver puts the pedal to the medal, the racecar goes faster and faster.

Just like the engines in planes, trains and automobiles, praise creates the enthusiasm we need to get things done.

Praise keeps us excited along life's journey. It encourages us as we walk through life's valleys. It emboldens us as we strive to reach the top of life's mountains.

But more than that, praise is a source of spiritual cleansing and healing. As we praise the Lord, it creates a supernatural stirring in our innermost being. This stirring of the spirit removes bad attitudes, negative outlooks, destructive emotions, heartfelt hurts, and deep regrets buried in our minds and subconscious.

Praise rids our minds of the ungodly thoughts, words, desires, feelings, and emotions that can sink us in the storms of life. But, most importantly, as these unwanted thoughts and feelings are uprooted and flowing out of our lives by our praise; God is entering our lives and releasing His power, presence, protection and provisions into it.

Now I can see why the psalmist said, *"I praised Him more and more each day" (Psalms 71:14)*. The psalmist knew the more we praise God the better we feel. I am convinced there are two reasons we feel better. The first is *God inhabits our praise (See Psalms 22:3)*. The second is *where the Spirit of the Lord is there is liberty (2 Corinthians 3:17)*.

It's simple.

More praise, more presence.
More presence, more power.
More power, more prosperity
in every area of our
lives!

Pushed Into Praise

As previously noted, in 1 Samuel 1 we are given the account of Hannah who is unable to bear children. To make matters worse, she is being agitated, antagonized, and verbally assaulted by her rival, Penninah. Hannah wanted a child, but could not because the Lord had closed up her womb.

This must have been extremely frustrating as her rival, Penninah, repeatedly pushed, provoked and prodded her day after day (1 Samuel 1:6). After all, Penninah had what Hannah wanted. Hannah wanted a child. In her bareness, Hannah had to endure years of irritation from Penninah and the disappointment of not having a child.

Now Hannah is hurting, humiliated, humbled and on the verge of emotional collapse. Like Hannah, there are so many people in the world who can relate to Hannah's frustration and pain. Like Hannah, they do not have the luxury of faking their prayers or playing church games. They need God to move in their lives right now.

Yes, Penninah's provocation increased Hannah's frustration and pain. But glory to God, instead of it pushing her down, it pushed Hannah into the presence of God. Once she got into His presence, Hannah got down to the business of praying and praising.

For Hannah, it was not about Penninah. In fact, it was never about Penninah, nor is it ever about your enemies. Other than praying for those that despitefully misuse you it is a misuse of your prayer time to ramble on-and-on about what your enemies are trying to do to you.

Hannah never mentioned Penninah in her prayer. She did not waste time talking about what Penninah was doing to her. Hannah wisely acknowledged God's greatness and prayed for what she needed from the Lord. She prayed:

Lord Almighty, if you will only look on your servant's misery and remember me, and not forget your servant but give her a son, then I will give him to the Lord for all the days of his life (1 Samuel 1:11).

In verse 17 God answered her prayer when Eli said, *"May the God of Israel give you what you have asked him for."* At that moment, the Lord was bringing an end to her frustration and pain. Hannah's bitterness was gone and now filled with joy she got her praise on when she declared:

How happy I am because of what God has done! I laugh at my enemies; how joyful I am because God has helped me! (1 Samuel 2:1).

But do not forget, it was Penninah's continuous pestering that provoked Hannah. It drove Hannah into the house of God with unrelenting purpose and passion. Because of the frustration, pain and grief of her rival, Hannah prayed her way into a miracle.

Yet, I wonder what would have happened if Penninah had not irritated and provoked Hannah. Would Hannah have been in the house of God praying with the same level of intensity, focus, and passion? I often wonder the same things about the Body of Christ.

Maybe this is why we all have Penninahs in our lives. I am sure you can think of a few Penninah's in your life right now. Just thinking about them makes your blood boil, your heart rate rise, your skin crawl and your eyes twitch.

So often, God will use your Penninahs and their attacks and ill-treatment to push you into passionate prayer and praise. For this reason, as odd as it may seem, you should thank God for your Penninahs. I know I do.

The agitation and aggravation of your Penninahs may frustrate you. However, they also make you pray more and praise God more. They unwittingly drive you into God's presence and they ultimately push you into your destiny.

ANOTHER TEST AND TESTIMONY
Strange Praise

On the day I got the worst news one could imagine that my wife to be was dying, I received the greatest revelation that her injuries are not unto death. These conflicting realities had strangely woven together both pain and praise.

The facts said she was dying and it crushed me emotionally. Try as I might, I could not stop the tears from welling up in my eyes. However, God said she would live and spiritually I was rejoicing. I felt like dancing. How strange is that?

Stranger still, what I really wanted to do was find the boy who did this to us and break his neck. The *"old me"* would have broken the boy into tiny little pieces, stomped on the remains, and did a happy dance in the immortal words of Lionel Richie *"all night long."*

Ironically, the joy of the Lord would not let these vindictive and ungodly feelings take root in me. The *"new me"* was walking in forgiveness, freedom, faith, favor and was on fire for the Lord. Trust me when I say it was nobody but God that made this strange change in me a reality.

As you can imagine, these conflicting feelings made no sense at all to me. I felt strange as an odd union of pain, petulance and praise formed in my life. Instead of rage, revenge and a ravening desire to rip the boy apart, I felt a steadily increasing joy that was unspeakable and full of glory (See 1 Peter 1:8).

The Blood of the Lamb was now covering me, the Holy Spirit had filled me, and God's word had changed me. Truly, 2 Corinthians 5:17 had taken root in my life:

> *If any man be in Christ he is a new person. Old things have passed away and all things have been made new.*

Shift In The Atmosphere

Who could have imagined that during the darkest days of my life I would develop a new identity and a deep passion for praising the Lord? How strange is that? The truth of the matter is life in Christ Jesus is full of strange things. We are after all, peculiar people serving an indescribable God.

However, when you consider that God turned the Death Angel away and spared my wife's life, I had plenty of reason to get my praise on. God was moving in my wife's life in a miraculous way and He revived her right before my very eyes.

Her prognosis quickly improved from 24 hours to live, to 48 hours to live, 72 hours to live, and so on. Her condition steadily improved from critical, to stable, to fair, to good. Day by day, the hospital staff removed the machines that were keeping her alive.

Now each visit to the hospital had a completely new feeling. My visits were no longer emotionally draining, physically exhausting, and spiritually taxing walks along the tenuous tightrope of life and death. Now each visit was a celebration of life, of God's power, and of God's goodness.

As the psalmist said, God had turned my lamentation into joyful dancing. He had taken away my clothes of mourning and clothed me with joy, that I might sing praises to Him and not be silent. O Lord my God, I will give you thanks forever! (See Psalms 30:11-12)

Over a period of three months, God moved her from the point of death to being discharge from the hospital. In so doing, God had taken us from planning a funeral service to preparing a welcome home party. We went from the devil destroying our lives to God giving us the victory.

With this new lease on life, it was time to take our lives back. It was time to take the fight to the devil using...

The Weapon of Praise

The devil was mad at my family and I. Considering all that we had gone through, the last thing he wanted to hear was my wife and I praising God and I should have known he would not go away that easy. The Bible says that every moment of ever day he is seeking people to destroy (1 Peter 5:8).

Every day we are fighting *against the ruler of the kingdom of the air, the spirit who is now at work in those who are disobedient (Ephesians 2:2)* and every day we are wrestling *against principalities and spiritual wickedness in high places (Ephesians 6:12).*

The bottom line is the world is full of demonic strongholds and wickedness (See Matthew 24:12). Make no mistake about it; their evil mayhem is directed at the body of Christ.

So what is Satan using to launch his vicious attacks? Some of his primary weapons are despair, depression, delays, debauchery, discord, division, detours, doubts, and discouragement.

Two of his primary weapons against the body of Christ are doubt and discouragement. The following old short story gives us insight into the reason why. It goes something like this...

Illustration - Satan's Garage Sale

Once upon a time, Satan was having a garage sale. There, standing in little groups were all of his bright, shiny trinkets. Here were tools that make it easy to tear others down for use as stepping stones. And over there were some lenses for magnifying one's own importance, which, if you looked through them the other way, you could also use to belittle others, or even one's self.

Against the wall was the usual assortment of gardening implements guaranteed to help your pride grow by leaps and bounds: the rake of scorn, the shovel of jealousy for digging a pit for your neighbor, the tools of gossip and backbiting, of selfishness and apathy.

All of these were pleasing to the eye and came complete with fabulous promises and guarantees of prosperity. Prices, of course, were steep; but not to worry! Free credit was extended to one and all. "Take it home, use it and you won't have to pay until later!" old Satan cried, as he hawked his wares.

The visitor, as he browsed, noticed two well worn, non-descript tools standing in one corner. Not being nearly as tempting as the other items, he found it curious that these two tools had price tags higher than any other. When he asked why, Satan just laughed and said: "Well, that's because I use them so much. If they weren't so plain looking, people might see them for what they were." Satan pointed to the two tools, saying, "You see, that one's Doubt and that one's Discouragement — and those will work when nothing else will"

Illustration Application

When you consider the ruthless and relentless attacks of Satan, it may be best to refer to each day of our lives as *"D-Day"*. D-Day is a military term meaning the day on which a battle starts. Truly, every day we are in a battle against Satan.

But, do not get worried or walleyed by Satan's weapons and weird ways. Do not be troubled by any of his deceitful tactics. Do not be afraid of any of his antics. *Do not be surprised at the fiery trials you are going through, as if something strange were happening to you. (1 Peter 4:12)*

Remember, Satan only has the power that you give him. If you do not give into his evil ways, then he has no power over your life. In fact, the deeper truth is Satan should be afraid of you and here is why.

You are not helpless, defenseless, or weaponless in this war. Heaven is on your side and the weapons you have are mighty through God. As God has declared in His word, your weapons have divine power to demolish strongholds.

Moreover, Psalms 144:1 tells us *God is our strength and He is teaching our hands to war and our fingers to fight.* With God on your side, your hands are a weapon of praise, your voice is a weapon of praise, and your life is a weapon of praise. Maybe this is why the psalmist emphatically stated *clap your hands all God's people; shout unto God with a voice of triumph (Psalms 47:1).*

He knew that praise radically changes lives. Instead of going through life dreading its challenges, praise strengthens, energizes and prepares you for the battles of life. Praise is so powerful that even the praise of children *keeps us safe and secure from our enemies and stops them in their tracks (Psalms 8:2, Good News Translation).*

In Matthew 21:16 the disciples asked Jesus *do you hear what these children are saying?" "Yes," Jesus replied. "Haven't you ever read the Scriptures? For they say, 'You have taught children and infants to give you praise.*

Literally, your praise amplifies God's presence in you and around your family, and it destroys the work of the devil

WORDS TO THE WISE
The family that praises together, is a family that will stay together.

at the same time. It sets the stage for God's favor to move in your household. Now imagine your entire family praising the Lord. Your family will *"Thrive in the Fires of Life".*

In the past, praise may not have been your weapon of choice. However, once you try it and you see how well it works, you will never put it down again. Praise devastates the *principalities, powers, rulers of the darkness in this world, and the spiritual wickedness that is working against all of us (Ephesians 6:12).*

Instead of sitting back in suspense hoping Satan will leave you alone, your praise takes the fight to the enemy. Now instead of hoping Satan's plans will not affect you, with uplifted voices, uplifted hands and uplifted hearts your praise destroys the enemy's plans before they can cause havoc in your life.

The Battle of the Five Armies

Again, I say with uplifted voices, uplifted hands and uplifted hearts your praise destroys the enemy's plans before they can come to fruition. This is exactly what happened for King Jehoshaphat and the children of Israel in 2 Chronicles 20.

War was at Israel's door and they had nowhere to run and nowhere to hide. Surrounded by the armies of Ammon, Moab, and Mt. Seir, unless God intervened, everything they had would be desecrated or destroyed.

Put yourself and your family in their predicament. It would be like waking up in the morning knowing you are going to lose your home, your job, your family, and finally your life before the sun goes down. Everything that you love, own and worked hard for will be gone before the day is over. What would you do?

The children of Israel chose to praise the Lord and it was their praise that changed the balance of power on the battlefield. Now, instead of four armies fighting in battle, Ammon, Moab, Mt. Seir against Israel, their praise enlisted a fifth and far more powerful army...

...the Army of the Lord

It is an Army whose Commander in Chief is the *King of kings and the Lord of Lords (Revelations 19:16)*. John the Revelator described the Commander of Lord's army in this magnificent scene in Revelations 19 when he wrote:

> *11 And I saw heaven opened, and behold a white horse; and he that sat upon him was called Faithful and True, and in righteousness he doth judge and make war. 12 His eyes were as a flame of fire, and on his head were many crowns; and he had a name written, that no man knew, but he himself. 13 And he was clothed with a vesture dipped in blood: and his name is called The Word of God. 14 And the armies which were in heaven followed him upon white horses, clothed in fine linen,*

white and clean. 15 And out of his mouth goeth a sharp sword, that with it he should smite the nations: and he shall rule them with a rod of iron: and he treadeth the winepress of the fierceness and wrath of Almighty God. 16 And he hath on his vesture and on his thigh a name written, King Of Kings, And Lord Of Lords.

Joel 2:11 states, *"The Lord thunders at the head of his army; his forces are beyond number, and mighty is the army that obeys his command"*. King Jehoshaphat wisely enlisted the Lord's army when he *appointed singers unto the Lord, and that should praise the beauty of holiness, as they went out before the army, and to say, Praise the Lord; for his mercy endures forever (2 Chronicles 20:21).*

The Bible tells us that *"a choir"* went first into battle, clothed in sanctified garments and singing the song *"His Loving-Kindness Is Forever"* as they walked along praising and thanking the Lord!

They did not grab weapons, they did not seek the safety of shelter, and they did not retreat. They grab their faith, their musicians, their instruments, and their praise. The Bible says they bowed their head with their faces to the ground as *all of Judah and the inhabitants of Jerusalem fell before the Lord, worshiping the Lord (2 Chronicles 20:18).*

Now, as spiritual as we are, we must admit it takes a whole lot of faith to go to war with choir members, musical instruments and a handful of hymnbooks. That is exactly what the children of Israel did.

Instead of engaging in all-out war, they went to war by lifting up the Lord in praise. This single act of spiritual bravery changed the balance of power. Their praise restructured the battlefield in their favor and it armed the power of heaven on their behalf.

You see where there is heartfelt praise there will be an increase in God's presence. Now the armies of Ammon, Moab, and Mt. Seir were marching into a setup. It was a setup put in place by Israel's praise.

It was in this atmosphere of praise that God launched a surprise attack on Israel's enemies. The Bible in 2 Chronicles 20:22 says as Israel *began to sing and praise, the Lord set ambushes against their enemies and their enemies were defeated.* The battle was over. That's the power of praise.

Your Secret Weapon

If you really want to take the presence and power of God working in your life to another level, in addition to praising your way through, walk in humility. Humility is lowliness of mind and a deep sense of one's own unworthiness in the sight of God.

Micah 6:8 says *"the Lord has told you what is good, and this is what he requires of you: to do what is right, to love mercy, and to walk humbly with your God."* The following scriptures sum up Humility's power:

> *If my people who are called by my name will "humble" themselves and pray, seek my face, and turn from their wicked ways, then will I hear from heaven, forgive their sin, and heal their land (2 Chronicles 7:14).*

> *Humble yourself under the mighty hand of God He will lift you up (James 4:10; 1 Peter 5:6).*

God Fights for You

Humility says to God, *"I give my life to you. I replace my plans with Your plans".* Humility acknowledges that God's ways are greater than ours are and His thoughts are far superior to ours (See Isaiah 55). Humility keeps you from getting ahead of God and it allows the plan of God to unfold in your life.

Numbers 12:3 says *Moses was a very humble man, more humble than anyone else on the face of the earth.* However, Moses was not perfect. He had a number of shortcomings. He made mistakes, he doubted God, and he even mocked God in front of the people (See Numbers 20:1-12, Exodus 17:4, Numbers 11:10-15).

Nevertheless, Moses experienced some of the greatest moves of God recorded in the Bible. He spoke to God face-to-face as a friend (Exodus 3:1-6). We have an example of this at the burning bush, when God turned the rod in his hand to a serpent and when God healed Moses' hand of leprosy.

Don't forget about the move of God that happened when he used Moses to release a series of unprecedented plagues upon the Egyptians (Exodus 7-11). Furthermore, we have the instance when God used Moses to divide the Red Sea (See Exodus 13-14)

In the wilderness, God used Moses to feed a whole nation with quail, manna from heaven, and water flowing from a rock (See Exodus 16-17) and God even met with Moses in the mountain to give him the Ten Commandments on tablets of stone (See Exodus 31; 34).

If that's not enough, in Numbers 12 when Miriam defiantly confronted Moses, Moses did not have to fight back, because God fought for him. Instantly Miriam was stricken with leprosy. That's the power of humility. When you are humble, God fights for you.

Access to God's Glory

Exodus 33 and 34 provides one of the most powerful accounts of God interacting with man in the Word of God. Moses asked God to *"Show me thy glory." (Exodus 33:18).* In Chapter 34 verses 5-6 God grants his request as the Bible records *the LORD descended in the cloud, and stood with him there, any proclaimed the name of the Lord. The Lord passed by him there.*

Those who understand humility understand the power of God that manifest when we humble ourselves under His mighty hand (1 Peter 5:6). We are not concerned with mischaracterizations of humility as weakness. Many may see it as a weakness. However, to us who know better it is one of the fastest ways up and into God's presence when life is holding you down.

Satan knows when you are humble, God will lift you up and no power in hell can hold you down. He knows when you are humble, God fights for you and no one can defeat you. He knows when you are humble, God will give you the victory and no one can take it away.

Satan knows that praise and humility are too much for him to handle. It puts him in his rightful place – disarmed, defeated, dethroned, and under your feet where he belongs.

Hitting Satan with a lethal combination of humility and praise is like poison on the tip of an arrow. If the arrow does not kill the enemy, the poison on the dart most certainly will. That is what humility and praise are to Satan. Again, I say humility is spiritual might, not physical weakness.

Your Evil Nemesis

Pride is man's evil nemesis and it is lethal. It is having a deep pleasure or a warped sense of satisfaction from one's own achievements. It is having excessive self-esteem and an inflated self-perception.

Pride redirects your praise and worship from God to yourself. It makes *"you"* number one in your life, not God. It makes *"you"* the center of attention in your own mind, not God.

It also makes you vulnerable to Satan's attacks as it creates a demonic doorway into your life. Unfortunately, in an age of arrogance, individuality, and over confidence at the highest level, people are more concerned with praising themselves, not God. That's got problems written all over it.

I am a firm believer that, *"You are what you praise".* Jeremiah the prophet said of the children of Israel, instead of following God *they followed worthless idols and became worthless themselves." (Jeremiah 2:5).* Pastor Jack Hayford said:

> *"Worship changes the worshiper into the image of the one worshiped".*

In other words, we are what we worship. Those who *"worship God"* in spirit and in truth will display godlike characteristics and more importantly *the Father is looking for people like that to worship him (John 4:23).*

However, those who *"worship themselves"* will have ungodly characteristics as pride fills their heart with darkness and it changes their very nature. In the book of Jeremiah, the children of Israel began to act like what they praised. Over time, they developed characteristics of what they paid tribute too.

For these reasons, Satan would love nothing more than for pride to fill your life. Satan knows pride feeds your ego. He knows a Christian filled with pride is full of self. He knows praise ushers in God's presence, but pride pushes God's presence out.

Satan knows where there is praise God fights for you, but where there is pride God works against you. He also knows where there is pride there will be increased bondage, burdens, brokenness and other bad things.

That is why Satan wants you arrogant, egotistical and overly confident. He does not care what you have, what you do, or what you know. He does not care about what you drive, where you live, or what you do for a living. As long as pride fills your life, Satan is satisfied.

The Devil's Demise

Satan knows from his own experience the lethalness of pride. The Bible says Satan's pride lifted him up and God threw him out of heaven. Jesus in speaking about Satan's demise said in Luke 10, *"I saw Satan fall like lightening."*

Isaiah 14:12-14 reads:

> *How you have fallen from heaven, O star of the morning, son of the dawn! You have been cut down to the earth, you who have weakened the nations! But you said in your heart, 'I will ascend to heaven; I will raise my throne above the stars of God.*

Ezekiel 28:16-17 reads:

> I destroyed you, O Guardian Angel, from the midst of
> the stones of fire. Your heart was filled with pride because
> of all your beauty; you corrupted your wisdom for the sake
> of your splendor. Therefore, I have cast you down to the
> ground.

In verses 18-19 God said:

> I brought forth fire from your own actions and let it burn
> you to ashes upon the earth in the sight of all those
> watching you. 19 All who know you are appalled at your
> fate; you are an example of horror; you are destroyed
> forever.

Illustrations –Pride Kills

Pride is to the Christian what kryptonite is to
Superman. It zaps your God given power, leaving you
weak, defenseless and vulnerable. It has a negative impact
on your thinking, your body, your soul, your spirit, your
relationship with God and everything about you.

Pride is like a powerful python, a deadly boa
constrictor, or a massive anaconda. Once it has a grip on
you, it will slowly wrap its coils around your life, until it
crushes, suffocates, and then devours everything good and
godly in your life.

Pride is like a bite from a poisonous black mamba, a
venomous viper or a lethal rattlesnake. Its fast acting
venom will make your salvation shaky, your ability to
breathe in the breath of God extremely difficult, and it will
make your heartbeat out of rhythm with God's timing.

A person infected with pride will have a toxic soul. A
person infected with pride has a disillusioned mind. A
person infected with pride has a contaminated and
comatose spirit.

If left untreated it will culminate in spiritual paralysis
and death. Once again, I must reiterate pride is lethal. It is
one of the fastest ways to destroy your destiny in God.

Illustration Application

The aforementioned scriptures and illustrations draw attention to the dire consequences of pride in our lives. Had Moses walked in pride, only God knows what impact it would have had on the entire nation of Israel enslaved in Egypt and wandering in the wilderness.

However, here is what we do know from looking at the life of Satan, pride can take us from positions of prestige and power, and put us

WORDS TO THE WISE
Pride is demonic, destructive, and deadly. Avoid it at all cost. If you do not it just might cost you your life.

on the path of devastation and defeat in a matter of moments.

Matthew 23:12 makes it clear that those who lift themselves up in pride will be brought down. The Bible says, *"Pride goes before destruction, a haughty spirit before a fall"* (*Proverbs 16:18*). Proverbs 29:23 says, *"A man's pride brings him low"*.

However, it will not be Satan bringing you down or causing calamity to come your way. It will be God. He says in Isaiah 13:11 *"I will put an end to the arrogance of the haughty and will humble the pride of the ruthless"*. Remember what happened to King Herod in Acts 12:21-23:

> *Wearing his royal robes, he sat on his throne and delivered a public address to the people. The people shouted, "This is the voice of a God, not of a man." Immediately, because Herod did not give praise to God, an angel of the Lord struck him down, and he was eaten by worms and died.*

Benson's Commentary tells us God will not delay when it comes to defending His honor. King Herod did not give God the glory. He did not reject the blasphemous and offensive applause of men. He willingly received it and pride filled his heart. As a result, he lost his life. My friend don't let this be you.

Praise and Pain

I believe that praise without the experience of pain is just music. It is going through the motions. It is the repeating of words and the following of dance steps. It's learned behavior, its mimicry, its cognitive conditioning.

Almost anyone can learn the words to a song. Anyone can learn the moves to a particular dance. Therefore, singing and dancing in and of themselves are not the fullness of praise.

Now, please do not misunderstand me. I love gospel music. It is absolutely awesome. I love to hear a gathering of people all lifting up the name of the Lord in song and dance. It's powerful. I enjoy dancing and getting my praise on just as much as the next Christian does. The Bible says *let everything that has breath, praise the Lord." (Psalms 150:6).*

However, I believe that praise without the experience of pain is like preparing a meal without adding a critical ingredient. It is still a good meal, its edible, and it is good for you. But, it just does not taste the same.

Praise without a sprinkle of pain is missing something. It still sounds good. It is valuable. But, it just is not the same.

On the other hand, genuine praise that is born out of the pain, pressure and persecution of our past is powerful. It demonstrates itself in sincere and unfiltered appreciation and adoration to God.

In fact, our praise moves to a higher dimension through the experience of pain. This move is so profound and so radical that if Satan truly understood the impact that pain has on your praise he would leave you alone.

That is what happened for Paul and Silas in Acts 16:23-26. They had been beaten, chained and shackled, and thrown into prison. Now they had a choice to make.

They could complain, get mad at God, or even give up on their service to the Kingdom. After all, it was the work they were doing for the Lord that landed them in jail. Nevertheless, at midnight they choose to pray and sing praises to God.

The agony and discomfort of their imprisonment incubated their praise. They chose to use their pain and distress as the canvass upon which they painted their praise.

While they were praying and praising the Lord *suddenly there came a great earthquake, so that the foundations of the prison were shaken; and immediately all the doors were opened and everyone's chains were unfastened (Acts 16:26).* What a mighty move of God and it was initiated by their praise.

They were not just singing, going through the motion, or praying to get the mind off the situation. This was prayer and praise intensified by their pain. The results of their praise speak for itself as *"everyone's chains were loosed!"*

Don't Let It Steal Your Praise

"It" is anything, anyone or any situation that can so affect you that you are unable to complete the task that God has given you. They come in many different shapes, sizes and colors. The death of a love one, a debilitating disease, the loss of a job, getting passed over for a promotion, a bitter divorce, long-standing sibling rivalry, family member battling a drug addiction, financial turmoil, or some other painful or difficult set of circumstances.

We all face demanding situations. Regardless of what *"it"* is, the reality is these situations will haunt, harass and hinder you if you let them. When you spend your time complaining, having a pity party, getting mad and fixated on getting even you have allowed the situation to steal your praise. When you engage in senseless nitpicking or discontented murmuring, the situation has robbed you of your praise.

My friend these are the moments in life Satan is waiting for because they open the door for him. After he steals your praise, he will steal other things as well such as your joy, your peace, and your faith. However, he will not stop there. He will continue his quest to kill and to destroy everything good and godly about you (See John 10:10).

However, for the Christian who understands the power of praise, it is a mistake of the enemy to hurt, harass, or harm you. These experiences will ignite our passion and give potency to our praise. In so doing, we turn our attention away from the pain and problems and we put it on God.

This is important because you will embrace, emulate and emanate the characteristics of what you focus on. Said differently, you will:

- *"Accept" the things that you give your attention to*

- *"Attach" yourself to those things that occupy your mind*

- *"Act" out those things that influence your thinking*

For example, in Matthew 14:22-33, when the Apostle Peter focused on the Lord he walked on the water. He embraced the impossible. He accepted the opportunity given to him. He acted upon God's power by doing the impossible. He defied gravity and the laws of physics by walking on the water.

However, when his focus changed and he took his attention off the Lord immediately he started to sink. When he gave his attention to the storm the power of God, cease to operate in his life. Then, as he was sinking in the storm, he regained his focus and said *Lord save me.* Immediately Jesus lifted him up.

The difference in Peter walking on the water and him sinking in the storm was his focus. When he focused on Christ, miracle-working power operated in his life. When he was not, instantly the power was gone.

Similarly, when we focus on Jesus and we are drawn into His presence, we are empowered to do the impossible. That is just one of many reasons why perpetual praise is paramount to your success. It keeps you focused on God through the storms of life.

So once again, I must reiterate. Do not let the things you go through and the pain you endure steal your praise. In the time of trouble, don't dwell on the devil's shenanigans, let your life, your lips and your light *"Shout unto God with a voice of triumph!" (Psalms 47:1)*

In Concluding This Chapter

The Bible says there is a time for everything under the sun. There is a *"time to weep, and a time to laugh, a time to mourn, and a time to dance" (Ecclesiastes 3:4).* I submit for your consideration that any time is the right time to praise the Lord.

David knew this when he wrote *I will bless the Lord at all times and his praise shall continually be in my mouth (Psalms 34:1).* He goes on to say *I sought the Lord and He heard me and delivered me from all of my fears (Psalms 34:4).* He continues by saying *many are the afflictions of the righteous but the Lord delivereth him of them all (Psalms 34:19).*

While David focused on God, the problems, issues, and challenges in his life became minuscule in comparison to the greater presence of God working in his situation. Similarly, in Acts 16 the Apostle Paul praises the greatness of God and in 2 Timothy 3:11 he wrote that *"he endured persecutions and afflictions: out of them all the Lord delivered him."*

David and Paul were praisers. David was known for his psalms that magnify the Lord and Paul was known for his prayer and praise that shook the foundation of the earth and broke open the doors of his prison. It did not matter what time, day or night; or what the situation was, good or bad – they praised the Lord.

My advice to you is don't foolishly wait until after you receive a blessing to give God the praise. If you do, your difficult situations may last longer than they should. If you do, you will delay the manifestation of miracles. If you do, you will miss the essential encounters that you need with the Lord.

Instead of waiting to praise the Lord, I encourage you to glorify God in all things and at all times. I encourage you to praise your way through the

WORDS TO THE WISE

Every time you enter into God's presence with praise, God enters your life with more power!

storms of life. I am convinced that the intensity, focus, and timeliness of your praise directly effects:

- *The magnitude of your breakthrough and deliverance*

- *The level of your blessings and favor*

- *The extent of the divine transformation of your life*

One of the fastest ways to bring about your deliverance is to respond with a spirit of praise in the storms of life. The key is to praise God until the move of God you are waiting for in your life happens. But you can't stop there, your praise must be perpetual.

As King David said, you must bless the Lord at all times and His praise must continually be in your mouth. As Psalms 71:14 reads, *I will hope continually and will praise God yet more and more.*

Chapter 8

Activating Your Anointing

LETTING GOD'S POWER STRETCH OUT IN YOU

"You have an unction of the Holy One"
(1 John 2:20)

WE NEED POWER and power can come from a variety of sources. For example, when my wife was in the intensive care unit at Bayfront Medical Center, life support machines provided the power she needed to stay alive. There was a ventilator for her breathing, heart monitors, pulse meters, oxygen, temperature meter, pulmonary artery catheter, arterial lines, chest tubes and a host of other medical gadgets.

My wife's life was totally dependent upon these machines and the machines were totally dependent upon a continuous supply of power to work properly. If the power supplied to the ventilator were turned off her life would be over. Thus, an uninterrupted supply of power is critical to a hospital's infrastructure. Patient's lives are dependent upon it. My wife's life depended on it.

Divine Power Supply

Just as my wife and other patients were dependent upon the machines and power, we are dependent upon God's presence and His power. Take these away and life as we know it will cease. Thankfully, our God is everywhere at all times, all power is in His hands, and His power is always available unto us (See Exodus 15:6; Job 26:14; Psalms 62:11).

To some, God is known as Elohim, the God who has all power. Others call him Jehovah, the God of everything. Still others know Him as Jehovah Jireh, the God who provides, Jehovah Nissi, the God who protects us and Jehovah O'saynu, the God our Maker.

When Moses prepared for his meeting with Pharaoh, he asked God who should I say sent me. God replied, tell him *I AM sent you (Exodus 3:14).* In other words, tell Pharaoh the God in which no name, no word and no phrase can fully define sent you.

In fact, He is so powerful that He can *"ride"* the heavens (See Deuteronomy 33:26). Job says God:

> *Spreads out the northern skies over empty space; he suspends the earth over nothing. 8 He wraps up the waters in his clouds, yet the clouds do not burst under their weight. 9 He covers the face of the full moon, spreading his clouds over it. 10 He marks out the horizon on the face of the waters for a boundary between light and darkness. 11 The pillars of the heavens quake, aghast at his rebuke. 12 By his power he churned up the sea; by his wisdom he cut Rahab to pieces. 13 By his breath the skies became fair; his hand pierced the gliding serpent. 14 And these are but the outer fringe of his works; how faint the whisper we hear of him! (Job 26:7-14)*

Job further acknowledges God's power when he said *I know that thou canst do everything, and that no thought can be withholden from thee.* The Living Bible reads *I know that you can do anything and that no one can stop you. (Job 42:2).* Job then asks the question *"Who then can understand the thunder of His power?"* Similarly, Moses asked the question *who is like unto thee, O Lord, among the Gods? Who is like thee, magnificent in holiness, fearful in praises, doing wonders?" (Exodus 15:11)*

God is the highest authority over all things, at all times and in all places. The Bible says *Our God is in the heavens, and he does as he wishes (Psalms 115:3). If he snatches away, who can stop him? Who can say to him, 'What are you doing?' (Job 9:12).* God is absolutely awesome and stands in a category all by Himself.

Thus, the answer to the questions asked by Job and Moses are answered in 1 Kings 8:23, *there is no god like our God (See 1 Kings 8:23).* His power is beyond comprehension, His might is unknowable and His magnificent greatness is unfathomable. The bottom line is power belongs to God!

Activating God's Power

When God's power is working in our lives, we can *"do all things through Christ who strengthens us. (Philippians 4:13)* Thus, we are who we are and we do what we do because of God's presence and power in our lives. Jesus confirms this in John 15:5 when He said *apart from Me you can do nothing.*

The questions you and I must answer are what good is life without the power of God to overcome its struggles? With trouble pressing you on every side, what value is there in *"knowing"* about God's power and not *"having"* it at work in your life?

In James 4:7 God gives us a strategy to turn on His power in our lives. *"Submit yourselves to God. Resist the devil and he will flee from you."* It's just that simple.

The first and most critical step is *to "submit"* yourself to God. It begins with salvation and continues as we daily yield or surrender to God's authority. Submitting yourself to God means giving your body as a living sacrifice and allowing God to transform your mind (Romans 12:1-2).

This leads into the second step, you must *"resist"* the devil. Resisting the devil is the conscious, deliberate action on your part to say no to ungodly behaviors, to cast down evil imaginations and rebuke sinful desires in your life (See 2 Corinthians 10:5). Resisting the devil means refusing to give him any place in your life. It means choosing to live a good and godly life (See 2 Timothy 3:12).

Simply knowing James 4:7 is not enough. Submitting to God is not the end of our requirements. The onus is on you and I to resist the devil and no one can do this for us. It is a vital part of your life as a Christian.

At the City of Refuge Christian Church of Florida, we believe that a person who becomes a believer no longer pursues the appetites of this world. Additionally, we believe in the sanctifying power of the Holy Ghost by whose indwelling Christians can live a holy life.

Living according to James 4:7 will turn God's power on in your life. His light begins illuminating your life. Your dominion over Satan is established. Satan's attacks against you lose their effectiveness and he has no choice but to flee from you.

This is a Biblical truth, it is a spiritual law that you can activate in your life right now. James 4:7 does not require a lengthy explanation, nor does it require deep revelation. It only takes the willingness and determination to apply these two life changing steps given to us by God in the book of James.

Illustration - Flip the Switch

One day I was sitting in my bedroom working on this book. It was a beautiful day outside. The sun was shining bright and there was not a cloud in the sky. The curtains were open and the natural light of the sun provided the perfect ambiance for working on this book.

I had been typing for several hours and was totally engrossed in my work. I was so focused on getting this project done that I did not realize the sun had gone down. The room had slowly grown darker as the light of the sun had gradually gone away.

I could have continued to work in the darkness. I could have kept typing, but it would have been much harder and some things would have been impossible. I would be unable to read the books and resource materials or to enjoy all the room had to offer. It was obvious that I needed more light.

Now, it would make no sense to ask God to bring the sun back up or for God to fill the room with light. Could He do it, yes He could. But, some things are common since, have practical solutions and should not be over complicated with weird acts of spirituality.

I simply got up from my chair, walked over to the light switched, flipped the light switch on *"and there was light."* Problem solved. There was nothing deep, mystical or super spiritual about that. It was a conscious decision to do something that was in my power to do. I merely flipped the switch.

Illustration Application

James 4:7 is your light switch. There is no need to complicate the issue of God's power in your life with elaborate, extensive, flamboyant prayers. Sadly, such actions are more often than not a parading of the flesh.

More often than not, they are attention getters. They are misguided attempts at spirituality. They make for tantalizing television, and entertaining church services, revivals, camp meetings, and similar church events.

The way I see it there is no sense in over complicating the issue. You need God's light. You need God's power. You need victory over Satan. James gives you and me a simple formula to do just that.

- *Submit yourself to God*

- *Resist the devil's temptation*

- *He will flee from you*

When you do, you turn on God's power in your life. Instantly His light begins shining in your life and the devil and the darkness and thoughts of doom he brings are gone. Problem solved. That was easy!

Welcome Holy Spirit

I do not argue that we all need power. I do not argue there are different sources of power. However, the power that trumps all and that we must have can only come from the *"Ruach HaKodesh"* also known as God's Holy Spirit. It is an *"Incomparably great power for us who believe (Ephesians 1:19)* and it is:

> Far above all rule and authority and power and dominion, and every name that is named, not only in this age but also in the one to come (Ephesians 1:21).

Thus, any power that seeks to replicate God's divine power supply is an imitation, inadequate, inappropriate, ill fated, and illegal. Knowing this, Jesus told his disciples to *"wait"* in Jerusalem until they received the power of the Holy Spirit. The disciples knew the Word of God and they knew their assignment.

However, knowing the word and knowing what to do are not enough. There was to be no preaching, no teaching, and no laying-on of hands *"until"* they received God's power. In Luke 24:49 they are directed to stay in the city until the Holy Spirit comes and fills them with the power from heaven. In Acts 1:4-5; 8, He commanded them that they:

> Should not depart from Jerusalem, but wait for the promise of the Father, which, saith he, ye have heard of me. For John truly baptized with water; but ye shall be

baptized with the Holy Ghost not many days hence. But ye shall receive power, after that the Holy Ghost is come upon you

Likewise, we must do the same. Knowing the Word of God is not enough. Knowing your assignment is not enough. There should be no preaching, no teaching, and no laying-on of hands *"until"* we receive God's power.

God knows we need it. Jesus died so we could receive it. The Holy Spirit has come to release it. Finally, in Acts 2:2 the promised manifestation of the Holy Spirit occurred when *suddenly a sound like the blowing of a violent wind came from heaven and filled the whole house.*

At that moment, the promised presence and power of the Spirit of God was released. At that moment, the Holy Spirit filled, empowered, and set the disciples apart. At that moment, the New Testament Church in all of its splendor was born and the gates of hell cannot prevail against it.

Regarding the filling of the Spirit, Micah the prophet declared, *"I am filled with power, with the Spirit of the Lord."* We call this filling, the anointing or the baptism of the Holy Spirit. The scriptures confirm this act of divine empowerment:

- *Receive the Holy Spirit*
  (John 20:22)

- *The Holy Spirit abides with you and will be in you*
  (John 14:17)

- *Jesus will baptize you with the Holy Spirit and fire*
  (Matthew 3:11)

- *You will be baptized with the Holy Spirit*
  (Acts 1:5)

- *The disciples were all filled with the Holy Spirit*
  (Acts 2:4)

- *They were all filled with the Holy Spirit*
  (Acts 4:31)

- *The Holy Spirit fell upon all those who heard the word*
  (Acts 10:44)

- *The Holy Spirit came on them*
  (Acts 19:6)

- *Be filled with the Spirit*
  (Ephesians 5:18)

Once the disciples received God's power in Acts chapter 2 there is an explosion of miracles, signs, wonders, and other supernatural manifestations and revelations:

- *Peter heals a lame man*
  (Acts 3:1-11)

- *Ananias and Sapphira are exposed*
  (Acts 5:1-10)

- *People healed by Peter's shadow*
  (Acts 5:12-16)

- *Peter heals Eneas of a palsy*
  (Acts 9:33-34)

- *Tabitha is raised from the dead*
  (Acts 9:36-41)

- *Sorcerer smitten with blindness*
  (Acts 13:6-11)

- *Paul heals a cripple*
  (Acts 14:8-10)

- *Spirit of divination cast out*
  (Acts 16:16-18)

- *Paul and Silas freed from prison*
  (Acts 16:25-26)

- *Multitude healed by special miracles
  (Acts 19:11-12)*

- *Paul raises Eutychus from the dead
  (Acts 20:9-12)*

- *Paul bitten by viper and felt no harm
  (Acts 28:3-6)*

- *Paul heals the father of Publius and others
  (Acts 28:7-9)*

Additionally, there will be manifestations of the Fruit of the Spirit, which are *Love, Joy, Peace, Long-Suffering, Gentleness, Goodness, Faith, Meekness, and Temperance (Galatians 5:22-23).* Furthermore, there will be manifestations of the Gifts of the Spirit, which are *Wisdom, Knowledge, Faith, Healing, Miracles, Prophecy, Discernment, Tongues, Interpretation of Tongues, Administration, and Helps (1 Corinthians 12:8-11)* .

Moreover, the Holy Spirit will establishes and seal you in Christ Jesus (2 Corinthians 1:21-22). He will destroy the yokes of bondage in your life (Isaiah 10:27) and strengthen your mind, fortify your soul and quicken your spirit.

These benefits of the Holy Spirit are vital because Satan is crafty. He is a master at usurping authority, controlling a person's mind, stealing their soul, and crushing their spirit. These are the areas that Satan is most interested.

He does not want your house, your car, your money or similar things. He may use these things to launch his attack, but he does not want these things. What he really wants is your mind, soul and spirit. He does not want your stuff. *Satan desires to have you (Luke 22:31)*

This is why Jesus told the disciples to *"stay in the city until you have been clothed with power from on high." (Luke 24:49).* The disciples would have been no match for Satan without God's power. Likewise, we are no match for Satan without God's power. We need the *Ruach HaKodesh*, the Holy Spirit.

Now that we have the power of the Holy Spirit, we must walk in it. That's what the disciples did. That's what the Apostles did and that's what we must do as well.

Spiritual Dyne-o-might

The Holy Spirit changes everything when He enters our lives. Not only does He build us up (See Jude 20-25), but His power destroys the work of the devil (1 John 3:8).

We often refer to the Holy Spirit's power as *"Dunamis"* power. The word dunamis appears more than 120 times in the New Testament alone. According to Strong's Concordance, it is the empowerment to succeed in all things through the supernatural gifting of God.

When you consider the trials we face and the weakness of man, it is easy to see that the Holy Spirit and the power that He brings are paramount for our success. The Apostle Paul knew this when he said his *faith was not built upon the wisdom of man, but in the power of God (1 Corinthians 2:5).*

If I had simply listened to the wisdom of man and not trusted in the power of the Holy Spirit, I would recommended taking my wife off life support hours after the car accident and buried her a few days later. My daughters Keona and Kenya would have never been born.

This is why you can never stop believing in the Holy Spirit and the miracles, signs and wonders of God. We see this in Acts 19:11-12. Surrounded by a group of sick and hurting people, the Holy Spirit worked:

> *Extraordinary miracles" through the Apostle Paul so that even handkerchiefs or aprons that had touched him were brought to the sick, and the diseases left them and the evil spirits went out of them.*

Dunamis power is spiritual dynamite and Satan does not want you to possess it. He does not mind you attending church, singing in the choir or dancing. He does not mind you having money, success, fortune and fame. He does not mind you being popular, pretty or prestigious.

However, the last thing he wants is for you to operate in dunamis power. But, there's nothing he can do to stop it from happening once the Holy Spirit has come upon you (See Acts 1:8).

Illustration – Check Your Connection

One day I brought my wife a new Apple laptop computer. It came with the latest software, bells and whistles. I quickly set it up for her so she could get started on her newest book *"Get Delivered from the Saints"*.

Girlfriend was excited like a kid on Christmas. She pressed the power button and to her dismay, nothing happened. That's not good!

I double-checked that the AC adapter was connected to the computer. Sure enough, it was. I checked to ensure it was plugged into the wall outlet. Sure enough, it was. Again, I pressed the power button and nothing happened. This brand new computer was useless.

Before calling Apple, I took one more look at the connections. Ah ha! The AC power cord connection was not secure. They looked as if they were connected. However, when I took a closer look, there was a tiny break in the connection preventing the flow of power. Once I secured the connection, she pressed the power button, and the computer came on. Problem solved.

Illustration Application

Just as a computer with a bad power cord connection is useless, the same is true of Christians. If our connection with God is bad or broken, then we are no different from a computer without power. We are useless and of little value to the Kingdom.

In fact, a Christian with a poor connection and no power will do more harm than good. There are no ifs, ands, or buts about it. Just look around the world and the

Church today, the impact of misguided, disconnected, powerless Christians is readily apparent.

Instead of rebuking sin and walking in righteousness, many are approving and participating in Satan's evil ways. Even worst, they are encouraging others to do the same. It is an indication that their connection with God is broken and His power is not actively flowing in their lives.

Thus, we can have the best intentions. We can have the best plan. We can have the best support. However, if we do not have a good connection with the Holy Spirit and His power flowing in our lives, there is nothing we can do to overcome Satan's attacks. He can easily disrupt our days, destroy our dreams and devastate our destiny.

Fight Power With Power

The New Testament reveals a steady increase in demonic power. We can see this during the earthly ministry of Jesus Christ. *"A great deal of Jesus' ministry was devoted to exorcising evil spirits or demons." (Betty, 2005, p. 13)*

One could argue that during Jesus' three and a half year ministry, there were more references to demonic activity, influence, oppression and possession than in all of the Old Testament books combined.

The level of cruelty, suppression, and torment is noticeably increased. On one occasion, a demonic spirit in a possessed man told Jesus *my name is Legion because there are so many of us inside of him (See Mark 5:9; Luke 8:30).*

It is an indication of the magnitude and severity of demonic warfare that was manifesting in the earth at that time. Matthew Henry Concise commentary in discussing the demonic possession in these scriptures reads:

> *A legion of soldiers consisted of six thousand men, or more. What multitudes of fallen spirits there must be, and all enemies to God and man, when here was a legion in one poor wretched creature!*

But, this is just one example of one man possessed by an untold number of demons. Now consider these evil spirits are still at work in the world today. The evidence of this evil activity is staggering.

In a 2001 article researchers noted that incidents of demonic interference since 1960 have become *"virtually an explosion."* In a 2015 article, it is noted:

> There is mounting evidence today that evil spirits do oppress and occasionally even possess the unwary, the weak, the unprepared, the unlucky, or the targeted (Betty, 2005, p. 14)

In Revelations 12:12, the Apostle John warned us of such evil activity when he wrote *woe to the earth and the sea, because the devil has gone down to you! He is filled with fury, because he knows that his time is short.*

Critics would argue that demonic activity is a myth. That demonic power, influence, oppression and possession are the stuff of fairy tales. I say the proof is in the pudding. Just look around our world today. It does not take a doctorate in theology or advanced training in demonology to see Satan's evil ways are running amuck in our society.

But it takes power to fight power. It takes the power of the Holy Spirit to defeat demonic powers. There is no doubt in my mind, there is a greater level of demonic power, activity, influence and possession today, than any time in human history. This is one reason why we need the power of the anointing.

So, imagine a person without the power of the Holy Spirit flowing in their life trying to fight against Satan. Imagine a person with nothing more than *"a form of godliness"* trying to rebuke demons.

Imagine a person who is not walking in James 4:7 trying to challenge evil spirits. Because they *"are not"* submitted to God, they *"cannot"* resist the devil. As a result, Satan *"will not"* flee from them. That has got problems written all over it.

Instead of fleeing from them, Satan will get more involved and his evil ways more pervasive in their life. He knows that any effort to fight back in our own might, typically ends up in a good old fashion, sons of Sceva beat down (See Acts 19:11-20). *The evil spirit jumped on them and overpowered them all. The attack was so violent that they ran out of the house, naked and wounded.*

Don't Be Fooled

Do not be naïve, demonic powers such as magic and witchcraft are widespread in the world today (See Colossians 1:3; Ephesians 6:12; Luke 22:53; 2 Corinthians 4:4). They may appear to be harmless games and people who are using these *"dark powers"* may seem helpful.

The truth is Satan is using things that look good, feel great or seem right to entice people away from God. All while he is slowly persuading them to let their guard down. Do not be fooled. Playing with such things is risky, costly and deadly.

Sadly a growing number of people think influence, oppression and possession by demonic powers is not real (Malia as cited by Stafford Betty, 2005, p 14). That is because we have mistakenly associated demonic possession with a person's head spinning around, spitting up profusely, their bed violently shaking, and their bodies levitating in the air.

Don't be fooled, this isn't Hollywood. The power of darkness is real. Just because a person is not showing physiological issues (Matthew 12:12), or unusual habits (Luke 8:27), is not out of control (Matthew 8:28) or they are not acting violently (Acts 19:16) does not mean they are not demonically influenced, oppressed or possessed.

My advice to you my friend is don't play with it. Even if something that is sinful looks harmless, spiritual or even beneficial, it isn't. Sin is sin, evil is evil, and wrong is wrong regardless of how right they may seem in the minds of men.

Unfortunately, demonic activity often goes undetected because many in our society consider devilish, diabolical and demonic things nice, normal and necessary. Many people consider dark powers, magic, witchcraft, mediums, palm readers, clairvoyants, spiritualists, tarot card readers, and people involved in similar activities to be helpful. How demonic is that?

Regardless of what men may think, God forbids it. His word says:

> *Let no one be found among you who sacrifices their son or daughter in the fire, who practices divination or sorcery, interprets omens, engages in witchcraft, 11 or casts spells, or who is a medium or spiritist or who consults the dead. 12 Anyone who does these things is detestable to the Lord; because of these same detestable practices the Lord your God will drive out those nations before you. (Deuteronomy 18:10-12). See also Exodus 22:18; Leviticus 19:31; 20:27).*

Not only does God outlaw such practices; but also playing with such things has devastating consequences. It will:

- *Darken your heart*

- *Doom your spirit*

- *Destroy your testimony*

- *Dilute your anointing*

- *Damage your life*

- *Devastate your destiny.*

Nevertheless, that did not stop the wayward King Saul who visited the witch at En-dor in 1 Samuel 28:7. The Bible says:

Saul said to his servants, "Seek for me a woman who is a medium that I may go to her and inquire of her." And his servants said to him, "Behold, there is a woman who is a medium at En-dor." Then Saul disguised himself by putting on other clothes, and went, he and two men with him, and they came to the woman by night; and he said, "Conjure up for me, please, and bring up for me whom I shall name to you.

What about the woman in Acts 16:16. The Bible says as the Apostles were going to the place of prayer they were *Met by a female slave who had a spirit by which she predicted the future. She earned a great deal of money for her owners by fortune telling.*

The Apostle Paul recognized the demonic spirit at work in her life. He became so annoyed by the evil spirit that he put an end to its work when he declared *in the name of Jesus Christ, I command you to come out of her! (Acts 16:18)*

The Apostle Paul acknowledged the presence of the dark spirit working in her, he took authority over its power and he stopped the evil spirit by the power of the Holy Spirit at work in his life. The Bible says *at that moment, the spirit left her.*

How Did Satan Get In

We must always be on the lookout for Satan's handy work. This was God's message to Cain in Genesis 4:7 when He said to him *watch out! Sin is crouching at the door, eager to control you.*

Remember, Jesus' warning to the Apostle Peter *"Satan desires to have you."* By *"have you"* it does not mean he wanted Peter to be his friend or to join his team. It means he wanted to have his way with Peter. It means he wanted to violate him, abuse him, humiliate him, and ruin him (See Luke 22:31).

Similarly, Satan has the same warped desires for you and me. He wants to shake our lives apart. He wants to separate us from Christ just as a farmer separates wheat from husks (God's Word Translation). He wants us disconnected from God's power and trusting in his demonic, deceptive, destructive and deadly ways.

When Satan's evil ways are manifesting in your life, an important question that you must ask yourselves is *"How did Satan get in?"* Satan is slick and subtle (See Genesis 3:1), his words can be smooth as butter (See Psalms 55:21) and his appearance can be captivating and deceiving. The Bible says *Satan disguises himself as an angel of light (2 Corinthians 11:14).*

For these reasons, we need to:

> *Watch and pray that we enter not into temptation (See Matthew 26:41).*

The Apostle Peter was a close disciple of Jesus and a central figure in the birth of the New Testament church. It was to Peter that Jesus said, *"Upon this rock I will build my church and the gates of hell will not prevail against it" (See Matthew 16:18).*

When Peter spoke in the upper room, the Holy Spirit fell (See Acts 2 and Acts 10). It was Peter in Acts 9 who knelt down and prayed, and turned to the lifeless body of Tabitha and said arise. Instantly, by the power of God, she opened her eyes and she sat up.

Yet, Satan still found a door of opportunity into Peter's life. Once inside He used his demonic prowess and craftiness. He influenced Peter to speak against Jesus' assignment on the cross. The Bible says *Peter took Jesus aside and began to rebuke him. "Never, Lord! He said. "This shall never happen to you!" (Matthew 16:22).*

Just That Quick
Satan Got In.

Knowingly or unknowingly, Satan's deceptive ways and destructive attacks affect all of us. Genesis 3:1-5 provides the first instance of such an attack when Satan attacked Eve in the Garden of Eden:

Now the serpent was more crafty than any of the wild animals the Lord God had made. He said to the woman, "Did God really say, 'You must not eat from any tree in the garden'?" The woman said to the serpent, "We may eat fruit from the trees in the garden, but God did say, 'You must not eat fruit from the tree that is in the middle of the garden, and you must not touch it, or you will die.'" "You will not certainly die," the serpent said to the woman. "For God knows that when you eat from it your eyes will be opened and you will be like God knowing good and evil

So, how does Satan get in? One of the ways he enters our situations is when we do not take a few moments to look at the things we do and say to ensure they are in accordance with the Word of God. Do not let this be you.

Regardless of what you hear or see, before you do it or believe it, you must...

Examine It!

If you do not examine what you do and say, you may be doing and saying things that are crippling the anointing in your life. You must know, just because something sounds good, does not mean it is from God. Just because something looks and sounds *"Churchy"*, does not mean it is godly.

Just because many *"Church"* people are doing something or saying something, does not mean God approves of it. Remember, Matthew 7:13 says *wide is the gate and broad is the road that leads to destruction, and many enter through it.* Said differently, a whole lot of good people are heading to a bad place. Don't let this be you.

In addition to being on the lookout for Satan's handiwork, you must be careful whom you allow to teach, train, mentor or speak into your life. Some life coaches are life criminals, con artist, or charlatans. Some overseers are outrageous and outlandish orators. They are robbing people of the promise, purpose and plan of God for their lives.

Wake Up, Wise Up, And Rise Up!

This is not a game or a land of make believe. I am not the Wizard and this is not Oz. You are not Alice and this is not wonderland. The powers of darkness are real and we are in a fight for our lives. Remember, Satan is coming to:

> *Steal, kill and to destroy.*
> *(John 10:10)*

We must wake up and wise up. This is imperative since the margin for error on the journey of life is small and the risk of going astray is too great. Matthew writes:

> *Narrow is the way, which leadeth unto life, and few there be that find it" (verse 14).*

Dear friend, do not believe everyone who says that they have the Spirit. Instead, examine them *test them. See whether the spirit they have is from God, because there are many false prophets in the world. (1 John 4:1, God's Word Translation).*

You cannot simply believe everything you see and hear. You cannot do something just because everyone else may be doing it or saying that it is right. You need to know who you are following and what you are doing. It is the only way to know where you are going. To do this you must:

> *Examine everything carefully; hold fast to that which is good (1 Thessalonians 5:21)*

This is true of what you are told in the church, read in a book, or hear in the world.

John 17:17 says God's *word is truth.* Psalms 33:4 says, *"The word of the Lord is right and true."* Thus, it is vital that you judge all things in the light of God's word, not the law of the land, the opinion of others, or the naughty needs of people. Your destiny depends on it.

This is where Eve went wrong. She let Satan interpret the word for her. She did not examine his words in the light of God's commandments. As a result, she now saw that the fruit of the tree was good for food and *pleasing to the eye, and also desirable for gaining wisdom, she took some and ate it. She also gave some to her husband, who was with her, and he ate it. (Genesis 3:6)*

Because they did not examine what they had seen and heard, Satan was able to talk Adam and Eve into doing something that God had forbidden. Just that quick Satan usurped their authority, disrupted their fellowship with God, and stole their power.

Satan's deception and destructive ways led them astray. It is not until we read in verse 13, that Eve admits, *"The serpent deceived me".* She did not recognize the attack until it was too late.

Satan's ways are still the same today. Just look around. People are deceived and they are unabashedly opening the doors of their lives to Satan. They are doing things that are contrary to the Word of God and teaching others to do them as well.

This is one reason why it is important that you know the Word of God. It is through the Word of God that we recognize and steer away from errors, ungodly habits, heresy, and bad teaching when you hear or see it (See 2 Timothy 2:15).

My friend I offer you this warning. If you do not take a few moments to examine what you see, hear, do and say in the light of God's word, you will end up like Adam and Eve. Powerless and Deceived!

Kick the Devil Out

Unlike Eve in Genesis 3, Jesus quickly took authority over Satan. How did Jesus do it? He did it by speaking the Word of God with power and authority. Jesus said to him *get out of my way, Satan! (Matthew 16:23, God's Word Translation).*

Jesus recognized Satan working his way into the conversation and he quickly took authority over it by the power of God. There were no long and drawn out lengthy prayers. There was no dancing, shouting or speaking in tongues. No one got drenched in anointing oil. He simply spoke the word powerfully and precisely.

When He did, Satan was defeated. Just that quick, Jesus gave Satan the boot. Reminds me of the song we sang in Church:

> *I can feel God stretching out in me.*
> *I can feel God stretching out in me.*
> *He opened up my mind and kicked the devil out.*
> *I can feel God stretching out in me.*

Just thinking on the words of the song emboldens me. I can feel God's mighty power as I am writing. Thank you Holy Spirit!

Remember, as a child of the King, God is fighting on your behalf. Regardless of Satan's destructive ways and work manifesting in and around your life, if God allowed it to happen, please know that He has the power and a plan to bring you through it. *He is the Alpha and the Omega, the Almighty (Revelations 1:8).*

My friend it is time to kick the devil out and slam the door shut. Every time he comes back, you have been anointed to kick that joker out...

...Again, Again and Again

Jesus gives us another example of how we should kick Satan out of our lives with the word. It was after Jesus had fasted 40 days and 40 nights the Bible says Satan showed up. The following discourse between Satan and Jesus ensued (Matthew 4:3-10).

First Kick

If thou be the Son of God, command that these stones be made bread. But Jesus answered and said, It is written,

Man shall not live by bread alone, but by every word that proceedeth out of the mouth of God.

Second Kick

"Then the devil taketh him up into the holy city, and setteth him on a pinnacle of the temple, And saith unto him, If thou be the Son of God, cast thyself down: for it is written, He shall give his angels charge concerning thee: and in their hands they shall bear thee up, lest at any time thou dash thy foot against a stone. Jesus said unto him, "It is written again, Thou shalt not tempt the Lord thy God".

Third Kick

Again, the devil taketh him up into an exceeding high mountain, and sheweth him all the kingdoms of the world, and the glory of them; And saith unto him, All these things will I give thee, if thou wilt fall down and worship me. Then saith Jesus unto him, "Get thee hence, Satan: for it is written, Thou shalt worship the Lord thy God, and him only shalt thou serve."

With each attack, Jesus kicked Satan by declaring, *"It is written"*. Unlike Eve who allowed Satan to speak into her life and interpret the Word of God for her (Genesis 3), Jesus spoke the Word of God to Satan. Repeatedly He replied, *"It is written"* and Satan was defeated.

When Satan could not take it anymore, the Bible says the devil left and angels came and ministered unto Jesus (Matthew 4:11).

Just Like Jesus

Jesus said in Luke 10:18-19 *behold, I have given you authority to tread on serpents and scorpions, and over all the power of the enemy, and nothing will injure you.* So, when Satan and his sinful ways are manifesting in your life rebuke them, denounce them, and kick them out. This is why you need God's anointing.

God has anointed you to take authority over Satan's work just as Jesus did (See Matthew 4:1-11; Luke 11:14). He has anointed you to speak His word powerfully, precisely and authoritatively just like Jesus. When you do, you will literally feel the power of God stretching out in you.

In another example in Acts 13:10, the Apostle Paul took authority over the evil spirit working in Elymas the sorcerer when he said to him *you are a child of the devil and an enemy of everything that is right! You are full of all kinds of deceit and trickery. Will you never stop perverting the right ways of the Lord?*

Then in verse 11, the Apostle Paul declared *now the hand of the Lord is against you. You are going to be blind for a time, not even able to see the light of the sun.* The Bible says *immediately mist and darkness came over him, and he groped about, seeking someone to lead him by the hand.*

Consider what happened to the disciples in Luke 10:17 when they said, *even the demons obey us when we speak in the name of Jesus!* The same is true in our lives. You have the same authority and dominion as Christ and the disciples over demonic spirits

Touch Not My Anointed

It goes without saying that Satan preys upon powerless Christians (1 Peter 5:8). These are Christians that have weak prayer, weak faith, and a weak walk with the Lord. Just as a wounded gazelle captured on the African plain, Satan's predatory attacks easily ensnare them.

But to God be the glory, many of us once held in a trap by the devil to do what he wanted us to do are now free from Satan's grasp and have God's power flowing in our lives (See 2 Timothy 2:26, New Living Translation).

Illustration – Can't Touch This

Many years ago old school rapper MC Hammer said, *"U Can't Touch This!"* The song became a global sensation.

People all over the world were dressed up and dancing like MC Hammer. With a fancy beat that made you move your feet and lyrics that could motivate a dead man he shouted, *"Can't touch this"*.

One day I heard my oldest daughter Kendra, playing this song. I was like *"O' snap!"* It almost made me jump up out of my seat, break out into the Hammer dance and shout, *"Stop! Hammer time!"* Okay, I'm back. I had a quick flash back as I was writing.

Obviously, I was being facetious with the references to MC Hammer. On a more serious note, God was the first to say, *"Can't touch this"* when He declared *"Touch not my anointed and do them no harm (Psalms 105:15; 1 Chronicles 16:22).*

Clearly, there are inherent dangers in touching the things of God. Consider this example in 2 Samuel 6:6-7:

> *When they came to Nachon's threshing floor, Uzzah put forth his hand to the ark of God, and took hold of it; for the oxen shook it. And the anger of the Lord was kindled against Uzzah; and God smote him there for his error; and there he died by the ark of God.*

The Ark of the Covenant is a chest designed by God and it was made of wood and overlaid in gold. It contains the Ten Commandments given to Moses, Aaron's rod that budded, and a jar of manna from heaven (See Hebrews 9:4). God spoke to Moses from the Ark of the Covenant.

Number 7:89 reads *when Moses entered the tent of meeting to speak with the Lord, he heard the voice speaking to him from between the two cherubim above the atonement cover on the Ark of the Covenant law. In this way the Lord spoke to him.*

In essence, the Ark of the Covenant is the presence of God. As we see in the account of Uzzah in 2 Samuel 6, touching the things of God unwisely can be catastrophic.

Illustration Application

When God said touch not my anointed, He was dropping the hammer or should I say He was sending a message throughout all eternity and putting every living creature on notice. Keep your hands off my stuff.

The Bible says in 2 Corinthians 6:16, *we are the temple of the living God; just as God said, "I will dwell in them and walk among them."* As a child of God, those who are touching you must understand they are touching the Spirit of God working in you. By touching, I mean disrupting the plan of God for your life.

Thus, your enemies are taking the same risk as Uzzah when they are touching, or disrupting the plan of God for your life. God deposited His word and other items in the Ark and defended it vigorously and just as God defended the Ark of the Covenant, He is defending His children who are filled with His presence.

King David knew this when he declared to his servants:

> *"Why weren't you afraid to up and kill God's anointed?" Right then he ordered one of his soldiers, "Strike him dead!" The soldier struck him, and he died. "You asked for it," David told him. "You sealed your death sentence when you said you killed God's anointed." (2 Samuel 1:15-16).*

How much more will God do for us who are filled with His presence, His word, His Spirit and are doing His will, when people are touching or attempting to disrupt His plan for our lives. Only God knows and He gives this ominous warning. *It is a fearful thing to fall into the hands of the living God (Hebrews 10:31).*

Now That's Good Stuff

Allow me to share a few final thoughts on power and the power of God. The Bible says *the power of life and death is in your tongue (Proverbs 18:21).* Therefore, you must be mindful of the words that come out of your mouth. Your words shape the world *"you"* live in. Your words have power and with them, you can:

- *Create problems or solve them*

- *Build up mountains or pull them down*

- *Dig a valley or climb out of one*

- *Darken your day or brighten it*

The words that come from our own mouths often ensnare us (See Proverbs 6:2). With your own words, you could be binding yourself to ungodly commitments, establishing unwise obligations, or creating problems that God never purposed for your life.

Satan is a master at using your words to set traps for you. If you continue to speak destructive words over your life, you will find

WORDS TO THE WISE
If you don't have something good and godly to say about your life, then don't say anything at all.

yourself dealing with all kinds of problems. Problems God never purposed for your life. Instead of making your life harder with the words that come out of your mouth, use the power of your words to put you in position to receive God's anointing. Instead of speaking words that cancel the power of God in your life, use your words to promote and uphold them.

Stop saying what you can't do, instead proclaim what you are doing, can do, and will do by the power of God. Stop talking about who you can't be, instead declare who you are and who you will be by the power of God. Stop professing what you don't have, instead give thanks for the blessings you have and the blessings that are on the way.

The songwriter said, *"What God has for me it is for me. I know without a doubt that He will bring me out. What God has for me it is for me."* Hearing yourself speaks such powerful, prophetic, bold, positive, faith filled statements will strengthen your inner man. It will boost your faith. It will activate the anointing in your life.

Remember, *faith cometh by hearing (Romans 10:17)*. The biblical application is what you consistently hear is what you will ultimately believe. Remember, what you believe is a very good indication of what you will receive.

It is important that you hear yourself speaking the promises and blessings of God over your own life. Preaching is great and prophecy is powerful. However, there is nothing quite like you hearing yourself declare the power, purpose and plan of God over your own life.

When you are consistently hearing words that reinforce your faith, the way you think is aligned with God's will for your life. You will literally feel God's power stretching out in you. You will feel the God in you arise and your enemies will be scattered (See Psalms 68:1).

That's power.
That's activating the anointing.
That's good stuff!

Chapter 9
Boldly Believing Through Life's Battle

FACING WHAT FRIGHTENS YOU

"When they saw their courage…
they took note that these men had been with Jesus"
(Acts 4:13)

COURAGE IS THE willingness to face what frightens you. It is bravely confronting the challenges that each day brings. It is boldly taking action in spite of your nervousness or the uncertainty. It is declaring in your darkest moments, in the face of your biggest critics, and in the hardest of seasons in your life, *"I'm coming out of this".*

Courage is from the Greek word *"Tolmáo".* It means to be bold, to demonstrate the bravery necessary to complete a task, assignment or mission. It is the preparedness to do what must be done even when the task appears to be too difficult, dangerous, or daunting.

In discussing courage, Nelson Mandela said:

> *I learned that courage was not the absence of fear, but the triumph over it. The brave man is not he who does not feel afraid, but he who conquers that fear.*

Muhammed Ali said:

> *He who is not courageous enough to take risk will accomplish nothing in life.*

Winston Churchill said:

> *Success is not final, failure is not fatal: it is the courage to continue that counts.*

For the Christian, courage means to put it all on the line for God and having the faith to believe He will see you through. It is hearkening diligently unto the voice of the Lord your God in the midst of the storm. It is standing strong in the Lord and in the power of His might.

Like Peter, it means walking on water a second time after you have failed. Like the woman with the issue of blood, it means pushing through the crowd standing in the way of her miracle. Like Paul, it means going back into a city to keep preaching after you have been stoned and left for dead.

Courage is getting back up again when you did not get the promotion. It is getting back up again when your friends, coworkers, or boss has pulled you down. It is getting back up again when you did not get the loan. It is getting back up again when your marriage did not work.

It is getting back up again when the doctor says there is nothing more he can do for you. Courage is getting back up again when you have lost a loved one. It is getting back up again when your heart has been broken in a relationship.

Life can hurt you. People can hurt you. But, you owe it to yourself to demonstrate the determination and courage to get back up again. This is important because your victories are often on the other side of what frightens you and courage is the road that God has given you to get to them.

ANOTHER TEST AND TESTIMONY
Have No Fear

Many years ago, the Lord spoke to me and said, *"Have no fear, I AM here."* Those words from God are forever etched in my mind. Jesus confirmed these words to the body of Christ in Matthew 28:20 when He said:

> *I AM with you always,*
> *even to the end of the ages.*

But, notice what the Lord did not say to me. He did not say, *"Have no fear because I have stopped all your storms."* He did not say, *"Have no fear because I have gotten rid of all your pain, your problems, or your plight."* He simply said, *"Have no fear, I AM here."* He never mentioned what I was going through. He simply assured me that He would be with me.

The words that God spoke to me were similar to the assurance Joseph had in Genesis 39:2 which reads, *"The Lord was with Joseph."* Not only was God with him through his trials, the Bible says in spite of the trials he endured Joseph, *"became a successful man"*.

So you are probably thinking, *"Dr. Jordan is the man. Since the Lord spoke that word into his life he has never again been afraid."* As good as that sounds, I can assure you, nothing could be further from the truth. I still experience moments in life that leave me frenzied, frightened, and flustered.

But, do not get it wrong. Do not get confused. I am comfortable admitting that because everyone will be frightened by something. If you have not, keep on living. There are more trials coming your way.

Mountains, Valleys, and Giants

I typically classify significant trials in my life in one of three categories: it's a mountain, a valley or a giant.

Mountains
Are serious significant unmovable issues, difficulties or obstructions that stand in your way

Valleys
Are low points in life when you are troubled on every side, stressed and feel isolated

Giants
Are problems that are unusually large, powerful and they follow you everywhere you go.

There are mountains of debt and even mountains of doom. There are valleys of depression, valleys of despair, valleys of darkness and valleys of death. There are financial giants, giants of sexual immorality, giants of addiction, pride, poverty, pain, lying, and giants that affect your health.

Mountains, valleys and giants can be strong, formidable, and intimidating. They are seemingly unconquerable. They look overwhelming and they make you feel nervous, timid, and afraid.

But, here are a few powerful truths I want to get into your spirit. *God has not given us a spirit of fear. But of power, love and a sound mind (2 Timothy 1:7).* Romans 8:15 reads *"This resurrection life you received from God is not "timid".* Psalms 3:6 reads, *"I will not be afraid of ten thousands of people who have set themselves against me round about."* Thus, nervousness, or being timid or afraid are not of God.

The truth of the matter is:

You cannot be timid and walk in the fullness of God.

When God says go to a timid person, they sit still like a bump on a log. When He says stand still, they run like the wind. When He says come, they about-face faster than a nervous soldier marching into battle.

Being timid makes the mountains look higher and wider, it makes the valleys appear darker and deeper, and it makes the giants seem bigger and stronger. It makes situations look worse than they are. It makes trials last longer than they should. It makes the storms of life feel more intense.

Being timid will keep you from giving your all. It will keep you from living each day to the fullest. It will keep you from stepping out when the time is right. It will keep you from taking action when God says move.

Thus, being timid results in a person being out of place and in missed opportunities. It limits the flow of the anointing, it hinders a person's response to God's word, it causes revelation to remain unseen and it culminates in promises going unclaimed.

I can assure you this is not the will of God for your life. God did not anoint us to be scared of the mountains, valleys and giants in our lives. He has anointed us to be bold, to face our mountains, valleys and giants, and to walk in victory.

Remember, what the Lord said about the mountains. Speak to them and they will move (Mark 11). Remember, his promise in the valley. He will be with you (Psalms 23). Remember, what happen to the giants. They all fall down (1 Samuel 17).

Don't Be Scared

God will often challenge you to do something that looks impossible, too good to be true, or that makes no sense. He will ask you to *"Give"* when your money is low, to *"Stand still"* when you feel like running and to *"Move forward"* when you see things in the way.

He will ask you to *"trust him"* when you cannot see Him, to *"Fight"* when you have been defeated and to

"Rejoice" when you are still hurting. He will even ask you to *"Be strong"* when you are weak and worn.

Remember, Jesus said to Peter *"Come"* walk on the water in the middle of a raging storm. I am sure Peter was afraid. I am sure Peter was probably thinking, *"What have I gotten myself into."* Nevertheless, he stepped out on the water anyway.

Just like Peter, in this life you will feel the numbing and immobilizing effects of fear. You will face difficult, dangerous, and daunting trials that cannot be praised or proclaimed away. Mountains, valleys and giants are coming your way and they are coming with or without your approval.

Yes We Can

Numbers 13 gives the account of Joshua, Caleb and the ten spies whom God sent to look at the promise land. When they returned from the land, *Caleb said, "We should by all means go up and take possession of it, for we will surely overcome it." But the men who had gone up with him said, "We are not able to go up against the people, for they are too strong for us."*

Please note, all the men heard the promise of God and all the men looked at the same land. However, ten of the spies saw the enemy and now they lacked the courage to walk in the will of God. They said *next to them we felt like grasshoppers, and that's what they thought, too! (Numbers 13:33)*

Joshua and Caleb on the other hand, said *let's go up and take control, because we can definitely conquer it."* The King James Bible reads *we are yet well able to take the land.*

I submit for your consideration you cannot be timid and walk in the fullness of God for your life. That's why Joshua and Caleb's encouragement to the people is so powerful. It resulted in them crossing over into Canaan and possessing the Land just as God intended.

Illustration – Facing What Frightens You

To live victoriously you must face what frightens you. More often than not, running away only makes matters worse. For example, a hunter in the woods who happens upon a black bear knows he must face his fear. Running away may trigger the bear's natural predatory instinct prompting an attack.

Similarly, a captain of a boat knows to turn the boat into the wind and waves when sailing into a storm. When the storm is too close, the captain cannot turn the boat around to out run the storm. He must face the storm, batten down the hatches and let her ride.

Illustration Application

It has been my experience that even when I have asked God to take me out of a frightful situation, He did not. However, what He did do is give me peace in the storm, grace to endure, and strength to overcome. To put it another way, He gave me what I needed to conquer my fears.

It was up to me in those moments to magnify God's power and presence with praise (See Psalms 34:3), to speak God's word with accuracy and authority (See Mark 1:22), to put on God's mighty armor (See Ephesians 6) and to let God's divine light shine (See Matthew 5).

If we walk in these truths, when Satan attacks he will hear our praise, feel its power and see our boldness. He will see God's armor, recognize God's light, and he will know that we are battle tested, covered by the blood, and walking boldly in the authority given to us *"...in the name of Jesus!"*

After all, to get to the place that God is taking you, you cannot let pain, persecution, people or the past deter you. You must be brave enough to try again when challenged to do something you previously failed to accomplish.

So what if you tried to move the mountain, make it through the valley, or to kill the giant and failed the test? That should have nothing to do with what you are doing right now. So what if the tasks given to you have never been done? You must be courageous enough to do what has never been done before.

So what if you have been challenged to go further than everyone else? You must be bold enough to go where no one has gone before. So what if people say you cannot overcome the troubles before you? You cannot be frazzled, flustered or made to forfeit your destiny.

If people could have helped you, they should have helped you a long time ago. Maybe someday in the future, they just might. However, as it stands right now, there is no sense in waiting around for their approval or support. You have work to do, a devil to defeat and a God to glorify. Be bold and just do it.

Sanctified Swagger

Sometimes people may see your boldness as arrogance, haughtiness, or even high mindedness. I call it *"Blessed Assurance"*. I call it the *"Unstoppable Spirit"*. I call it *"Sanctified Swagger"*.

When you know who you are in God you can hold your head up, stick your chest out and stand up confidently. Some might mistake your confidence for arrogance or pride. However, we are not talking about being arrogant. Arrogance is selfish and satanic, and it is one of man's greatest weaknesses.

Sanctified swagger on the other hand is radiating buoyancy. It's an ebullience that flows from the Spirit of God working in your life. It results in improved performance, a more joyful countenance, and a lot less stress. With it, you will bounce back faster when things knock you down and have more confidence in the storms of life.

Illustration – Whose Got Your Back

When I was a little boy, there were many instances when I stood up to someone or started some trouble with someone who was bigger, stronger and older than I was. You know why I did it. I did it because I had two big brothers on my side. I knew that for someone to get to me, they had to go through my brothers.

Knowing this, I was bold, cocky, and good at *"selling wolf-tickets"*. I made threats, criticisms, and insults to intimidate people. I frequently wrote checks that I knew my derrière could not cash – if you know what I mean.

I talked a good game, made bluffs and empty threats sprinkled with a few choice words to folks in the hood. As you can tell, I was a hot mess growing up. Thank God for salvation.

But, at that age, I knew and they knew they could have clobbered me. Nevertheless, I kept running my mouth because of my brothers. I had no fear. I believed that I could do or say anything. Why? Because I knew my brothers were there for me if things went south.

Now, I'm not suggesting that you should start trouble as I did back in the day. However, when trouble does find you, you need to know whose got your back. Spiritually speaking, you need to know God's got your back.

Illustration Application

I am convinced this is the knowledge that emboldened David's mighty men in 2 Samuel 23 and Shamgarah in Judges 3. I am convinced this is the message from the Apostle Paul to the body of Christ when he said, *"if God be for us, who can be against us" (Romans 8:31).*

Granted, you and I are not exempt from tear-jerking trials, messed up moments, demanding dilemmas or people problems. We are however, blessed with the protection of a God who is with us through it all. In this, we should be confident. As Psalms 27:1-3 reads:

> *The Lord is my light and my salvation; whom shall I fear? the Lord is the strength of my life; of whom shall I be afraid? 2 When the wicked, even mine enemies and my foes, came upon me to eat up my flesh, they stumbled and fell. 3 Though an host should encamp against me, my*

heart shall not fear: though war should rise against me, in this will I be confident.

David tells us in Psalms 23 even when he walked through the valley of death he had no fear *"because"* God was with him (See Psalms 23:4). That's what I call sanctified swagger.

Even though he faced a slew of huge obstacles, David was encouraged when others might have been discouraged. He was encouraged because, like a big brother watching over my shoulder, he knew the Lord was watching over him and it gave him...

...Boldness in the Battles of Life

In 1 Samuel 17, David faced a frightful situation when he fought Goliath. Consider what David is seeing as he prepares for this battle. Goliath is approximately 10 feet tall and some estimate his weight at more than 650lbs and unlike David, Goliath was a fighter and experienced in the art of war.

Goliath was big, boisterous and battle tested. He openly mocked and defied God and the armies of Israel But, none of this mattered. Although David was not experienced in the art of war, he was experienced in the art of trusting God.

But, moments before the fight, David had to contend with the discouraging words of King Saul who said *thou art not able to go against this Philistine to fight with him; for thou art but a youth, and he a man of war from his youth (1 Samuel 17:33).* So not only did he need courage to fight Goliath. David needed courage to overcome his doubters.

To his credit, his confidence was unshaken. What I like about David, is he did not let the doubters talk him out of the fight. He did not let the trial before him change his mind set.

David looked back at the testimonies God had given him. He remembered what the Lord had already done for him and used it as evidence that God would do it again. He replied to King Saul in verses 34-37:

> *Thy servant was keeping his father's sheep; and when there came a lion, or a bear, and took a lamb out of the flock, I went out after him, and smote him, and delivered it out of his mouth; and when he arose against me, I caught him by his beard, and smote him, and slew him. Thy servant smote both the lion and the bear: and this uncircumcised Philistine shall be as one of them, seeing he hath defied the armies of the living GOD. God delivered me out of the paw of the lion, and out of the paw of the bear, he will deliver me out of the hand of this Philistine.*

What is all the more impressive is, David volunteered for this fight. That's correct. David volunteered for the fight when he said to Saul *let no man's heart fail because of him; thy servant will go and fight with this Philistine (1 Samuel 1:32).*

David understood something that you and I must understand as well. His power and victory over his enemy would not come from his skills as a fighter, but through his faith in God. That's confidence. That's boldness. That's the Unstoppable spirit.

In spite of the opposition he faced, David, the untrained little boy used a stone, a sling and the name of his God to defeat Goliath. As noted in 1 Samuel 17:40-50:

> *He took his staff in his hand, and chose him five smooth stones out of the brook, and put them in a shepherd's bag which he had, even in a scrip; and his sling was in his hand: and he drew near to the Philistine....And when the Philistine looked about, and saw David, he disdained him: for he was but a youth, and ruddy, and of a fair countenance. And the Philistine said unto David, Am I a dog, that thou comest to me with staves? And the Philistine cursed David by his GODs. And the Philistine said to David, Come to me, and I will give thy flesh unto the fowls of the air, and to the beasts of the field.*

Stop Running, Start Fighting

The Bible tells us when all the men of Israel saw Goliath, they fled from him and were greatly afraid. They were terrified. They said one to another *have you seen this man who is coming up? "He comes out each day to defy Israel." (1 Samuel 17:24-25)*

The more they talk the more entrenched they were in the spirit of fear. As a result, these thoughts of darkness, doom and defeat in their minds had trapped them. Yet, this same phenomenon of being trapped by fear is happening around the world in the body of Christ today.

Too many Christians today are missing the blessings of God because of fear. It is holding them back. It is keeping them focused on the past, unprepared for what is happening right now and worried about the future.

They are afraid of what others might think. They are afraid of the magnitude, the gravity, or the pressure of the moment. They are afraid they will fail.

The quote of Paulo Coelho, Brazilian lyricist and novelist, adds some good perspective on being afraid:

> *There is only one thing that makes a dream impossible to achieve: the fear of failure.*

Knowing the effect of fear, God told Joshua *"Have I not commanded you? Be strong and courageous" (Joshua 1:9).* Likewise, He said to Solomon *be strong and courageous and do it. Do not be afraid and do not be dismayed, for the Lord God, even my God, is with you. He will not leave you or forsake you" (1 Chronicles 28:20).*

Faced with the task of facing Goliath, David could have acted like the other men in Israel and did nothing. However, he chose to move courageously. He acted immediately upon the Word of God working in his life because he believed the Lord would deliver Goliath into his hands.

Said differently, the word of the Lord for David was I have given you the power to defeat your enemy. With this word, David was emboldened. He trusted God to do what He said He would do and he moved in this *"right now"* word from God.

Now listen to David's confident and courageous words to Goliath before he defeated him. He is speaking with such an assurance that it must have sounded ridiculous to those that had gathered to watch the fight:

> *Thou comest to me with a sword, and with a spear, and with a shield: but I come to thee in the name of the Lord of hosts, the God of the armies of Israel, whom thou hast defied. This day will the Lord deliver thee into mine hand; and I will smite thee, and take thine head from thee; and I will give the carcases of the host of the Philistines this day unto the fowls of the air, and to the wild beasts of the earth; that all the earth may know that there is a God in Israel. And all this assembly shall know that the Lord saveth not with sword and spear: for the battle is the Lord's, and he will give you into our hands.*

Now watch the power of speaking your victory, of living with courage, of operating in the spirit of David:

> *And it came to pass, when the Philistine arose, and came, and drew nigh to meet David, that David hastened, and ran toward the army to meet the Philistine. And David put his hand in his bag, and took thence a stone, and slang it, and smote the Philistine in his forehead, that the stone sunk into his forehead; and he fell upon his face to the earth. So David prevailed over the Philistine with a sling and with a stone, and smote the Philistine, and slew him; but there was no sword in the hand of David.*

Immediately, he ran with boldness to meet Goliath. David knew God was with him and he did not let the clear and present danger of facing Goliath stop him. In the end, David got the victory and when the Philistines saw their champion was defeated, they fled (See 1 Samuel 17:51).

The lesson for you and I is David did not just give lip service, he fought Goliath. David talked the talk and he walked the walk. When the time came to fight, he ran toward Goliath. That's courage, that's boldness, that's the unstoppable spirit.

My message to you is do not run from the challenges in your life. Embrace the *"Spirit of David"*. Its bold, its bodacious, its brave and it is vital when the storms of life are bearing down on you. Like David, I challenge you to speak to your situations, to prophesy to your problems, and take action when the time is right. Then testify when you get the victory!

Don't Let You Stop You

If you are waiting for the days when the mountains, valleys and giants in your life are all gone, you will be waiting for a long time. That is why success in life takes courage and confidence in God as you keep working toward your destiny.

Will there be obstacles in your way. Most definitely! But, the biggest obstacle that must be conquered is the obstacle of *"self"*. Nobody knows you like you know you. You know your weaknesses, you know your shortcomings, you know your proclivities, you know your fears and you know your past.

But, don't let *"you"* stop *"you"*. Challenge yourself to take action. Dare yourself to take the mantle, to grab the bull by the horns, to take charge of your life. In other words, encourage yourself to take the first step even when you are mentally, physically, emotionally, and spiritually exhausted.

Consider these examples from scripture. In Exodus 10 after Moses, *"stretched out"* the rod in his hand the water divided. In Joshua 6 after they *"walked around"* Jericho the walls fell. In Matthew 14:29, after Peter *"stepped out"* of the boat he walked on the water.

Thus, when you stretch out, God will bring you out. When you step out, God will cause storms in your life to cease. When you walk it out, He will make the walls built up in your life fall down.

Prepared for Battle

God prepares us for the battle by giving us the gifts we need in the moments they are needed. These are special abilities and talents bestowed upon us by the Almighty. As Dr. Myles Monroe postulated:

> *God has put a gift or talent in every person that the world will make room for. It is this gift that will enable you to fulfill your vision. It will make a way for you in life.*

There are spiritual gifts such as knowledge, understanding, speaking in tongues, and wisdom. There are natural gifts such as preaching, teaching, singing and other artistic skills, as well as strength, endurance, and intelligence. Finally, there are ministry gifts such as apostles, prophets, evangelist, pastors, and teachers.

Illustration – God Giftedness

In Judges 7, the Lord reduced Gideon's army from more than 30,000 men down to just 300 before he went into battle. That's right! Before he went into battle, God got rid of 99% of Gideon's army. Gideon was probably thinking *"What in the...?"*

It would be like you having $10,000 to pay your bills for the month, then God allowing devourers to take $9,900 of it. Now you have $100 to pay your mortgage, make a car payment, pay your utilities, buy food, gas, and other essentials.

Originally, you had more than enough money. Now you have no idea how you are going to make the ends meet. You would probably be thinking *"What the...?"*

For Gideon this was not a small skirmish, a trivial fight or a quick dust up. The Bible says in 1 Samuel 17:12 *vast* armies of Midian, Amalek, and the other nations of the Mideast were crowded across the valley like locusts—yes, like the sand upon the seashore". Yet, by the power of God, Gideon's 300 men came out with the victory.

You ask how I know that Gideon is God-gifted. When you have successes that make no sense or victories that are just ridiculous, that is when you know God has gifted you.

That is what happened for David when he fought Goliath. David was an untrained warrior. Goliath was an experienced, well-trained, warrior. But, David was gifted by God and that is all that mattered.

Illustration Application

The story of David and Goliath would be like you or I showing up at a gunfight with a slingshot, or like trying to pay a five-hundred dollar light bill with five dollars, or like trying to feed a family of three with three dollars for three years. It goes without saying, without God's power, presence, and provision each would be impossible.

Before his fight with Goliath, David said I have fought and killed lions and bears. It was if David was saying by the power of God, I have fought and defeated things that should have easily killed me.

When it came time to fight, he did not grab armor, a sword or a spear. Instead, he grabbed a sling, a few stones, his courage and the name of the Lord. That was all David had and that was all he needed to win this fight.

The Bible says in 1 Samuel 17:51 *"when the Philistines saw that their champion was dead, they turned and ran."* That's God. That's being God-gifted. That's the unstoppable spirit!

The question you have to answer is *"What are you doing with your gifts?"* You see being gifted is one thing. However, using your gifts for God is another. When we use our gifts to advance the Kingdom of God, He empowers them.

That is when our gifts transcend our knowledge, abilities and understanding. That is when our gifts confound the wise. That's when we soar to a whole new level in our walk with God.

Dear reader, don't neglect the gifts that are in you. God will use them to light your path in the valley and to push you over the mountain. He will use them to move obstacles, to make a way out of no way, to open closed doors, and when necessary to kill giants.

Timing is Everything

Amos 3:3 asked the question, *"Do two people walk hand in hand if they aren't going to the same place".* The children of Israel were keenly aware of this truth. For forty years, they walked in the desert, following a cloud by day and a fire by night. The Bible records in Numbers 9:22-23:

> *Whether the cloud stayed over the tabernacle for two days or a month or a year, the Israelites would remain in camp and not set out; but when it lifted, they would set out. At the Lord's command they encamped, and at the Lord's command they set out. They obeyed the Lord's order, in accordance with his command through Moses*

The revelation for you and I is the children of Israel moved when God moved. They moved in the direction that God moved. They moved at the pace that God moved. If their timing were wrong, if their direction was incorrect, or if their pace was off, they knew the power of God flowing in their lives would be hindered or halted.

This is why the devil uses fear to disrupt your walk with God. He wants to immobilize you, interrupt you, and intimidate you. He wants to throw off your timing, direction, and pace with God.

He knows that if you move ahead of God you will do things that are unwise, ungodly, or unnecessary. If you move too late, you will miss the opportunities, endowments, provisions, and favor that God purposed for you in that moment.

But more importantly, Satan fears what will happen when you do move when God says move. He fears what will happen when you do what God says. That's what we see in David's fight with Goliath.

When David fought Goliath, timing was everything. David moved when God said move. When the time was right, David ran toward Goliath and God delivered Goliath into his hands. For lack of a better phrase, David was operating with a *"Do it right now, Getter done"* mentality.

The reality is David should not have won the fight if it were simply a matter of skill, experience and know how. But this was David's fight to win and God had promised him the victory. The time to fight was now.

David could not afford to put the fight off until the next day. He could not waste time trying to find someone else to fight in his place. This was David's fight. God had given Him a word of victory and gifted him to complete the task. It was now up to David to move in this anointing.

Likewise, God is present in your life and He has purposed to give you the victory over Satan's tricks and schemes. Deuteronomy 23:14 says *your God is present to deliver you and give you victory over your enemies.* Psalms 60:11-12 tells us *God will give us help against the adversary. Through God we shall do valiantly, and it is He who will tread down our adversaries.*

God's message to you is if you will move when I say to move, if you will move in the direction I say to move, your *"Goliaths"* will fall.

Illustration - Wrong Action, Wrong Time

Imagine a train conductor who puts on the brakes too late. The train will plow into the train station. Imagine an airplane pilot who puts down the landing gear too late. The plane has to endure a potentially deadly gear-up landing. Imagine the captain of a cruise ship that turns the helm too late. The cruise ship will run a ground.

Spiritually speaking, imagine a prayer warrior that chooses not to pray for someone in the moment they need it the most. Imagine a prophet who will not share a right now word in the moment God sent it. Imagine a person who God has anointed to heal, choosing not to lay hands on the sick when God said to do it.

The person in need of prayer may have missed a life changing experience with the Lord. The person in need of a message from God now has to wait for another person to do it or for God to reveal it through some other means. The person who is sick has to endure additional hours, days, weeks, or more for their healing.

Certainly, when a person chooses not to move, God can raise up someone else who will do it in their place. That is what Mordecai told Queen Esther when he said *if you persist in staying silent at a time like this, help and deliverance will arrive for the Jews from someplace else" (Esther 4:14).* That is what Jesus said to the Pharisees when He said *if we keep silent God is able to make stones along the side of the road cry out (Luke 19:40).*

The point is God's will, will be done. However, a divinely inspired moment may have been missed. Those in need may have to endure the consequences.

Please know this, the person that failed to take the right action, at the right time is not off the hook as they may miss out the most. As Mordecai told Esther if she did not move when God said move, *you and your father's family will perish" (Esther 4:14).* Don't let this be you.

Illustration - Right Action, Right Time

Now imagine the train conductor applying the brakes at the right time. The train stops, as it should. The passengers are able to get off the train without harm.

Imagine the airplane pilot that puts the landing gear down at the right time. The plane lands safely. The travelers are able to continue on their journey.

Imagine the captain of the cruise ship who turns the helm in the right direction at the right time. The ship continues sailing safely on the water. The passengers are able to continue enjoying their vacation.

Spiritually speaking, imagine a prayer warrior with the courage to pray for someone at the moment God ordained. Jesus said in Matthew 18:19 *If two of you on earth agree about anything they ask for, it will be done for them by my Father in heaven.*

Imagine a prophet who speaks at the moment God commands it. Psalms 107:20 says *God Sent His word and healed them, and delivered them from their destruction.* Imagine a person anointed to heal, and he or she courageously lays hands on the sick at the moment when God has released unto them the power to heal. James 5:14-15 says we should expect that:

> *By praying for him, and anointing him with oil in the name of the Lord, the prayer of faith shall save the sick, and the Lord shall raise him up; and if he has committed sins, they shall be forgiven him.*

Again I say, right timing and action means everything.

Illustration – When God Says "Wait"

When I was in the Army stationed at Fort Rucker in Alabama, my family and I were preparing for a road trip back home to Florida. We packed the car, gassed it up, and we were ready to hit the road. Before we could pull out of the driveway, the Lord spoke to my wife.

He told her that we should *"wait"* until the next morning to leave. It seemed a bit odd, nevertheless we said yes Lord. We went back into the house and called it a day.

The next morning it all made perfect sense. A severe storm had moved through an area that we would have driven through. The road suffered major damage. The flooding was so severe that it washed out an entire portion of the road. It was on the portion of the road that we would have been traveling had we left at the time originally planned.

Had we left the night before, we would have been on the same stretch of the road at the same time the flooding occurred. The storm swept a few cards off the road into the rising water. My thoughts and prayers go out to those families.

Illustration – When God Says "Go"

On another occasion, my youngest daughter Kenya got very ill. We took her to the Lyster Army Medical Center on Fort Rucker. The doctor gave us some prescriptions and sent us home. As we were leaving the hospital, the Lord spoke to us to take our daughter to Florida to see a doctor in our hometown.

We immediately packed the car and were on our way. The hospital tests revealed a rare illness. The illness caused inflammation of the arteries and veins throughout the body, to include those that carry blood to and from the heart. The doctor began intravenous treatment right away and within a few days, she had fully recovered.

Had we not listened to God and courageously did exactly what He said only God knows how the story would have ended for my baby girl. But to God be the glory she was completely healed. We heard the voice of God, did exactly what He said, and through God's divine providence we overcame yet another obstacle and have continued on our journey with the Lord.

Illustration Application

Life is full of critical moments. These are moments when you are tested and you have to make a decision. It is in these moments you do not have time to play games. Taking the right action at the right time is the only path to victory.

My friend, do not delay. Do not let people or the situations you are facing dissuade you. When it is in your power to do something, do it at the moment God said it should be done. Timing is everything.

There will be times when God will say *"hold still; and see the great deed which I will perform before your very eyes" (1 Samuel 12:16, The Complete Jewish Bible)*. In the previous illustration, we were eager to go on our road trip to Florida, but God said wait. Because we waited as the Lord directed, I believe the Lord kept us out of harm's way.

Conversely, there will be times when God will say, *"Why are you crying out to me? Tell the people to get moving" (Exodus 14:15)*. It is in these moments we must do as Jeremiah 7:23 says to obey God's voice, and He will be our God, and we will be His people; and we will walk in all the way which God has command us, that it may be well with us.

I must admit that it takes courage to obey the voice of the Lord. That is because when God speaks the way may seem hard, the road may look rough, and the path may appear difficult to navigate.

When my daughter was ill we had not planned on going to Florida, but God said go. Because we said yes to the Lord and went as He commanded, when were in the right places to receive our blessing when God released it.

They Better Recognize

In Act 4:13, the Bible says when the people *"saw"* the boldness of Peter and John they were astonished. Instantly, the people knew they knew they had been spending time with Jesus. What a powerful testimony.

Consider what life was like for Peter, John and the disciples when this was happening. After the resurrection, they were being hunted down like animals. Fearing for their lives, John 20:19 says some hid themselves in a room for fear of the Jews.

Now when we read scriptures like Acts 4:31 we can see the boldness of the disciples. They weren't hiding, they were boldly praying and *when they had prayed, the place in which they were gathered together was shaken, and they were all filled with the Holy Spirit and continued to speak the Word of God with boldness.*

They knew their lives were in danger. Yet, they came out of hiding and boldly declared the Word of God through signs and wonders.

Not only did other people recognize their boldness, there was an instant recognition of their boldness among the demonic spirits working against them. We see this same recognition in the life of the Apostle Paul. As one evil spirit testified in Acts 19:15, *"Jesus I know, and Paul I know."*

The evil spirit recognized the boldness and demonstration of the Holy Spirit's power, then went on record by saying I know the power of God when I see it. So let me reiterate, when we live boldly and courageously before the Lord, it is easily recognizable.

Therefore, if you want to take dominion of any evil spirits working against you, *proclaim the Word of God with all boldness and without hindrance (See Acts 28:31).* By so doing, you will kindle afresh the gift of God that is in you (See 2 Timothy 1:6). You will ignite the fire of the Holy Ghost.

We you do there will be an easily recognizable demonstration of God's power radiating from your life. As we see in the Word of God, it worked for the disciples. As I can testify in my own live, it is working for me and I can assure you my friend it will work for you.

Today is the Day

Looking at what happened yesterday will not help you and waiting for tomorrow is of no value. You cannot win today's fight waiting for tomorrow's anointing. Neither can you win by reminiscing on yesterday's favor, blessings or provisions.

Remember, the Apostle Paul writes in Hebrews 11:1 that *"Now faith"* not *"tomorrow's faith or yesterday's faith"* is the *substance of things hoped for, the evidence of things not seen."*

Now is the time to climb the mountains, walk through the valleys and defeat the giants that are confronting you. Please know this In spite of the trials in your life *"You Are Blessed"*

Bold Declaration

Today is the day and now is the time for me to walk in victory. I have victory over every mountain, valley and giant in my life. I even take authority over the small issues that are attempting to destroy the fruitful vines of peace, prosperity, promotion and promise that God has ordained for me.

I submit my life to the authority of God the father, His Son Jesus, and to the leading of the Holy Spirit. Through the power of God, I can do all things. I am who God says I am. I will do what God says I will do. I receive the blessings God has released over my life. My family is blessed, the work of my hands is blessed, and the plan for my life is blessed.

Satan you have no power. The trials that I am facing do not have power over me. I am a child of God. His power is above all powers. His name is greater than all names. His will shall be done in my life. Not tomorrow, not next week, not next year, not some time in the future. His will is being done in my life right now.

In Jesus name, AMEN!

Chapter 10

Living, Long-Suffering, and Loving It

COMING OUT OF THE STORM BETTER AND MORE BLESSED

"When He has tried me, I shall come forth as gold"
(Job 23:10)

FOR MANY PEOPLE overcoming the storms of life is a matter of will power, persistence, and positive confession. These things are important; but, as most soon discover will power, persistence, and positive confession will inevitably fail. They fail because we have limited strength, knowledge and abilities.

Jesus confirmed this truth in Matthew 26:41 when He said *the spirit is willing, but the flesh is weak.* In other words, there will be points in life when our strength and abilities will not be enough. They will fail us. Therefore my friend, do not be surprised when they do.

We've Been Exposed...

Dear reader the storms of life often bring to light our shortcomings. They uncover our vulnerabilities and they reveal our limitations. This exposure is one of many ways in which God works. In 2 Chronicles 32, King Hezekiah was prospering and doing well, when *God left him alone only to test him that He might know all that was in his heart (2 Chronicles 32:31)*.

This testing was not so God could know what was in Hezekiah's heart. God knows what is in our hearts. Jeremiah 17:10 tells us God searches the heart, so He knows what is in it. This testing was so Hezekiah could know what was in *"his"* heart.

I believe unknown aspects of a person's character, nature, identity and faith are disclosed when we are in the storms of life. When a person's back is against the wall, when trouble is at the door, or when it looks like he or she is about to fall or fail you really get to know who they are.

In fact, if you really want to know someone, watch them in the storms of life. Yes, fortune and fame can bring out the worst in a person. But, nothing exposes our true identity like the storms of life.

...In The Storm

Many people carry on and cut up like the biggest devils the world has ever seen when they are in the storms of life. Their countenance, character and the way they converse are just dreadful, distasteful, and downright despicable. With such behaviors, God is not pleased.

Instead of a halo, an angelic glow, a godly persona and living like a friend of God, it's like they have horns growing out of their head, a pitchfork in hand, a forked tail sticking from their backside and they are parading around like Satan is their pal.

If you want to know what areas in your life need fixing, watch your actions when your back is against the wall, when you are suffering, when things are not going your way, when you are in the storms of life.

Without the Holy Spirit and His power and presence in your life, old habits will come out of hiding when trouble hits your door. The truth of the matter is:

> *If you are not led by the Holy Spirit, the storms of life can make you act unseemly, unwisely and ungodly.*

In this God is not glorified. God is glorified when we are patient, prayerful, and persistent in giving Him the praise in the midst of our trials, troubles and tribulations. In other words, God is glorified in our Long-Suffering.

An Exposé on Long-Suffering

Long-Suffering is from the Greek word *"Makrothumia"*. The New Testament writers frequently used this word. Colossians 3:12 reads we have been *"Chosen of God, holy and beloved, and have put on a heart of compassion, kindness, humility, gentleness and patience."*

The word for patience is Makrothumia or Long-Suffering. It means patiently enduring the issues, problems or discomforts of life. However, it means more than that. It means to do it in a way in which God is exalted and the devil is defeated.

When we operate in Long-Suffering, we are empowered by the Spirit of God to control our anger, to resist the urge to lash out, and to keep from acting out of character when times are hard.

When we are operating in Long-Suffering, our hardships can last for one day, one week, one month, one year, several years or a life-time. However, through it all, God is still good and worthy of the praise. Why? Because it is not about how long we suffer or how much we suffer.

For the Long-Sufferer it is about trusting in God's plan and knowing He will see us through. It is about glorifying God in the process. Trust me when I say, it takes the Holy Spirit working in us to bring us to this level of faith, understanding and obedience.

I heard a colleague in the ministry say one day *"The body hates pain."* There's no argument from me on this point. The truth of this simple, yet profound statement resonated with me. It means there is an inherent dislike for pain.

Yet, the deeper truth is without Long-Suffering when our bodies hurt us, there is a demonically inspired desire to act out, lash out, and freak out. This is the evil spirit that must be conquered with the fruit of Long-Suffering.

We can see Long-Suffering in action in Acts 5:41, *after they had been beaten with whips and sticks they rejoiced because they were counted worthy to suffer for the name of Jesus Christ.* To endure such harsh treatment and to glorify God in the process is Long-Suffering in action.

Now, if you are like me we do not go through life looking to be whipped. We do not wake up each morning begging others to pulverize us. At least I hope not. However, so often in life, the world has the belt and it is beating our butts. For this, we need Long-Suffering.

I'll admit, no one likes suffering; but since we all must endure it, we might as well get the most out of it. The truth of the matter is we learn, we evolve, we grow, and we transform through the things we suffer.

Helen Keller noted:

> *Character cannot be developed in ease and quiet. Only through the experience of trial and suffering the soul is strengthened, ambition inspired, and success achieved.*

Swiss-American psychiatrist Dr. Elisabeth Kübler-Ross noted:

> *The most beautiful people we have known are those who have known defeat, known suffering, known struggle, known loss, and have found their way out of those depths.*

Famed poet Felicia Hemans said:

Strength is born in the deep silence of Long-Suffering hearts

Rewards of Long-Suffering

There is more to Long-Suffering than patiently going through the storms of life. Long-Suffering prepares you for elevation, manifestation, impartation and revelation from God. I mean levels that are beyond that typically seen in other people.

In fact, the degree of suffering is often a good indicator of the level of grace that is coming forth from God. It has been my experience that God graces people who come through unusually difficult hardships with unusual levels of promotion, power, and promise.

Higher Elevation

Consider Joseph, the son of Jacob (Genesis 37-50). Joseph brothers hated and betrayed him by throwing him into a pit. Shortly thereafter, merchants sold him into slavery. The wife of his slave master falsely accused of rape and the slave master through him into prison. Oddly, this all started because he had a dream and he shared it with his brothers.

The first time I read this story, I was like *"Really!"* His brothers hated him because of his dream. They betrayed him for something that was beyond his control. After all, it was God who sent Joseph the dream, this was not a trick conjured up by Joseph.

When he told his brothers, *"they hated him all the more."* Joseph's attacks were unusually difficult and the attacks made no sense. He simply had a dream from God and that dream of greatness sparked a series of unusual and egregious attacks.

Yet, the Bible says the *"Lord was with Joseph" (Genesis 39:2, 21).* During these attacks, God gave him extreme favor, insight and elevation. He endured his brothers' hatred, a pitiful pit, demoralizing slavery, treacherous lies, and false imprisonment and God promoted him to the second highest position in the land of Egypt.

That is the power of Long-Suffering. It prepares you to walk in greater levels of blessings. It keeps you ready to receive the favor of God, as you are making your way through low points in life.

Mighty Manifestation

Consider the relentless attacks on Job's life. In Job 1, unprecedented tragedy descended upon his life. He loses his children, property, possessions, wealth, his health and even his good name.

If anyone deserved a good life, a life that was free of hurt, harm and danger it would have been Job. In every way the man was perfect *(Job 1:1)*. Job was upright and devout before God and man. He was devoted to God, to his family, friends and his workers.

Even with this testimony, the Bible says *he was ruined without any reason (Job 2:3)*. He endured unprecedented loss, hardships, and suffering. But, to God be the glory, he came out of these trials with double for his troubles (See Job 42:10).

In the end, the Lord blessed the latter part of Job's life more than the former part. You may be asking why God blessed Job. I submit for your consideration, it was because of the spirit of Long-Suffering at work in his life.

Divine Impartation

The Bible tells us that King David's family thought little of him. His own family considered him unworthy and unfit for kingship. As Samuel looked upon the sons of Jesse to anoint as king, his father reluctantly mentioned his name to the prophet (See 1 Samuel 16).

To make matters worse, David was not even there to defend or speak up for himself. However, God was there and God's plan for David's life unfolded according to

God's plan. You see man cannot hinder God's divine impartation in a person's life.

David was destined for the anointing, he was bound for kingship, and he was heir of greatness. He had spent his life fighting bears, lions, and giants. These trials taught him to depend on the Lord and they prepared him to walk in the unmerited favor of God. Therefore, it did not matter what his friends or family thought of him. David did not need their approval.

Once he had the anointing and rose to be king, his battles did not stop. There were days when he wanted to give up. In Psalms 13 David said:

> *How long, Lord? Will you forget me forever? How long will you hide your face from me? How long must I wrestle with my thoughts and day after day have sorrow in my heart? How long will my enemy triumph over me?*

Nevertheless, in his suffering, David did not give up. He trusted in God and instead of quitting he rejoiced. In Psalms 13:5-6 he writes, *I trust in your unfailing love; my heart rejoices in your salvation. I will sing the Lord's praise, for he has been good to me.* That's the power of Long-Suffering.

Greater Revelation

Repeated hardships, mistreatment, rejection, sickness, and turmoil characterized the Apostle Paul's ministry. He recounts his suffering in service to the Lord in 2 Corinthians 11, when there were times when he became weary, wounded and downright worn out.

In the midst of his pain and suffering, God caught him up into the third heaven. He showed him miraculous thing that are unlawful for a man to see *(*See 2 Corinthians *12:2).* The Apostle Paul enjoyed unprecedented revelation and insight into the realm of the spirit.

We see in the life of the Apostle Paul that Long-Sufferers are going through with power from on high. We are going through with the promise of increase. We are going through with the intent to glorify God. We are going through to do God's will, to grow in Christ, and to get to the place that He has prepared for us.

This is not something that happens overnight. Nevertheless, a little progress each day produces big results. Dr. Martin Luther King Jr., said:

> *Every step toward a goal requires sacrifice, suffering, and struggle.*

Now It's Your Turn

Like King David, Joseph, Job and Paul maybe you are suffering, facing rejection or dealing with an unusually difficult trial. Like King David in Psalms 13, you may be questioning God. Why so much pain? Why so much disappointment? Why so much defeat?

But I have come to tell you that your suffering, rejection and pain are not in vain. The truth of scripture is *if we suffer with Christ, we shall also reign with him (2 Timothy 2:12)*.

WORDS TO THE WISE

Don't be surprised when you suffer. But more importantly, don't be surprised when God brings you out of it much better and more blessed.

Suffering prepares you for levels of manifestations that you cannot handle right now. It prepares you for uncommon power, authority, and dominion in the realm of the spirit. I believe they will steadily increase in your life as you allow the fruit of Long-Suffering to have its way in your life.

You see suffering is the catapult of increase. Suffering is the incubator of growth. Suffering is the school in which we master the trials and tribulations on one level, and it prepares us supernaturally for the next level of manifestation, impartation and revelation.

To throw a wrench into this process Satan will prod you to operate in a spirit of bitterness, hatred and fear. He knows Long-Suffering will bring you out of the storms of life wiser, stronger, and more gifted in God. He knows Long-Suffering will reshape your identity, develop a new attitude in you, establish a new outlook for your life, and give you renewed purpose and perspective.

Regarding the importance of perspective the Apostle Paul wrote in the book of Colossians:

> *Look up, and be alert to what is going on around Christ—that's where the action is. See things from "his perspective." (Colossians 3:4)*

It is seeing the storms of life from God's perspective that transforms you in times of suffering. In Romans 12 the Apostle Paul calls it the renewing of the mind (See Romans 12:2). The word transform is from the Greek word *"Metamorphoo"* or metamorphosis.

It means changing, transfiguring, or converting. It is much like the metamorphosis of a caterpillar into a butterfly. It enters its cocoon restricted to crawling upon the earth, but emerges from its cocoon with abilities it did not have before it went in.

I believe a similar endowment of abilities happens to us as God transforms us in the storms of life. I believe that you my friend are being transformed at this very moment. I believe the words shared with you in this book are assisting in the transformation of your life right now. For this, I give God the praise.

Long-Suffering and Grace

Do you know what can happen when God blesses us beyond measure? Do you know what can take place when we experience increase manifestations or walk into abundant favor? Do you know what can occur when God bestows His gifts upon us?

We can become arrogant, proud and lose sight of God. We can become full of ourselves and empty of the Spirit of God. Such behaviors are a recipe for disaster and it will stop us in our tracks.

The Apostle Paul was a mighty man of God who saw and did many extraordinary things. Many consider him to be one of the most important people in the Bible. He wrote the majority of the New Testament.

God gave the Apostle Paul the privilege to see and know things about Heaven that no man on earth has ever seen or known. He was *caught up into paradise and heard things too sacred to be put into words, things that a person is not permitted to speak (2 Corinthians 12:4)*. As my daughters would say, the Apostle Paul was the *"Man"*. He was the *"Bomb"*.

In 2 Corinthians 12:7-10, the Bible reveals one of God's strategies for dealing with arrogance and pride in His people. The Apostle Paul said:

> *So I wouldn't get a big head, I was given the gift of a handicap to keep me in constant touch with my limitations. Satan's angel did his best to get me down; what he in fact did was push me to my knees. No danger then of walking around high and mighty! At first I didn't think of it as a gift, and begged God to remove it. Three times I did that, and then he told me,*

> > *My grace is enough; it's all you need. My strength comes into its own in your weakness.*

Once the Lord gave him this revelation, the Apostle Paul was glad to let it happen. He quit focusing on his handicap and the hardships and began appreciating them as gifts from God. That is the power of Long-Suffering and God's grace.

Now Paul:

> *Took his limitations in stride, and with good cheer, these limitations that cut him down to size—abuse, accidents, opposition, bad breaks. He just let Christ take over!*

And so the weaker he got, the stronger he became (See 2 Corinthians 12:9-19, The Message Bible).

Paul declares that in his time of suffering God's grace sustained him. He was able to endure, to continue on, and he was unstoppable because of the grace of God that was flowing in his life.

In short, Paul gloried in the tribulation and God strengthened him in his struggle. His repeated prayers for God to remove the pain did not result in the pain going away. It did result in God's great grace resting upon his life.

Similarly, our prayers may not remove the pain, stop Satan's attacks, or change the intensity or frequency of the storms that we face. However, God emboldens and fortifies us with Long-Suffering as we *fight the good fight, finish our course, and keep the faith (1 Timothy 4:7).*

Long-Suffering and Power

Where there is power, there must be Long-Suffering. Where power gives us the strength to do something, Long-Suffering ensures that what we do is wise, worth it, and in God's will when we are hurting. So, this leads me to a powerful lesson we all must learn:

*"Just because you have
the power to do something, does not
mean that you should."*

Long-Suffering is Holy Ghost empowerment to hold our peace and let God fight our battles. It keeps us from getting ahead of God and out of His will. Long-Suffering gives us the power to *"Stand still and see the salvation of the Lord" (Psalms 46:10).* So, this leads us into another issue worth discussing:

*What good is
power if you cannot control it
or use it wisely?*

I am convinced that people with power without the fruit of Long-Suffering are a danger to themselves and to others, and they hinder the work of the ministry.

When faced with situations that cause sorrow and suffering, difficulties and delays people with power and authority, without the fruit of Long-Suffering may do things haphazardly, heedlessly, and hastily. When there is an opportunity for personal gain, their actions are often seditious, senseless and self-centered.

For example, God promised Abraham and Sarah a son (See Genesis 17:19). When it was taking God too long, they concocted their own ill-fated plan. The consequences of their actions are still evident in the world today. This is why Long-Suffering is so important in the life of the believer.

Long-Suffering keeps us from being easily hoodwinked, hoaxed or hurried into acting untimely, unknowingly or unwisely. Long-Suffering brings our anxieties under control. You see where there is Long-Suffering we take comfort in knowing the challenges and delays of life are in God's hands.

It allows things to happen according to the will of God, not the desire of man. It keeps us still as God works through us to defeat the devilish schemes that are mounted against us (See Exodus 14:14; Romans 16:20). It equips us so that in all things, we can *"Wait on the Lord"*. It keeps us in *"good courage"* and by so doing, *"The Lord will strengthen our hearts"* (Psalms 27:14).

Long-Suffering and Love

Zechariah the prophet said Jesus' friends wounded him (see Zechariah 13:6). Said differently, those who knew him best brutalized him. Isaiah 52:14 says they beat him so ruthlessly and unmercifully that he looked appalling and ghastly. The NET Bible reads *He was so disfigured he no longer looked like a man (Isaiah 53:14)*.

Yet, by His actions, Jesus revealed the power of Long-Suffering and love. He could have asked the Father and the Father *would at once send more than twelve legions of angels to deliver him (Matthew 26:52-54)*. But Jesus' love kept Him on the cross.

He endured the pain, the humiliation and as a result, God strengthened Him in the struggle. Then He topped off this ultimate act of love when He proclaimed *Father forgive them for they know not what they do (Luke 23:34)*.

That is the power of Long-Suffering and love. With steadfast love, He saved the world through an ultimate act of lovingkindness on the cross (See Hebrews 12:2). When we were still powerless, and trapped in sin, Christ died for the ungodly (See Romans 5:6).

Thus, the love of God is so amazing. The Apostle Paul says, *"All the special gifts and powers from God will someday come to an end, but love goes on forever." (1 Corinthians 13:8)*. Verse 4 reads, *"Love is very patient"*. It goes on to say in verse 5-8:

> ...*love is kind, never jealous or envious, never boastful or proud, never haughty or selfish or rude. Love does not demand its own way. It is not irritable or touchy. It does not hold grudges and will hardly even notice when others do it wrong. It is never glad about injustice, but rejoices whenever truth wins out. If you love someone, you will be loyal to them no matter what the cost. You will always believe in them, always expect the best of them, and always stand your ground in defending them.*

As noted by Dr. Martin Luther King, Jr.,

> *We must discover the power of love, the power, the redemptive power of love. And when we discover that we will be able to make of this old world a new world. We will be able to make men better. Love is the only way.*

Life Without Long-Suffering

A person that lacks the fruit of Long-Suffering is more often than not short tempered. Their approach to solving problems is more often than not argumentative, apathetic and when those do not work its affronting and assaulting. All of which are counterproductive and contradistinctive to the will of God.

Satan knows this. He knows without Long-Suffering people are more likely to have outburst, to get angry and resort to violence in the storms of life. He knows they are easily enraged, misguided and waste a lot of time in destructive and vengeful behavior. He knows they are likely to give up on God when the going gets tough.

To make matters even worse, Satan knows they are like a firecracker with a short fuse. Once lit, they will explode before anyone knows what has happened.

As I have taught for years at the City of Refuge Christian Church, anger is a destructive emotion. It leads to destructive behaviors such as fights and quarrels, murders and covetousness (See James 4:1-2).

It leads to arguing, fussing and bickering which are divisive behaviors that will divide a house, ruin a marriage and destroy a person's destiny. Here is why. *When you are angry you are giving Satan the chance to enter your life (Ephesians 4:26-27, Good News Translation).*

I often hear people who are angry, fussing or bickering say *"I gave them a piece of my mind."* But, here is what they did not realize. By so doing, they also gave Satan an entry way and permission to enter their life.

We have seen what happens once he gets inside. He steals, kills, and destroys. That is why Satan would love nothing more than for you to go through life mad at the world and easily enraged.

Every time something happens to you, you turn into the *"Incredible Hulk".* Like the Incredible Hulk, nobody likes you when you are angry. In fact, you do not even like you when you are angry.

You are constantly smashing, breaking and destroying people, places and things. In the process, you are destroying your testimony, destroying your relationships, destroying your career, destroying your ministry, destroying your gifts, destroying your opportunities, destroying your destiny and destroying everything around you.

You can choose to live this way if you want to. But, let me warn you, it is one of the quickest ways to bring your life to a screeching halt. Remember, the Biblical standard for the Body of Christ is to:

> *If it be possible, as much as lieth in you, live peaceably with all men. (Romans 12:18)*

> *Follow peace with all* men, *and holiness, without which no man shall see the Lord (Hebrews 12:14).*

Don't Be A Fool

The Bible says *the anger of man does not result in the righteousness of God (James 1:20).* In fact, the Bible teaches us *anger resides in the bosom of fools (Ecclesiastes 7:9).* The psalmist says we should "*Refrain from anger, and forsake wrath! Fret not yourself; it tends only to evil*" *(Psalms 37:8).*

Unfortunately, there are people who are in jail or in the grave today because someone got angry. At this very moment, there

WORDS TO THE WISE

A quick temper can turn a wise man into somebody's fool. Don't be a fool.

are families, friends, coworkers, neighbors and even fellow church members who are moments away from hurting themselves or someone else because they are angry. These are just the types of situations that Satan is looking for.

Satan wanders, waits, and when he finds a person *"without Long-Suffering"* he works his evil ways. He knows when they are angry they are less likely to hear from God. He knows they are easily provoked into acting ungodly. That is the perfect time for him to launch his attack.

In fact, when a person is angry Satan does not have to do much to get them riled up. He knows it will take very little effort to alter their destiny, twist their desires and shatter their dreams. When a person gives into anger, with the slightest negative nudge, they will unwittingly throw their dreams away.

Yes, I know. It is frightening when you think about your life in these terms. Trials come to make us strong, not foolish. So do not be a fool.

In speaking of his trials, the Apostle Paul said it best in Acts 20:24 when he said, *"None of these things move me".* Said differently, he refused to be quick tempered. Their antics did not easily anger or emotionally charge him. The Apostle Paul's message to you and I is don't allow the foolishness, the harsh treatment or the traps of men to disrupt what God is doing in our lives.

Ephesians 4:16 give more insight into the Apostle Paul's message to you and me. *Don't sin by letting anger control you."* In verse 4:31 he says we are to *get rid of all bitterness, rage and anger, brawling and slander, along with every form of malice.* Without Long-Suffering, it is virtually impossible to walk in these scriptures.

Life With Long-Suffering

A person operating in the fruit of Long-Suffering is more often than not even-tempered, persevering and are not easily flustered in the storms of life. They are patient. They are keenly aware of the blessings that are manifesting as they wait, rely and lean on the Lord as He leads them through times of adversity (See Proverbs 3:5-6).

Long-Sufferers know that Long-Suffering is not waiting like a wimp for Satan to stop attacking. I can assure you that will not happen. But, the good news is it does not matter. Long-Suffering renders Satan's plans to anger and misguide you in the storms of life ineffective.

Long-Suffering gives us the opportunity to hear from God and to respond to the storms of life in the power of

His might and according to His will. It is absolutely astonishing how Long-Suffering leaves your enemies stymied, stupefied and looking silly.

Your enemies can hit you with their best shots. However, instead of getting angry and opening the door for Satan to come in, you patiently wait on the Lord. When the enemy attacks, you *Count it all joy when you fall into various trials, knowing that the testing of your faith produces patience (James 1:2).*

Instead of giving place to the devil in anger, you magnify God's presence and cast out Satan. In so doing, you slam the doors that Satan has used to enter into your life in Satan's face. Now, the devil does not know what to do to you.

When he attacks, you rejoice. If he leaves you alone, you give God the glory. So, no matter what he does, God is exalted, the devil is defeated and you win!

When Job lost his family, finances, and fitness, Satan must have thought Job would surely flip out God. Even Job's wife assumed as much. Nevertheless, Job walked in victory through Long-Suffering. The Bible says *in all that Job went through, he did not sin by blaming God (Job 1:21-22).*

He proclaimed *the Lord giveth and the Lord taketh away, but blessed be the name of the Lord.* In other words, Job gloried in his tribulation and he was strengthened in his struggle. That's Long-Suffering.

Illustration – That's My Momma

I can recall when my mother had an awful reaction to a medication. It decimated her skin from the crown of her head to the soul of her feet. For nearly two years, horrid infections, painful sores and ghastly blisters riddled her body.

In the waning years of her life, she went from being an independent and powerful woman of God to a frail, often incapacitated, shell of her former self. There were times when she could not stand, sit, or lay down without extreme discomfort and excruciating pain.

Yet, two things remained true. First, she never let go of God's unchanging hand. Second, God never let go of her throughout this trial.

In the final days of her life on the earth, I watched her as she rocked back and forth in the hospital bed speaking in tongues, calling on the name of the Lord, and giving God the praise for all He had done and was doing in her life.

The last time we spoke as I left her room, I said to her *"I love you momma"*. She took a quick break from her conversation with the Lord and said *"I love you to baby"*. I cannot tell you how good it felt to hear her voice.

But, there was something in her voice that let me know it would be the last time I would speak to her until we meet again in glory. Within hours of leaving the hospital, I received the call that she had taken a turn toward Beulah land.

The following morning she went home to be with the Lord. Through it all, she kept the faith. She was truly a virtuous, God-fearing woman that endured hardship as a good soldier (See Proverbs 31:10 and 2 Timothy 2:3). What a powerful testimony and what a mighty God we serve.

Illustration Application

For me it was one of the greatest examples of Long-Suffering. During those two years, I watched the Bible come to life right before my very eyes. She suffered without complaining. However, she did not do it through will power or determination. She did it through the power of the Holy Spirit.

She patiently endured knowing:

> *Blessed is the one who perseveres under trial because, having stood the test, that person will receive the crown of*

life that the Lord has promised to those who love him (James 1:12).

My momma showed me through the power of the Spirit that Long-Suffering is not about how long or how much we may hurt. Long-Suffering is not about relying on your own strength, or having the wherewithal or the determination to endure troubles. That is exhausting and it is futile.

She showed me that Long-Suffering is about glorifying God. It is about trusting in what God is doing *"through"* you by the Holy Spirit, and not giving into what the devil or life is trying to do *"to"* you. Its believing *"Not my will, but thy will be done"* Lord. That's what my momma showed me.

I always knew I had the world's greatest mom. She was absolutely awesome. Her final display of God's power in a time of sorrow was the icing on top of the cake for me!

Illustration - Abraham's Paradox

One of the greatest challenges we face is *"waiting"* on God. Particularly, when it seems He is taking too long. Too long to heal, too long to increase, too long to deliver, too long to promote, too long to avenge, just too long to do what we are waiting for God to do in our lives.

The songwriter rightfully stated, *"He may not come when we won't Him, but He will be there right on time."* In these times, patience is a virtue. Impatience on the other hand is a disastrous liability.

Consider for just a moment what the Bible says in Hebrews 6:14, when Abraham was 75 years old, God told him, *"Surely blessing I will bless thee, and multiplying I will multiply thee."* It was nearly 25 years later after Abraham *"patiently endured, that he obtained the promise"* (Hebrews 6:15). Abraham waited a quarter of a century for God's word to come to pass.

During this time he *did not waver through unbelief regarding the promise of God, but was strengthened in his faith and gave glory* to God *(Romans 4:20)*. When it looked impossible and it was taking God a long time to deliver, the Bible says, *"Abraham believed God" (Romans 4:3)*. That's Long-Suffering and it is essential when dealing with the storms of life.

Illustration - Application

We all want good things to happen in our lives. But, the issue for most of us is we want the good things to happen *"now"* not *"later"*. The fruit of Long-Suffering helps us hold out and hold our peace as we go through things right *"Now"* until the good things we know are coming *"Later"* manifest.

The Apostle Paul writes in 2 Corinthians 2:10 because of God's grace he was *"well content with weaknesses, with insults, with distresses, with persecutions, with difficulties, for Christ's sake"*. Then Paul says, *"For when I am weak, then I am strong."*

When we trust God enough to wait until He says move, we can endure our hard times as He leads us through what we are facing right *"Now"* until the blessings we are expecting manifest *"Later"*. That is the power of Long-Suffering.

Long-Sufferers know *weeping may endure for a night, but joy is coming in the morning" (Psalms 30:5)*. They know the *present troubles are small and won't last very long. Yet they produce for us a glory that vastly outweighs them and will last forever!" (2 Corinthians 4:17, New Living Translation)*

How Will You Go Through...

The children of Israel suffered centuries of harsh enslavement in the land of Egypt. When the time was right God brought them out with *"great substance"* (Genesis 15:14). Job suffered more than any other man and in the end, God blessed him with double for his troubles (Job 42:12).

Joseph faced rejection, mistreatment, slavery, and lies before his unprecedented promotion (Genesis 41:1-45).

Moses went through the Red Sea to get out of bondage (Exodus 14). Joshua had to go through Jericho to get to the promise land (Joshua 6).

Jonah survived being thrown overboard and swallowed by a fish (Jonah 2). Afterward, he went to Nineveh and preached the biggest revival recorded in the Word of God. David had to fight Goliath before he became king (1 Samuel 17).

Jesus endured rejection, brutality, the cross and received a portion among the great (See Isaiah 53:12). The Bible reads in Luke 24:25 *"It was necessary for the Christ to suffer these things and to enter into His glory."*

The Apostle Peter was moments from his execution when God freed him from prison (Acts 12:5-11). The Apostle Paul went through many trials to get to the place of great grace and unparalleled revelations seen by no other man. On one occasion, he survived a stoning. Afterward, he got back up and went back into the city and kept preaching (Acts 14:19-20).

As you can see from this selection of men in the Bible, God's people will go through trials and tribulations. However, it is not just a Christian thing to face trials. Even those who are not Children of God face the storms of life.

The question isn't *"will"* we go through storms. Storms are coming your way with or without your approval. The question isn't even *"when"* will we go through or *"where"* will we go through. The question that you and I must answer is *"how"* will we go through. You see, how you go through a trial makes all the difference in the world.

...With or Without Christ

The Bible promises in Romans 8:16 if you go through hard times with Jesus Christ, you will enjoy the good times with him as well. The Apostle Peter said *if you suffer for doing what God approves, you are blessed (1 Peter 3:14, God's Word Translation).*

The psalmist said:

> *Blessed is the one…whose delight is in the law of the LORD, and who meditates on his law day and night. That person is like a tree planted by streams of water, which yields its fruit in season and whose leaf does not wither and whatever they do prospers (Psalms 1:1-3).*

As noted in Psalms 1 God plants us *by the rivers of water (See Psalms 1:3).* It implies that God feds, fertilizes, fortifies and fixes us by His word. It paints a picture of a person with a strong foundation, who produces good fruit and can withstand the harsh conditions of life.

As the planted of the Lord, the Word of God ensures optimum growth, development and quality of life. Like a well-watered tree, we stick through the harshest of storms. The winds of change may blow and the rains of sorrow may fall. However, like a tree planted by a river of water we stand tall.

The bottom line is when we go through the storms of life with Christ we are *"blessed and are made better".* We rejoice as we go in one side of the storm and out the other. That's what I call living, long-suffering and loving it.

Conversely, for those that go through this life without Christ, instead of living, long-suffering and loving it, they are dead in the trespasses and sins, and storms bring out the worst in them. Just like a plant without water, they wither in the storms of life. As the psalmist said:

> *They are like chaff that the wind blows away. Therefore the wicked will not stand in the judgment, nor sinners in the assembly of the righteous. For the Lord watches over the way of the righteous, but the way of the wicked leads to destruction.*

I am sure you can see from the pericape of scripture in Psalms 1 the glaring line of demarcation between those who go through *"with Christ"* and those who go through *"without Christ".* Those without Christ are destroyed and those with Christ are restored.

Illustration – Thriving in the Fire

The world-renowned giant Redwood trees along California's coast are massive, mind-blowing and majestic. They are the largest living things on the earth. Some Redwood trees stand more than 300 feet tall, 30 feet wide, and weigh several million pounds with bark that is nearly 3 feet thick.

Some redwood trees are more than 3,000 years old. That means at the time I am writing this book, there are redwood trees that are alive today that were alive when David was the King of Israel. Consider for just a moment how many storms they have gone through and today they are still standing.

The roots of the large redwood trees can stretch out for more than 150 feet. Their roots intertwine and as a result, each redwood tree supports the trees standing next to it. As one unknown author wrote:

> *They are locked to each other. When the storms come, the winds blow, and the lightning flashes, the redwoods still stand. They are not alone for all the trees support and protect each other. Each tree is important to all the other trees in the grove.*

For these reasons, redwood trees can endure thousands of years of heat, storm winds and rains, and other disasters. They can withstand being toppled over because of the unity and strength. Some are even standing with roadways built through them and houses built in them.

But here is another amazing fact regarding redwood trees. Redwood trees *"need fire"* to grow and to reproduce. Yes, they need fire. Not only can they *"survive a fire"*, year after year, they *"thrive in the fire"*. That is what I call living, long-suffering and loving it.

Fire is essential to the redwood forest. The redwood seedlings usually require a seedbed prepared by fire. The fire removes unwanted debris and refuse that can hinder seed growth. Thus, fire is vital in continuing the life of new Redwood trees. The bottom line is redwood trees are awesome!

Illustration – Folding Under Pressure

Unfortunately, there are countless numbers of Christians who instead of standing strong like giant redwood trees, are falling to the ground like brittle twigs. In the pressures of life, they are easily broken and shattered and in the fires of life, they are easily ignited and burned.

Why is this? One reason is their lives are not watered by the Word of God. They are not being edified, enlightened, and energized in a healthy well-balanced church (see Ephesians 4:11). Don't let this be you.

Furthermore, the anointing is not activated in their lives. They are not being strengthened and renewed by the Holy Spirit. The fruit and gifts of the spirit are dormant or dead in their lives. As a result, they do not have the God-given endowments, enlightenment, and equipment that are essential for living the life God has purposed for them.

For these reasons, they are like brittle twigs. Their lives are fragile and when the slightest pressure arises, they are liable to break at any moment. They do not produce fruit that is pleasing unto God, nor can they endure the testing of the Lord or the storms of life.

They are spiritually unfruitful, unproductive, and unfulfilled. They are emotionally unstable and their attitude frequently changes without warning. They are often whining and complaining about something and every day is a bad day.

Unfortunately, brittle people are everywhere. We meet brittle people at church. We meet them at work. We meet them in hospitals, in offices, in stores, on college campuses, at the park, and in the gym. We meet them in every facet of life.

They range from doctors, executives, politicians, to entry-level workers, lay members, volunteers, and front-line staff, to police officers, firefighters and members of the military. There are brittle apostles, prophets, pastors, evangelist, and teachers. There are brittle people who are independently wealthy, members of the middle class and even among the poor.

Brittle people often miss, mishandle, and mistake opportunities from God. Time and time again God's opportunities are deemed impossible, inconvenient, or improbable. Consequently, it is easy to see why brittle people remain spiritually broken, busted and bankrupt. They are *like the chaff which the wind blows away and their ways shall perish (Psalms 1:4; 5).*

Illustration Application

My advice to you is to be leery of the brittle people in your life. Listening to them talk, is often unendurable, unfulfilling and it is definitely unwise. Emotionally, psychologically, and spiritually they will drain you.

From their perspective, nothing ever goes their way. When things do not work out it's always someone else's fault. Overtime they can have a destructive impact on your day, direction in life and your destiny.

On the other hand, some people are like Redwood trees. Redwood trees are a picturesque view of who we are both individually and collectively as Christians. We are the Body of Christ and *"the planted of the Lord".* As the plated of the Lord, we are cared for by *"The Almighty God.*

When we are watered by God's word, we grow like Redwood trees. We are prosperous in stormy situations and what we produce will not wither in the scorching fires of life. You see, just like redwood trees that need fire, Isaiah 43:2 says *when you walk through the fire, you will not be burned, and the flames will not harm you.*

I am convinced that fire and tribulation in the life of a Christian is a good thing. I am convinced that it exposes those hidden, deep rooted and inconspicuous issues that hinder our growth. I am convinced that fire makes us more fruitful and productive.

Maybe this is why Zechariah told us *God will put us into the fire, refine us like silver, and test us like gold. When we call on Him in the fire He answers and says, 'They are my people,' and they will say, 'The Lord is our God. (Zechariah 13:9).*

Malachi 3:3 says *God is as a refiner and purifier of silver; he will purify his children and refine them like gold and silver.* Proverbs 17:3 tells us *just like fire that tests the purity of silver and gold, the Lord tests the heart.*

For the Christian, there is no need to fear the fire and storms of life, nor should we be anxious in a year of drought. When the storm winds blow, we must stand together in the Lord. The Bible confirms this truth as *it is good for us to stand together in unity (Psalms 133:1).*

Thus, we are better together. Like the redwood trees, there is strength in numbers. In the storms of life, we must be united one to another and each of us must believe:

> *I shall not, I shall not be moved.*
> *I shall not, I shall not be moved.*
> *Just like a tree that's planted by the water.*
> *I shall not be moved.*

My advice is to find the redwoods in your life. Find the people who can hold you up, the people who are supportive of your dreams and are helpful, not harmful, in times of adversity. Find the people who will not leave you lost, lacking and lonely in the storms of life.

Unlike brittle people, you can rely on them in crunch time. They've been through a few storms and they are still standing. But, more importantly, they can tell you how they made it through. These are your redwood trees.

Blessed, Better, Not Bitter

Again, I say the pain of today and the experiences of your past are preparing you for your tomorrow. When you place them in God's hand the pain and experiences of the past serve as springboards launching you into your destiny.

As the psalmist said, *"Before I was afflicted I went astray, but now I keep Your word" (Psalms 119:67).* The psalmist goes on to say, *"It was good to me that I was afflicted so that I might learn God's statutes"* (Psalms 119:71).

Said differently, God in His infinite wisdom uses the storms of life for our good. For this reason dear reader I can confidently declare to you today that the storms of life will not destroy you, but position you for your blessings.

My friend, do not miss your miracle. Let God complete the work He is doing in your life. Be patient in your affliction. If you do you will be perfect, complete, and in need of nothing (James 1:4).

Job declared in the midst of his pain *"I shall come forth as gold" (Job 23:10).* This scripture from Job reveals two powerful truths I want you to get in your spirit. The first is that he would *"come out"* of the trial. The second is he would come out of it *"a much better man"* than he went in.

Similarly, the book of Exodus gives the account of the children of God who suffered through 430 years of harsh slavery in Egypt. They worked every day at the hands of a cruel taskmaster (See Exodus 1:11). Throughout their ordeal, they were praying and trusting God to deliver them from these atrocities.

In spite of their prayers, each year the level of cruelty and the demand placed upon them were increased. Instead of their plight getting better it was getting worse (Exodus 5:6-9). Many stopped believing God would deliver them as it was taking God too long to fulfill His promise.

After all, 430 years of patience and Long-Suffering is a long time to wait on God. In fact, depending on what you may be going through, 4 hours, 4 days, 4 weeks, 4 months, or even 4 years could be a long time to wait on the Lord.

In the end, the Bible says God's children came out of Egypt, out of the days of their tribulation with great substance (See Genesis 15:14). They did not limp out, wander out, or barely make it out. They came out with extreme favor and bountiful blessings. They came out better than they went in.

The Bible says He brought them out of Egypt *loaded down with silver and gold and the Bible says not one among the tribes of Israel even stumbled (See Psalms 105:37, New Living Translation).* God's promise to bring them out better than they went into their trial is for you too. Claim it today. Claim it right now. As the Lord has said *know that I am the Lord: those who hope in me will not be disappointed"* (Isaiah 49:23).

Final Thoughts on Long-Suffering

There are difficulties that we all must go through. But God is using these difficult times to mold us, to perfect us, and to prepare us for something even greater. Romans 8:18 teaches us *the suffering we are currently going through is not worthy to be compared to the glory that would be revealed in your life.*

Dear reader consider this. The grace and power of God that have kept you to this very moment are just foreshadows of the even greater manifestations that He has coming your way (See 1 Corinthians 2:9).

I realize we have all experienced moments when we were really impatient. Moments when the suffering felt like it was too much to bear. Moments when we grew tired of waiting on God to do something or for something to happen. However, I cannot stress enough the importance of waiting on God and to looking forward to the better days that are coming your way.

Long-Sufferers know there may be difficulties and delays in life, but their destiny will not be denied. And, when it comes to their destiny, a Long-Sufferer knows they are going through the storm, not dying in it and they shall come forth as pure gold.

Here is a powerful truth for your life:

There are mighty moves of God that will only manifest during the storm and others are scheduled to manifest after the storm is over.

My friend *"Be joyful in hope, patient in affliction and faithful in prayer."* God may not come when we want Him, but He will be there right on time. In the meantime, He is strengthening you in the struggle and when the time is right, *He will deliver you out of your distresses (See Psalms 107:6).*

Receive this truth in your life,
in Jesus Name,
AMEN!

Chapter 11

Expecting Mighty Moves of God

CREATING AN ATMOSPHERE FOR MIRACLES

"And he gave heed unto them,
expecting to receive something of them"
(Acts 3:5)

MIGHTY MOVES OF God happen when we expect them to happen. When we expect that the things that we ask for in prayer will come to pass, it sets in motion supernatural acts of God that cannot be stopped. That is the power of expectancy, it is in the Bible, and it is the springboard into the realm of the unstoppable spirit.

It's More than a Theory

Expectancy is from the Greek word *"Prosdokaó"*. It means to watch and wait with earnest anticipation. In addition to being supported by scripture, it is a well research theoretical construct. Hundreds of books and peer-reviewed articles have been written about the expectancy theory. Expectancy theory proposes:

> *A person will act in a certain way because they expect by so doing they will get a desired result.*

Said differently, if you *"believe"* something is going too happened it changes the way you *"act"*. It suggests that the higher your expectation, the harder you will work to achieve your goals and dreams.

Dr. Victor Vroom, professor in the school of business at Yale dedicated a considerable amount of time studying expectancy and its influence on the actions and outcomes in a person's life. According to Dr. Vroom, the level of expectancy is a good predictor of the effort a person will put forward to achieve their goals *(Work and motivation, 1995)*.

Dr. Albert Bandura, one of the most frequently cited psychologist, inferred in his 1997 work *"Self-efficacy: The exercise of control"* that a person with high expectations is better prepared mentally to deal with the trials they face in life.

In completing my professional doctorate degree, I dedicated more than two years to an advanced qualitative phenomenological study of the expectancy theory. In reading more than 300 books and scholarly articles and interviewing a slew of research candidates, the analysis of the candidate responses and the literature support the premise that:

> *What we expect effects what we will and will not do and thereby what we will and will not receive.*

What researchers call expectancy theory, the body of Christ calls *"faith"* in God. Where expectancy theory is based on how *"bad"* a person wants something and that by *"working hard"* they will get what they want, expectancy for the Christian is decidedly different and far greater.

Our expectations are not founded upon what we want or what we do. Our *"expectation is from God" (Psalms 62:5)*. After all, it is God and God alone who makes all things possible. Therefore, within every moment of every day is an opportunity for a miracle, so:

> *Don't be discouraged. Don't be upset. Expect God to act! For I know that I shall again have plenty of reason to praise Him for all that He will do. He is my help! He is my God! (Psalms 42:11, The Living Bible)*

Miracles are Everywhere

A miracle is a supernatural act of God that cannot be explained by nature, science or the wisdom of man. They defy logic, they leave the intellectual speechless and they confound the wise. Also known as *"signs and wonders"*, they are undeniable evidence of God's presence and they increase our awareness of God's power and His magnificence.

Just look around. Miracles are everywhere. Our universe is a massive, ever expanding supernatural act of God. It is not a big bang. It is a big miracle. It is beyond scientific exploration or explanation. In fact, the more we discover about the universe the more we realize just how miraculous it is.

The Milky Way Galaxy that we live in contains more than 300 billion stars. But, that is just one galaxy among the billions of galaxies in the observable universe. Most Astronomers estimate the observable universe has more than 100 billion galaxies.

There are estimates that as many as 70 billion trillion stellar populations exist in the observable universe. Now consider this. Only God knows how much more exist in the great unknown. Thus, the heavens contain more miracles than we can count, calculate or comprehend.

Yet, the Hand of God created each stellar body and everything that exist in them (See Genesis 1:1-28. Isaiah 48:13 says God:

> *Laid the foundation of the earth and His right hand spread out the heavens. When He called them, they all appeared.*

Jeremiah 32:17 says:

> *Ah Lord GOD! Behold, You have made the heavens and the earth by Your great power and by Your outstretched arm!*

Hebrews 11:3 reads *"by faith we understand the world was formed by the Word of God."* David wrote in Psalms 19:

> *The heavens declare the glory of God, and the sky displays what His hands have made.*

During Jesus' thirty-three and a half year ministry on the Earth, He performed countless miracles. There are nearly 40 miracles performed by Jesus recorded in the gospels. The Bible says He healed a paralytic man (Matthew 9:1-8). He restored a man's withered hand (Mark 3:1-6) and He even pulled money from the mouth of a fish (Matthew 17:24-27).

He did other amazing things as well. In fact, if every miracle performed by Jesus had been written the world would not be big enough to support the book that would be created (See John 21:25).

If that is not enough, even the disciples performed miracles (Luke 10:1). They cast out demons (Mark 9), they healed the lame (Acts 3), and did great wonders and miracles (Acts 6:8). In Acts 19, we are told they did:

> *Extraordinary miracles so that handkerchiefs or aprons were even carried to the sick, and the diseases left them and the evil spirits went out (Acts 19:11-12).*

Additionally, to see evidence of God's miracle working power we need not look any further then our own creation. *God formed man of the dust of the earth and breathed into his nostrils the breath of life and man became a living soul (Genesis 2:7).* You and I are walking, talking, living and breathing miracles.

The questions I have for you are *"Do you believe in miracles?"* I pray that you do. *"Are you expecting miracles in your life?"* I hope you are. I am convinced God wants miracles to manifest in your life.

The Miracle Worker

Miracles are vital in our understanding of the magnificence of our Maker. Jesus said *believe the miracles that I do so that you may know the Father (John 10:38).* Miracles reveal that God is not the figment of our imagination, nor is He some distant disinterested deity hiding in the clouds. They are proof that God cares for us, He visits us, and He is actively involved in our lives (See Psalms 8:4).

Furthermore, miracles are not random, whimsical acts of God. They are purposeful, well-calculated supernatural interventions of the Almighty. They happen in our lives when divine opportunities are released in an atmosphere of expectancy.

ANOTHER TEST AND TESTIMONY
Undeniable Evidence

I can recall talking to the doctors, hospital staff, police officers, paramedics and others in the days after the accident. Based on their experience our survival was nothing short of a miracle. They were absolutely amazed.

At speeds in excess of 90 miles per hour, everyone should have died on impact. If we survived the impact, the side effects of the crash certainly should have ended our lives. But, glory to God we survived!

One day when I was working on this project, the Lord reminded me of this miracle when He pressed these words upon my heart:

The day of the accident you, your wife and your daughter should have died. You are alive today because I intervened. Now go tell others about the miracle I have done for you.

Trapped in a comatose state like a bird snared in a hunter's net, it seemed her days were numbered. But, God's miracle working power was not done yet. He was just getting started. Several days later, her eyes opened as she awoke from the coma.

At that moment, I felt like a king with a fancy new castle. Like Superman with a shiny new cape and a big "S" on his chest. Like a guardian angel with a new set of magnificent wings.

What God had done in saving her life, my life, my daughter's life and the life of the young man that caused the accident was mind-boggling. Through special displays of His power, God kept us alive. Some might call it luck, chance, or good fortune. But, from my perspective, the evidence is undeniable – these were miracles.

Illustration – Jesus Took the Wheel

Years later on a rainy night, my family and I were driving home when for no apparent reason and without warning, a huge semi-truck swerved into our lane. It happened so fast that I did not have enough time to react. Instantly, I felt the steering wheel turn in my hands on *"its own accord"*.

I am convinced it was nobody but God or one of His angels. Had it not been for God's divine intervention, I know that truck would have crushed us and our lives would have ended that day. But for reasons I cannot explain, God said not so.

It is just further proof that as the psalmist said of God, *My times are in Your hand" (Psalms 31:15).* In this instance, by God's miracle working power our lives were spared. I was totally amazed.

Illustration – Warned in a Dream

One another night I was fast asleep and had a dream. In the dream, a man dressed in dark clothing was preparing to break into our home through an unlocked door. Suddenly in the dream, an Angel shouted, *"Go lock the door!"* Instantly I woke up.

I immediately checked the back door of our home. Sure enough, it was unlocked so I locked it. I then looked out the window and saw someone walking pass the pool enclosure.

So, while I was asleep and totally unaware of my surroundings, the Miracle Worker was watching over my family. As Psalms 121:3 says *He who watches over you will not slumber.* Psalms 41:2 says *the Lord will protect him and keep him alive, and he shall be called blessed upon the earth; And do not give him over to the desire of his enemies.*

I was so shaken by the dream, that I slept by the door the rest of the night. I shudder to think what might have happened if the Lord had not spoken to me in my dream. But He did. I was totally amazed.

Illustration – Riding on Empty

One day I was driving home from work. The gas was nearing empty and the fuel low light had been on for a few miles. I pulled into the gas station to put some gas in the car. To my dismay, I had mistakenly left my wallet and my cell phone home that morning.

At that moment, the Lord spoke to me and said, *"Everything will be alright"*. With these words, I drove more than 50 miles to my home on an empty gas tank. But, check this out. When I pulled into the driveway, my gas tank was no longer on empty. I had a *"half a tank of gas"*.

Abraham called our God *Jehovah-Jireh*, meaning the Lord will provide (See Genesis 22:14). Isaiah said *His ways are beyond our ways and His thoughts are beyond our thoughts. For just as the heavens are higher than the earth, so are Gods ways* higher than ours, and His thoughts than ours. (Isaiah 55:8-9). In that moment, He certainly proved it to me. I was totally amazed.

Illustration – Rear View Mirror

One day, my wife, my oldest daughter Kendra, and I were returning home from a trip to the mall. We were traveling on a single lane highway when suddenly all of the cars ahead of us started slowing down. A car ahead of us was making a left turn so the traffic was stopped as we waited for the road to clear.

My wife glanced in the rear view mirror and noticed a car barreling down the road behind us. It must have been traveling at least 60 miles per hour and it was not slowing down. It was only seconds away from slamming into the rear of our vehicle, when at the last possible moment the car veered to the right narrowly missing us.

As I watched this event unfold in the review mirror, it appeared as if the car had been pushed to the side just before it would have smashed into our car. Maybe this is just a small example of what 2 Samuel 22:3-4 proclaims:

> *My God, my rock, in whom I take refuge, my shield, and the horn of my salvation, my stronghold and my refuge, my savior; you save me from violence.*

With a nudge from above, the car came screeching to a halt in the grass on the side of the road. When we looked at the driver in the car, he had the most puzzling look on his face. You could tell from his expression he had no idea how he avoided the crash.

He was puzzled, I was thankful praying. He was perplexed, I was giving God the praise. I knew *"what the Lord had done!"* (See Psalms *118:23*). I was totally amazed.

Illustration Application

One of the many ways that God makes His presence known is through miracles, signs and wonders.

Nicodemus said to Jesus *"truly God is with you because of the miracles you do (John 3:2)*. Moses, after seeing the wondrous act of God at the Red Sea sang:

> *Who is like you O' Lord. You are glorious in holiness, awesome in glorious deeds, always working wonders. (Exodus 15:11)*

Experiences like those noted in the aforementioned illustrations and in the Word of God have taught me to live every day expecting miracles. This is important because once you have experienced a miracle you began living each day *"expecting"* God to do more. It is this sense of expectancy that fuels the atmosphere for supernatural things to *"happen"* in your life.

This is powerful because when God moves in miraculous ways it changes the way we see the world around us. It changes how we deal with the obstacles and opportunities we face. Most importantly, these miraculous moves of God help us to grasp in the natural the all-powerful, all-knowing, always present God.

What Would You Do

Expectancy is easier to muster up when things look possible. However, the reality of life is many things look impossible. It is in these moments when things look impossible, and faith seems foolish and nothing makes sense that we are left with the perplexing question *"What do you do when you don't know what to do?"*

What do you do when you know you are blessed, but you feel cursed? What do you do when all of the opened doors around you are being slammed in your face? When the friends that are for you are fewer than the enemies that are against you?

What do you do when you have more problems than you can solve? What do you do when you have to make a decision and every option looks bad? What do you do when you don't know what to do? What do you do when you are afraid to go forward and you dare not turn back?

In these moments what do you do? Like the children of Israel in Exodus 14, they were trapped at the Red Sea. Pharaoh's army was behind them and the Red Sea was in front of them. Make no mistake about it Pharaoh had evil intentions on his mind.

Like the children of Israel, we are often trapped by our circumstances. But consider the Word of God to the children of Israel:

> *Do not be afraid. Stand firm and you will see the deliverance the Lord will bring you today. The Egyptians you see today you will never see again." (Exodus 14:13).*

What a powerful promise and the only thing Israel had to do was stand on the Word of God.

Or, consider King Jehoshaphat and the children of Judah who faced certain destruction (2 Chronicles 20). They were surrounded by the armies of Moab, Ammon and Mount Seir, which had galvanized their forces and were closing in to destroy Israel.

This was an unsolvable, unavoidable, catastrophic mess waiting to happen. They were faced with a fight they could not win. The entire nation was looking to him for an answer.

To make matters worse in 2 Chronicles 20:12, King Jehoshaphat said *we do not have the strength to fight the armies that are coming to destroy us.* He confessed, *"We don't know what to do".* Now anyone that was looking to the king for answer or a word of encouragement must have been disappointed.

Therein is the danger of putting your trust in people and not in God. Inevitably, we all have face problems that a man cannot solve. We all will have situations in life that will leave us dazed and dumbfounded.

So the question remains, "What do you do when you don't know what to do?" Here's what you should do...

...Step Back, Watch God Move!

By King Jehoshaphat's own admission, they did not have the strength or weapons to win this battle. Jehoshaphat admitted fighting the enemy with conventional weapons of war would be futile. He admitted unless God stepped in his entire nation would be destroyed.

However, instead of quitting, giving up or surrendering he said to God, *"Our eyes are upon you"* (2 Chronicles 20:12). In so doing, he gave this unsolvable and unavoidable problem to God. The Bible says *Jehoshaphat bowed his head with his face to the ground: and all Judah and the inhabitants of Jerusalem fell before the Lord, worshiping the Lord.*

He turned his attention and the attention of the entire nation to God. Faced with an unsolvable problem, and certain defeat King Jehoshaphat took the quickest path to victory, he humbled himself. James 4:10 says *if we Humble yourselves before the Lord, he will lift us up.*

Thus, the answer to the mystifying question, *"What do you do when you don't know what to do?"* is to humble yourself under the mighty hand of the Miracle Worker. The answer is to look to the hills from which cometh your help (Psalms 121:1). King Jehoshaphat and the children of Israel did just that.

God said to the king *fear not, nor be dismayed; tomorrow go out against them: for the Lord will be with you. (See 2 Chronicles 20:17-18).* In verse 22 as *they began to sing and praise, the Lord set ambushes against the men of Ammon, Moab, and Mount Seir who were invading Judah, and they were defeated.*

When they humbled themselves, God defeated their enemies. When they stepped back, God moved in a mighty way and made a way out of no way.

Facts, Truth or Faith

Admitting that you do not know what to do does not mean you are unintelligent, unspiritual or uninformed. To admit that you are at a lost, confused, afraid, sick, in pain, or nervous is not an indictment against your faith. Talking about the facts that are stacked against you or the truth that suggests you are not going to make it, does not mean you accept them.

The fact is somebody has just been diagnosed with cancer. The fact is someone's spouse just filed for divorce. The fact is someone has just lost a job.

The truth is someone's child is using drugs. The truth is someone's home is in foreclosure. The truth is someone's family is in disarray.

The truth is what it is, *"the truth."* The facts are what they are, *"the facts".* They are no more and no less than that. However, the reality is:

> *Facts and truth*
> *are not greater than*
> *faith.*

In Matthew 20:32 Jesus asked two blind men *"What do you want me to do for you?"* The two men knew the facts and the truth. The facts are they were blind. The truth is there was no known cure for the condition.

However, they also knew they wanted to see. They acknowledge the facts. They understood the truth, but they spoke in faith when they said, *"We want to see."*

They did not deny the facts. They did not ignore the truth. They accepted the facts and they acknowledged the truth. Nevertheless, they were united in their faith.

They believed Jesus could heal and they expected Him to do it. And, He did. The Bible says, *"Jesus had compassion on them and touched their eyes. Immediately they received their sight."*

That is what I call getting the facts straight. That is what I call the unstoppable spirit. That is what I call...

Expecting Your Miracle

The songwriter said it like this, "*I anticipate the inevitable supernatural intervention of God. I expect a miracle*". To

"*Anticipate*" means to have a sense of excitement as you wait for something to happen. The word "*Inevitable*" means something that is guaranteed or that will happen at some point in time. Finally, the term "*Supernatural*" means something that is so mystical or magical, that it is unexplainable.

Thus, the songwriter is saying he is looking forward to an amazing move of God that must happen. Not that it "*might*" happen or that it "*could*" happen. He is looking for a supernatural move of God that "*must*" happen. It is inevitable. It is guaranteed. It is simply a matter of time.

Like the lame man in Acts 3 who looked at Peter and John expecting to receive something, or the two blind men in Matthew 20, we must look to God anticipating His supernatural intervention in our lives. Not just on Sunday morning. Not just at Bible study. But every day and at all times.

This mindset sets the atmosphere for the manifestation of miracles. The Bible says the lame man looked at them "*...expecting to receive something*". Even though he endured years of living crippled, his sense of expectancy was still alive and well.

In this atmosphere for a miracle, the apostles declared, *"In the name of Jesus Christ rise up and walk."* The Bible says, *"Immediately his feet and ankle bones received strength (Acts 3:7).* Then he leaped to his feet and went into the temple *walking and leaping and praising God (See Acts 3:8).* The brother was getting his shout on!

In another example of expectancy in Acts 14, the Apostle Paul was in the city of Lystra and there sat a man who was lame. He had been that way from birth and had never walked. As the man listen to the preaching of Paul, Paul looked directly at him and *saw that he had faith to be healed (Acts 14:9).* That's expectancy.

He had faith to be healed. He anticipated it happening to him. He refused to let his predicament undermine his faith and by the power of God, he was made whole. Paul immediately challenged the man to *"stand up on your feet!"* and at that moment, the man jumped up and began to walk.

In yet another example in Acts 20:7-12, the Apostle Paul was preaching up a storm. The Bible says he kept on preaching until midnight. Now, that is what you call a long-winded preacher. But, I digress.

As a man named Euticus heard the Word of God being preached, he *"fell"* into a deep sleep. The brother was sleeping so hard that he *"fell"* from the third floor of the building and died. How horrible is that? He died in the middle of a good sermon.

Immediately, the Apostle Paul *"fell"* on him and embraced him. Said differently, he laid his hands on him and prayed for him. Moments later, he said to the crowd *"do not be troubled he is now alive."*

Paul expected a miracle, stood in faith, and God moved in a mighty way. Had the Apostle Paul not prayed, if he did not believe in miracles, this man's life would have been lost. Instead, Paul believed in miracles, he expected God's miracle power to manifest and Euticus' life was spared.

The Heart of the Matter

The examples of expectancy in Acts 3, 14, 20 and throughout the Bible have been written down for our learning (See 1 Corinthians 10:11). However, reading them in a book is one thing, benefiting from them is another. To profit from them you must embrace this miracle mindset.

You see life is full of mountains that are too high, valleys that are too low and rivers that are too wide. Therefore, having a miracle mindset must be a part of your thinking, your psyche, your mental make-up. It truly is the heart of the matter.

The Bible says, *"As a man thinketh in his heart, so is he"* *(Proverbs 23:7)*. You see what you believe in your heart fuels the words that come out of your mouth. So, if you believe that you will climb the mountain, make it through the valley, cross the river, or overcome the storm, then talk about it.

Jesus said *out of the abundance of the heart, the mouth speaks* (*Luke 6:45*). Understanding this truth is vital because the words that come out of

WORDS TO THE WISE

If you believe in miracles, confess them, profess them, so when God releases them you will possess them!

your mouth sets the atmosphere that "*you*" live in and it is the atmosphere that "*you*" live that influences the manifestation of miracles in "*your*" life. Make some sense?

Unlocking Your Miracle

As my wife, Pastor Kisha says, "*God is the God of the impossible. He is the God of miracles.*" This truth is confirmed by the psalmist who declared, *You are the God who performs miracles (Psalms 77:14).*

The aforementioned psalm is simple, succinct and it requires no further explanation. The only thing we need to do to unlock this truth in our lives is to "*mix*" it with faith. Just hearing a word is not enough. Just knowing the word is not enough. The Word of God must be "*mixed with faith*" for it to manifest in your life (See Hebrews 4:2).

Mixing It Together

The question then is "*How do we mix the Word of God with faith?*" It's simple. The more you hear the Word of God, the more your faith will increase (See Romans 10:17). Then as you walk more and more by faith and not by sight (2 Corinthians 5:7), you are mixing the word with faith.

We have a powerful example of people mixing the word with faith in Luke 17. In desperate need of a miracle, the ten lepers cried out *"Jesus, have mercy on us."* Jesus responded, *"Go, show yourself to the priest"* (Luke 17:14).

They asked for a miracle, but what they got was a word. Now the lepers were left with a choice. They could do what Jesus said or they could ignore it. They were moments away from their miracle and the only thing preventing the manifestation of the miracle was their decision to mix the word from Jesus with their faith.

This same dynamic unfolds in our lives every day. We may not have leprosy but we do have needs. Needs that can only be met by a miracle from the Lord. Just like these ten lepers in need of a miracle, God often sends us a word.

When the men with leprosy heard the word from Jesus, they began walking toward the priest as Jesus had instructed them. In so doing, they were mixing the word with their faith. The Bible says, *"As they went, they were cleansed."*

In other words, when they started walking in accordance with the word the miracle they needed was unlocked. As they moved in faith, they were healed.

In another example, in Acts 16 Paul and Silas are locked in jail. The Bible says they had been placed in the inner most part of the prison and their feet and hands were chained and shackled. Yet Paul and Silas were not discouraged by their predicament.

Beaten, bound and belittled, they still believed in the miracle working power of God. Instead of complaining or having a pity party, they moved in faith. As they *"prayed and sang praise unto God"*, suddenly, the place was shaken by a violent earthquake. The prison doors opened and everyone's chains came loose. Thus, mixing the word with the faith set their miracle in motion.

Don't Mess It Up

On the other hand, when God's word is sent to people with no faith, there are missed opportunities and unclaimed miracles. As a result, divinely inspired moments for a miracle are messed up. We have an example of people messing up their blessing in Matthew 13.

We are told that Jesus was in a city and *"He did not do many miracles because of their unbelief."* *(Matthew 13:58; see also Mark 6:5-6)*. A widespread, deep-rooted lack of faith had settled into the minds of the people. Jesus had the power and desire to heal. Unfortunately, without faith the miracle power did not manifest in their lives.

I am not suggesting that Jesus did not have the power to perform miracles. Such a statement would be sacrilegious and blasphemous. Isaiah prophesied that Jesus would come to save us, to open the eyes of the blind, the ears of the deaf, and so the mute tongues could shout for joy (See Isaiah 35:4-6).

However, in Matthew 13 the people who needed the miracle did not *"expect it"*. As a result, with the exception of a few folks, most went home the same way they came, in need of a miracle. They messed up their divine moment for the supernatural intervention of God. Now all they had to look back on was a missed opportunity. Don't let this be you.

God Will Make It Work

When God's word meets faith God moves in amazing ways to make things work out for our good. We see an example of this in Acts 27-28 when the Apostle Paul and his shipmates were shipwrecked. All onboard were moments from death.

Yet, the Apostle Paul knew he would not die. In fact, he knew no one onboard the ship would die. How did he know this? He knew it because of the word he received from God. *Do not be afraid, God has granted safety to everyone who is sailing with you"* *(Acts 27:24)*.

Paul held onto the word that God had spoken into his life. From the moment this word was released into Paul's life, it did not matter what happened during their voyage.

No one aboard the ship would die because Paul *"mixed"* the word with faith.

He knew that if need be, God could *"make"* a new ship, or *"make"* a means for their survival, or *"make"* a way out of no way. He knew God would *"make it work"* out for their good.

Given the gravity of the moment everyone onboard the ship should have died. But, glory to God, *"they all made it safely to land" (Acts 27:44)*. The Bible says some jumped overboard and swam to land. Others grabbed planks and debris from the broken ship.

My friend that is what I call God making a way out of no way. My friend that is what I call a miracle. It was a miracle the Apostle Paul expected.

He heard the word, he mixed it with faith, and God did the rest. The Apostle Paul did not have to understand it or explain it, he only had to *"mix it"* with faith and leave the situation in the Hands of the Lord.

The Miracle Mindset

Just like the miracles during our horrendous car accident in 1989, against the odds we all survived. Everyone in the accident should have died. But God *"made"* it work together for our good.

Even to this day, I look back at that moment and remind myself of the miracle working power of God. I know that since He did it back then, He will do it again. It is this knowledge of God's greatness that fuels the unstoppable spirit.

In 1 Samuel 17, as David prepared to fight Goliath, King Saul told him he was not able to defeat Goliath. Given the facts, what King Saul said was the truth. David could not win this fight. After all, David was just a boy (See 1 Samuel 17:33).

David's belief in the miracle working power of God was put to the test. To everyone's surprise in verses 32-36, he told King Saul:

*Let no man's heart fail because of Goliath; thy servant
will go and fight with this Philistine...34 Thy servant
was keeping his father's sheep; and when there came a
lion, or a bear, and took a lamb out of the flock, 35 I
went out after him, and smote him, and delivered it out of
his mouth; and when he arose against me, I caught him
by his beard, and smote him, and slew him. 36 Thy
servant smote both the lion and the bear: and this
uncircumcised Philistine shall be as one of them.*

David knew it would take a miracle for him to defeat
Goliath. Therefore, he did what we all must do. He put
this battle in the hands of the Miracle Worker. He said:

*God delivered me out of the paw of the lion, and out of
the paw of the bear, he will deliver me out of the hand of
this Philistine".*

That's the miracle mindset. David looked back at what
God had already done for him, and then he testified about
the miracle he knew was on the way. With this miracle
mindset, David took action.

For David it did not matter how big Goliath was or
how much experience Goliath had as a warrior. David
knew this was his moment, his day, and his opportunity to
walk in victory. He knew a miracle was on the way.

David knew that if you believe in miracles no
mountain is ever too high, no problem is ever too
complex, no news is ever too bad, the enemy can never
win, the best is always yet to come, and every round goes
higher and higher.

David knew if you believe in miracles the sky is the
limit and all things are possible. He knew it only takes one
word from God and faith to turn any situation around.

In 1 Samuel 17:46 David said *this day the Lord will deliver
you into my hand... and the whole world will know that there is a
God in Israel.*

David's courage, confidence and conduct are inspiring.
His unshakeable faith is invigorating. What I like about

David, is that he did not wait to move. He believed and acted immediately upon the Word of God working in his life.

David did not wait for the miracle to manifest. He did not wait for *"evidence"* that he would win. He knew he needed a miracle, he *"expected"* God to do it, and he moved in faith. That's the unstoppable spirit.

In verse 40, we are told:

> *He took his staff in his hand, and chose him five smooth stones out of the brook, and put them in the shepherd's bag which he had, even in his wallet; and his sling was in his hand: and he drew near to the Philistine.*

No one, not even his fellow Israelites believed he had a chance to succeed. But David believed it and in 1 Samuel 17:50-51 we are told that:

> *David triumphed over the Philistine with a sling and a stone; without a sword in his hand he struck down the Philistine and killed him.*

That is what happens when live with a miracle mindset. It does not matter what you are going through, or what you are facing. It does not matter where you came from or where you have been. What matters most is your mindset.

David believed in the limitless possibilities that exist in God. As a result, he did what others would not do. He did what others said could not be done. He faced, fought and finished off Goliath.

You're Just Right for a Miracle

That is the power of the miracle mindset. It turns certain defeat into improbable victories. It turns frustrating failures into amazing feats. It turns depressing valleys into mountain top experiences. It turns dark nights into delightful days. It turns gloomy and doomy prognosis into divine destinies.

As Bishop G.E. Patterson said, *"When your back is against the wall and it feels like you're about to fall. You're just right for a miracle."* Here's the lesson for you and me in the words from Bishop Patterson and from David in his fight with Goliath. If you believe in miracles, then talk about them. Confess them, profess them, stress them and when God presents you with miracle opportunities you will possess them.

When You Can't See It
"Receive It"

In Luke 5:1-11, the Apostle Peter and his friends after fishing all night and catching nothing had given up. They were frustrated. They were tired. They were heading home empty-handed.

I cannot say I blame them for giving up. Most people faced with the same situation would probably have done the same thing. But a divine opportunity was presented to them by a word from the Lord. *Get back into the boat and let down your nets for a catch.*

Even though they could not see the fish, they needed to take their focus off the disappointments of last night and trust the word they received from Jesus.

For you and I that means we must, take our eyes off our failures and misfortunes. We must focus our attention on the good things that God has spoken into our lives. I am convinced that miracles manifest when we expect good things to happen.

The disciples did not need a bigger boat, better fishing gear, or bounteous friends. Jesus knew this and He sent them something even better. They needed another opportunity and renewed expectations. So, Jesus sent them a word. He spoke an opportunity into their lives.

When Jesus sent His word to the disciples, He was not concerned with their toiling all night and catching nothing. That was in the past. Instead, He sent them an opportunity to do it again when He said *get back into the boat, launch out into the deep and let down your nets.*

There was no lengthy discussion about their past, there was no drawn out reflection on their failure. There was no talking about or crying over spilled milk. He did not even give them a motivational, rah-rah speech. He spoke a message of hope into their lives.

The message to them was last night is over. Today is a new day and I am giving you a new opportunity. Now, the burden was on the disciples to receive it and walk in it.

Similarly, your Bible holds God's messages to you. Every time you open it, you have the opportunity to read those messages. My

WORDS TO THE WISE
Every time you read God's word, God is sending opportunities into your life.

friend, *"You've Got Mail"* Read your bible. Receive them and walk in them.

When You Can't See It
"Expect It"

In Luke 5:1-11, a huge school of fish was waiting beneath their boat and now it was time for Peter and his friends to go fishing again. It was time for action. It was time for them to demonstrate the unstoppable spirit.

They had received the word and as they were mixing it with faith. The Bible says, *it was no sooner said than done— they caught a huge haul of fish, straining the nets past capacity.*

That is the power we walk in when the Word of God is released in an atmosphere of expectancy. The disciples heard the word, heeded the word, and hastily walked in the word. When they did an atmosphere for a miracle was created and it resulted in the great blessing they received.

Now, instead of walking away defeated and empty handed, instead of walking away from the blessing they could not see, their entire day was miraculously turned around. But God was not done just yet.

Not only were Peter and his friends on the boat with him blessed, but the men in the other boat were blessed as well. The Bible says *they waved to their partners in the other boat to come help them. They filled both boats, nearly swamping them with the catch.*

Said differently, the blessing was so great that they did not have room enough to receive it. How did this happen? Why did this happen. The answer is easy.

They received the word spoken to them. They expected the word to manifest in their lives and now they had *"more"* blessings than they could handle. That is the power of expectancy.

Right Message, Right Mindset

You may be tired, frustrated, knocked down, and even shedding tears. But, the word of the Lord to you today is *"Get back into your boat! You have miracles to catch."*

God has great things in store for you. Yes, I'm talking to you! I'm not talking about your brother, sister, neighbor or someone else. He has great things in store for you and your sense of expectancy is the God ordained trigger to release them into your life.

Not tomorrow, not some day in the future, but right *"Now!"* Yes, right now. It is this right now dimension of expectancy that stretches the limits of your imagination. It expands your faith, broadens your horizon and keeps you perfectly position for God's supernatural release into your life. This should be your mindset.

A Message from Jabez

Jabez was a dreamer, a prayer warrior and a man of faith. Like so many people, he was a good man born into a bad set of circumstances. The Bible says in 1 Chronicles 4:9-10:

> *Jabez was a better man than his brothers, a man of honor. His mother had named him Jabez (Oh, the pain!), saying, "A painful birth! I bore him in great pain!"*

Jabez needed a miracle to turn his life around. He knew what he wanted, he expected God to do it, and he prayed a prayer of expectancy that set his miracle in motion:

> *Jabez prayed to the God of Israel: "Bless me, O bless me! Give me land, large tracts of land. And provide your personal protection—don't let evil hurt me.*

Jabez asked for supernatural increase, greater influence, divine protection, and victory over the evil intentions of men. Jabez asked for a big blessing, for divine strength, God's presence and His guidance. He asked for a miracle that would give his life a total makeover.

No one knows how many times Jabez prayed this prayer. But what we do know is God answered this one. We also know that Jabez did not let his situation change his expectations in God. The Bible says, *"God gave him what he asked."*

The message gleaned from the story of Jabez's life is that mighty moves of God are released by the prayer of a man who expects God to move. Jabez that teaches us the principle of scripture found in Matthew 7:7-8 keep on asking, and you will receive. Keep on seeking, and you will find. Keep on knocking, and the door will be opened to you.

That is the message in the wisdom of Jabez. In spite of the difficulty of our days, we must keep on keeping on. We must keep on praying. Keep on believing. Keep seeking the supernatural intervention of God in our lives.

A Message from Apostle Paul

The Apostle Paul's life was littered with adversity. In 2 Corinthians 11:23-29 the Apostle Paul recounts the trials of his life. In one instance, he was stoned and left for dead. To the surprise of everyone he got up, dusted himself off and went back into the same city and continued preaching (See Acts 14:19-28). That is what I call the unstoppable spirit.

On another occasion, after surviving a shipwreck in the middle of a raging storm, he was bitten by a poisonous snake. Once again, everyone expected him to die. But he shook off the viper and suffered no harm (See Acts 28:3). That is what I call letting nothing stop you.

The Apostle Paul was a real *"go-getter"* and in spite of the opposition, obstacles and obstinate people he faced he kept pressing on to reach the end of the race and receive the heavenly prize for which God, through Christ Jesus, is calling us (Philippians 3:14, New Living Translation).

The undeniable truth that resonates throughout the Apostle Paul's life is he faced each trial with determination and faith. With the help of the Lord, he repeatedly overcame the difficulties in his life and he completed the assignment God had given him.

As the Apostle Paul noted, *"Having therefore received help from God I have continued on to this day"*. What is all the more impressive is he made this statement when he was still a prisoner and people were trying to kill him (See Acts 26:20-22). It was as if he was saying to his persecutors, public enemies, and other mean spirited people *"You can't stop me!"*

If the Apostle Paul were here right now, I am sure he would tell you and me we are unstoppable. . He would tell us God is working things out for our good. He would tell us every day we wake up, to stand up, square our shoulders and face the storms of life head on.

A Message from Dr. *G*

My friend, my message to you is simple, yet profound. When you expect God to move all things are possible. Whenever we fully embrace this truth and live our lives by it, an atmosphere for miracles is created around us and the God of miracles turns our dreams and desires into reality (See Psalms 37:4-5).

Jesus said in Mark 11:23 *"If you have faith as small as a mustard seed, you can say to this mountain, 'Move from here to there,' and it will move. Nothing will be impossible for you."*

For me that meant, using the little bit of faith I had, and looking at my wife on her deathbed and speaking only those words that said she would get up. I visualized the impossible. I dreamed of the miraculous. I expected the unexpected and I believed the unbelievable.

This mindset moved me out of the realm of despair and defeat and into the realm of joy and victory. It moved me out of the realm of doom and gloom and into the realm of happiness, peace, divine power and invincibility.

In making the *"The Most High my shelter"* God's protective Hand, His loving Heart and His precious Holy Spirit became much more pronounced in my life. In those days I began to understand *no evil will conquer me; no plague will come near my dwelling." (Psalm 91:9-10).* As noted in Verse 11 I could feel *His angels protecting me wherever I go."*

In the face of insurmountable odds, this change had awakened in me an *"Unstoppable"* spirit. Even to this day, I refuse to let the unstoppable spirit in me die or become dormant. I live by the mantra:

> *I've got one life to live*
> *so I might as well make*
> *the most of it!*

Now I live everyday earnestly anticipating mighty moves of God. Now I live everyday confident that I have the victory in all things. Now I live everyday knowing that I have the help of God and His help has empowered me to continue unto this day.

And, as the songwriter said:

I don't believe
He brought me this far
to leave me!

I want this mentality to flow in your life as well. Having read the truths, insights, revelations, and life lessons within the pages of this book, I pray it has birthed in you a renewed focus and mentality. I pray that the *"Unstoppable Spirit"* has been awakened in your life.

Conclusion: The Choice is Yours

WALKING IN VICTORY

"Your ears will hear a voice behind you, saying,
"This is the way. Walk in it."
(Isaiah 30:21)

ONE GOOD DECISION can turn your life around. Therefore, every moment of every day has the potential to be the greatest moment or the greatest day of your life. You see right now, with one good decision your life could move to a whole new level in God. Regardless of what you have been through or are going through, one good decision will change your life for the better, forever.

An unknown author wrote:

> *Sometimes the smallest step in the right direction ends up being the best step of your life.*

Again, I am reminded of the Prodigal Son in Luke 15:18. No one would argue that he got exactly what he deserved. He had made a series of poor choices. He had squandered his inheritance and he was now living, eating and sleeping with pigs. *"Ugh, that's Just Nasty!"* However, with one good decision he turned his life around.

Refuse to Live In Defeat

With one good decision during a critical moment in his life, his situation and his destiny were changed. He said, *"I will arise and go to my father's house."* That is all it took and instantly the unstoppable spirit was awakened in him.

The Prodigal Son refused to accept a life that was less than what was possible. He did not let the poor decisions in his past or the despair of his current situation stop him from turning his life around.

He did not let the thought of what people might say when they saw him return home looking like crap and smelling like pig droppings stop him. He did not let fear of failure or rejection, doubters, and ridicule stop him. Neither should you.

We all wrestle with thoughts of failing, being rejected, and we all face doubters and ridicule. The truth is people may laugh at your dreams, scoff at your destiny or undermine your efforts. People may think you are crazy, they may even talk about you behind your back and they may even scandalize your name.

My response to people who do or say such things is *"So what!"* The way I see it, if people were going to help me, then they could have helped me a long time ago. Since they have not helped me, I refuse to let them stop me.

Remember what Jesus said to his friend Peter when Peter stood between him and the cross *Get behind me Satan (Matthew 16:23).* Remember what Jesus said to the Pharisees when they opposed Him *you are of your father the devil (John 8:44).*

Jesus did not let his relationship to those who stood in the way of His destiny stop him. He rebuked His detractors, He rebutted His doubters and He kept moving forward when devilish-minded people tried to derail Him. That's the *"Unstoppable Spirit"*.

If people tried to stop Jesus, the prophets, and others before us, then I know people are trying to do the same things to you and me. However, there is nothing we can do about that.

But, here is what we can do. Overlook their weird ways and wicked words. Move past their madness, their mean spirit, and their malignant motives. I have often said of people who mean me no good:

> *The world was turning*
> *before I met you.*

In other words, life goes on and time will keep ticking. I have better things to do with the time God has given me than focusing on people who mean me no good. After all, time is the most precious commodity that I have.

I pray for such people. I share God's word with such people. But, I refuse to let the work of God in my life cease for the sake of misguided, mean spirited, monstrous people. I encourage you to adopt a similar philosophy.

If there are people in your life that are hindering your assignments, sabotaging your destiny, and troubling your spirit, then you owe it to yourself to seek the Father's power and wisdom to conquer the storms they are creating. Your destiny depends on it.

The Prodigal Son finally realized this when he really needed some help and, *"no one would give him anything."* *(Luke 15:16)*. However, when no one would help him, he helped himself. With one good decision, he recovered from the wastefulness, waywardness and wantonness of his past.

He had no one else to blame for his place in life. Nevertheless, with one good decision, he broke free of his deplorable situation. With one good decision, he put himself in position to live a better life. With one good decision, his life was forever changed.

Nothing Can Stop You

Regardless of what you are facing, it can be ridicule, wickedness, temptation, deception, or deceit. No matter where you are to face it, it can be at work, in the store, in your home, in a relationship, or in the community. And, no matter what impact it is or is not having on your life, your outlook must never change.

The truth of the matter is:

You Shall Overcome.
Not someday, but today!

"Today is your day and now is your time." It is time for you to arise. It is time to move into the overflow. It is time for an even greater anointing. Looking at what happened yesterday will not help you and waiting for tomorrow is of no value. The time to act is now!

That is exactly what the Apostle Paul did. In the face of certain death, the Apostle Paul was unyielding in his faith and confident in his God. Even with his life in jeopardy, he still opened his mouth and proclaimed, *I stand here and testify to small and great alike (Acts 26:22).*

He made up in his mind and he was not going to be deterred, distracted, delayed or denied. The passion, power and purpose to complete his God given assignment were greater than the storms that were before him. That is the Unstoppable spirit.

It is my prayer that the unstoppable spirit has been ignited in you. This mindset fuels the undefeatable, never quit, steadfast, triumphant, opportunistic and optimistic spirit that is essential for reaching the goals that God has set before you.

Once we truly embrace the fullness of what having God in our lives means, our passion for praise is ignited, the anointing is activated, and boldness flows from our lives like living water and our expectations soar to new levels.

Do you believe this? If you do and you are ready to receive it, then it is time to make it official. It is time to confess it, profess it, so you can possess it. Remember, there is great power released into your life when you can hear yourself declaring the blessings, favor and power of God.

Say this with me.

> *I shall arise. I shall live and not die. I shall come forth as gold I am more than a conqueror. I am healed, delivered and set free. I am bold, blessed and coming out better. And God's plan for my life shall come to pass!*

Unstoppable

Once again, I ask you, *"What does it take to be unstoppable?"* My friend it requires you receiving and believing the revelation that you are undefeatable. It requires a never-quitting, steadfast, triumphant, opportunistic, and positive mindset. It requires a passion for praising the Lord, living in the anointing, walking with boldness, long-suffering, and high expectations in God.

This mindset serves as the genesis for this book. Unstoppable was written to strengthen and encourage you in your journey with God. It was written to draw your attention to powerful truths throughout the Bible.

> *Unstoppable is a*
> *Holy Spirit inspired mentality*
> *that will change your*
> *reality!*

Satan will use a montage of tricks, tactics and traps to stop you from reaching your God ordained destiny. But, for every diabolical scheme he concocts, God has given us a plethora of strategies, scriptures and so much more to overcome them. Like the Apostle Paul,

> *Having received help of the Lord we have continued on to this day (See Acts 26:22).*

In spite of the trials of this life, it is a journey filled with bountiful blessings and great opportunities if we will keep moving forward in Christ Jesus. I challenge you to keep moving forward, I promise you your best days are yet to come!

ONE FINAL TEST AND TESTIMONY
Let His Light Shine

God saved my family from darkness, destruction and certain death. In the process, He armed us with a powerful testimony. It's a testimony that He has all power in His hand and that He is the God that heals (See Exodus 15:26).

Now we bore the responsibility of showing forth the glory of God. As noted in the Word of God, it is because of His great work and presence in our lives that:

> *Our faces shine with God's brightness. We have been transfigured much like the Messiah. Each day our lives must become brighter and more beautiful as God enters our lives and we become more like him"* (See 2 Corinthians 3:17, The Message Bible).

What better way to let God's light shine than by walking in faith when things look impossible and by refusing to quit when times get hard. You see people are always watching the body of Christ, particularly when our backs are against the wall and it looks like we are about to fall. They would like nothing more than to see you and I give up when the going gets tough. However:

> *When the going gets tough,*
> *God's people keep on going!*

In the face of an endless stream of bad news from doctors, nurses and hospital staff, we held onto God's word. I am not suggesting the doctors, nurses, and hospital staff was the enemy. Nothing could be further from the truth.

Their knowledge, skills and expertise were instrumental in the blessings of God that were beginning to flow into our lives. I am forever grateful for their efforts. But, any information that contradicted the revelation of God in our lives had to be rebuked, rebutted and resisted.

As previously noted, doctors feared if my wife got pregnant, both her and the baby would die. But I was crazy enough to believe that God would dispatch an angel to hold the baby in place until the baby was born.

Not only did God bless my wife to carry a baby full term. He blessed us with a third child a year later. Now I have three miracle daughters: my oldest daughter Kendra who survived the car accident with my wife and I, and my two younger daughters Keona and Kenya who were born after the accident.

The facts suggested my younger daughters should not have been born. But we believe God is still in the miracle working business and I am so grateful that He is. My life would not be the same without my daughters. I am forever blessed because of them.

Its stories like these that prove we are unstoppable. We should let go and let God have His way. The Bible says:

> *"Don't worry? God is with you on this journey."*
> *(Judges 18:6)*

Its stories like these sprinkled throughout our lives that we have continued to share. We share them to show forth the greatness of our God. Our lives should have ended that infamous and dreadful Christmas day of 1989. But God saved us and set His light within us.

As the Apostle Paul said:

> *For God, who said, "Let there be light in the darkness,"*
> *has made this light shine in our hearts so we could know*
> *the glory of God (2 Corinthians 4:6).*

It's Your Time to Shine

God's light shines in darkness and darkness cannot conquer it. It cannot be put out, it cannot be denied, and it cannot be destroyed. It cannot be overcome, extinguished, comprehended, or conquered (See John 1:5).

By God's own design He has *"Made this light shine in our hearts" (2 Corinthians 4:6)* In Matthew 5:14 Jesus said *you are the light of the world. A city that is set on a hill cannot be hid (Matthew 5:14).* In Matthew 5:16 he states *let your light so shine before men, that they may see your good works, and glorify your Father which is in heaven.*

And, like stars in the heavens, our light appears brightest in the darkest of times. Once God's light is lit within you, it cannot be hid. You have to let it out!

Unfortunately, we live in a world in which people love darkness more than light (See John 3:19). We live in a time in which the body of Christ is under a violent attack and vicious people (See Matthew 11:12).

Nevertheless, the light of Gods' Holy Spirit shining through us will prevail. It always has and it always will. It is unstoppable and my friend, it is time to let it shine.

Remember Your Destiny

Your life is not an accident or a mistake. You were born at the right time. You were born in the right place and you were born to succeed. Consider for just a moment. The next moment could be the moment you have been waiting for. Are you ready for it?

When you are discouraged, remember your destiny. When you want to give up, remember your destiny. When the odds are stacked against you, remember your destiny. When others say you will not make it, remember your destiny. When your heart is heavy, remember your destiny.

This simple act of reminding yourself of the promises of God that you are moving toward will strengthen you in your current situation. It will lift you up when you are feeling down. It will point you in the right direction when you drift off course. It will keep your ears open to the voice of God in your life.

After the car accident, destiny lifted us up. There were financial setbacks. There were medical and physical setbacks. There were mental and psychological setbacks. There were setbacks in the workplace and even in ministry.

But, we refused to be discouraged. We refused to be distraught and downhearted, and here is the reason why. For us, each set back was simply a set up for something greater. Every closed door was just a sign that God had already opened other opportunities that were even better.

Remember Your Brother

What good would it be to live with an *"unstoppable"* spirit and not use the strength, power, favor and blessings of God flowing through your life to help someone else? Remember the instruction that Jesus gave to Peter, *when you have been restored, turn around and strengthen others (See Luke 22:32).*

The reality is we often find ourselves with opportunities to help others. I believe it is by God's design. The Bible says the strong must bear the infirmity of the weak (See Romans 15:1).

Galatians 6:1 reads *if another believer is overcome by some sin, you who are godly should gently and humbly help that person back onto the right path (New Living Translation).* The Apostle Paul noted in Romans 15:1, *those with strength have an obligation to bear the infirmities of the weak.* 19th Century author Charles Dickens said:

> *No one is useless in this world*
> *who lightens the burdens of another.*

The truth of the matter is in the morning you may be on the mountain looking down at others, but by mid-day, you may be down in the valley in need of a helping hand. Ironically, the person you help while you are rejoicing on the mountaintop just might be the person God will use to help you when you find yourself weeping in the valley of life.

That's just a
little something to think about.

Praying for Others

When the Apostle Paul got discouraged and distraught, God said to him *"I am with you, and no one is going to attack and harm you, because I have many people in this city."* *(See Acts 18:10).* I am sure many of these people the Apostle Paul had never met. However, by the power of the Holy Spirit, God had connected him to a network of believers.

In Acts 18, it is safe to assume God was using their prayers, provision, and so forth, to support the Apostle Paul as he completed his assignment for the Lord. It is safe to assume the same is true today. God has people around the world who are praying, promoting, and prepared to provide for your success. Likewise, most of these people you have never met.

But that does not matter. What matters is the great power in the network of believers. What matters is the great power in praying, promoting and providing for the success of one another.

This was the Apostle Paul's prayer in Colossians 1:9-13:

> *We have not ceased to pray for you and to ask that you*
> *may be filled with the knowledge of His will in all*
> *spiritual wisdom and understanding, so that you will*
> *walk in a manner worthy of the Lord, to please Him in*
> *all respects, bearing fruit in every good work and*

increasing in the knowledge of God; strengthened with all power.

Consider the powerful miracle that was released in Job's life when he prayed for his friends. The Bible says *the Lord restored the fortunes of Job when he prayed for his friends. (Job 42:10)*

The portion of the verse is *"When he prayed for his friends".* In other words, when Job prayed for someone else, the Lord blessed him. As theologian and author Samuel Rutherford said:

> *I have benefitted by praying for others; for by making an errand to God for them I have gotten something for myself.*

In another example, at the end of Genesis chapter 20 and the beginning of Genesis chapter 21, we are told that Abraham prayed for Abimelek's wife that she might conceive. This is important because Abraham is praying for Abimelek's wife to receive the blessing that he and his wife Sarah are still waiting for.

Verse 17 reads, *Abraham prayed to God, and God healed Abimelek, his wife and his female slaves so they could have children again.* Then we are told in the next verse in Chapter 21:1-2

> *Now the Lord was gracious to Sarah as he had said, and the Lord did for Sarah what he had promised. Sarah became pregnant and bore a son to Abraham in his old age.*

Thus, when Abraham prayed for someone else to receive the blessing that he and his wife were in need of, God answered his prayer and He simultaneously released the blessing that Abraham and Sarah need as well. That's powerful.

The lesson for you and I is, even in our pain or when our blessings seem delayed, when we pray for someone else we can rest assure that God is bringing the things we are expecting to pass. I pray that you catch that revelation. If you do, it will radically change your prayer life and the manifestation of God's miracles.

In another example in Acts 12, the Apostle Peter was locked in Jail and moments from his execution. Unbeknownst to him prayer was being made on his behalf. In Acts 12:5, the Bible says, *earnest prayer was going up to God from the church for his safety all the time he was in prison (The Living Bible).*

Because of their prayers, the Lord dispatched an Angel and Peter was delivered from death. Days before his execution:

> *Suddenly there was a light in the cell and an angel of the Lord stood beside Peter! The angel slapped him on the side to awaken him and said, "Quick! Get up!" And the chains fell off his wrists! 8 Then the angel told him, "Get dressed and put on your shoes." And he did. "Now put on your coat and follow me!" the angel ordered.9 So Peter left the cell, following the angel.*

If the power of praying for someone else was true for Paul, Job, Abraham, and Peter, then it is also true in my life and in yours. So here is an important question you should ask yourself, *"Who have I prayed for lately?"*

Now consider this. The miracle you are waiting for could be tied to the miracle in someone else's life and your prayer could be the tool that God is waiting to use to release it.

That's just another
little something to think about.

Selah!

Think Beyond the Grave

The message encapsulated in this book is about more than overcoming the trials, tests, and tribulations of this life. In addition to those things, the unstoppable spirit is about conquering the fear of death, hell and the grave.

This is important because "*if only in this live we have hope, then we are men most miserable*" *(1 Corinthians 15:19-20)*.

We all have at least one more major challenge awaiting us. We all have one more river to cross. But when you fully embrace the *"Unstoppable Spirit"*, the way you think about these things is revolutionized. "*Life without end at last*" will truly be yours.

You see death is not the end. It's just a transition. It's a new beginning. Psalms 116:15 tells us that it is *"Precious in the sight of the Lord the death of his saints."* The problem is we are looking at death from the wrong perspective. We see death as someone leaving. God sees death as one of His children coming home!

When this revelation was unlocked in my spirit, the way I saw everything around me changed. Even in death, I knew I had the victory. I no longer saw death for the child of God as someone being defeated; I now knew it to be God's deliverance and a vital step in our divine destiny. As the Apostle Paul put it, *"to die"* in Christ is gain (Philippians 1:21).

Through the door of death, we step into a new world. We enter into a new season with new opportunities. That is what Jesus told the thief on the cross *Today you will be with me in paradise (Luke 23:43)*.

Thus, to grasp the fullness of this book you must think in these terms. To grasp the fullness of this book you must think beyond the grave. Paul gave us a glimpse of life beyond the grave in 2 Corinthians 12:2-4 when he told us of being *caught up to paradise and heard inexpressible things, things that no one is permitted to tell.*

Jesus gave us a glimpse of life beyond the grave in John 14:2-3 when He said:

> *In my Father's house are many mansions: if it were not so, I would have told you. I go to prepare a place for you. And if I go and prepare a place for you, I will come again, and receive you unto myself; that where I am, there ye may be also.*

Someday, I will take my last breath in this world and move to my new home in heaven. But please know I have not been stopped. Like you my friend, I am unstoppable and on the other side of death's door, I am still running on for the Lord. Nothing and no one, not even death, hell or the grave can ever hold us down.

The Choice is Yours

Remember dear reader, your victory is not determined by the magnitude, the ferocity, or the frequency of your trials. Your victory is determined by your faith in God and the inner working of the Holy Spirit being activated in your life.

It does not matter what did or did not happen in your past. Right now, you have the opportunity to choose life, to choose victory, to choose God's way, to choose the unstoppable spirit. It is a choice that you have to make and no one can make it for you.

I encourage you to embrace the unstoppable spirit today! I declare the abundant life of God's blessing is released upon your life. Jesus said in John 10:10, *I have come that you might have light and life more abundantly (John 10:10)*. I decree this is your moment to claim it in Jesus name.

In Summation

With God on your side, you are *"Unstoppable"!* If anyone has a problem with that, tell them to take it up with God. After all, *"It's Lord's doing and it is marvelous in our eyes." (See Psalms 118:23; Mark 12:11)*

I encourage you to commit this scripture to memory.

> *Having therefore obtained help of God,*
> *I continued unto this day.*
> *(Acts 26:22)*

I encourage you my friend to stay in the Word of God and to stand in faith, in the power of the Holy Spirit, and in the Blood of the Lamb. They are your ray of hope, your

light in darkness, your strength in the time of need. They are your reason to believe.

Your Declaration of Victory

I am victorious. I accept and fully embrace the strength that God has given me to crush the enemy under my feet. I will not lose. I cannot lose. I refuse to accept failure. I may be delayed but I will not be denied.

I have victory in every area of my life. Victory in my mind, victory in my body, victory in my soul, and victory in my spirit. I have victory in my finances, victory in my family and I speak victory over my friends.

Satan I declare to you that all of your plans to defeat me are null and void. I send them back to the pits of hell. They are rendered powerless and by the power of my God who lives in me your work in my life is done.

I heed the voice of God in my life. I have ears to hear what God is saying to me. I have the strength of the Holy Spirit to complete the tasks that I have been assigned to me by God. Having received help from the Lord I have made it to this moment, and I will keep moving forward.

I refuse to be defined by my circumstances. Regardless of my situations, I am victorious. I have the victory through the finished work of Jesus Christ on the cross. I embrace my victory in Him right now. His victory is mine in Jesus name. Amen!

It is my prayer that you will pronounce this declaration over your life. Remember, with God on your side *"Nothing Can Stop You"*.

Sincerely,

Dr. Jerome D. Jordan, *D.B.A., M.M.*
"Be Blessed!"

In My Prayers

Thousands of people are killed or injured in car accidents each year. In 1989, the year my wife, my oldest daughter and I were almost killed in the horrific car accident discussed in the book, the National Highway Safety Traffic Administration reported 45,582 people were killed as a result of a car accident in the United States. From 1989 through 2012 at total of 971,606 people were killed in a car accident, an average of 40,000 a year. I shudder to think what the numbers are today. My thoughts and prayers are with those families that have lost love ones or have loved ones that have been seriously injured in a car accident.

May God's grace be with you.

Keep Moving Forward...You Can Do It

In Jesus Name...!

About The Author

Dr. Jerome D. Jordan, also known as Dr. $\mathcal{J}$., is a graduate of St Petersburg College with an associate's degree in computer technology and a bachelor's degree in technology management. He holds a master's degree in organizational management and a professional doctorate in business administration.

Dr. $\mathcal{J}$. has extensive training and experience in marriage and family counseling, ministry leadership training, spiritual growth and development, performance and behavioral counseling, career counseling, financial and managerial accounting, budgeting, organizational behavior and analysis, project management, motivational and team building strategies, business management, church administration, legal writing and research, computer automation and networking.

Dr. $\mathcal{J}$ is a no-nonsense preacher with an emphasis on the practical application of the Word of God in our daily living. He believes every Christian should be a shining example of Christ in the home, in the community and in the church. He is a family focused man, who has given his all for his wife, family and the ministry.

References

Betty, S. (2005, Spring). The Growing Evidence for "Demonic Possession": What Should Psychiatry's Response be? *Journal of Religion and Health*, *44*(1), 13-30.

Bandura, A. (1997). *Self-efficacy: The exercise of control*. New York: W. H. Freeman and Company.

Eveleth, R. (2003, August 2). In 1916, Georgia Tech Beat Cumberland College, 222 to 0. *Smithsonian*. Retrieved from http://www.smithsonianmag.com/smart-news/in-1916-georgia-tech-beat-cumberland-college-222-to-0-22745905/?no-ist

Jordan, K.G. (2013). Stronger Than You Think [Video file]. Retrieved from Youtube website: https://www.youtube.com/watch?v=BbFvT9ih3po&feature=share

Kisner, J. (nd). Victorious Attitude., Retrieved from http://www.ellenbailey.com/poems/ellen_237.htm Satan's Garage Sale. (nd). Retrieved from http://www.inspirationalarchive.com/1379/satans-garage-sale/ Vroom, V.H. (1995). *Work and motivation*. New York: John Wiley & Sons.

Satan's Garage Sale. (nd). Retrived November 17, 2016 from http://www.inspirationalarchive.com/1379/satans-garage-sale/

Walter, Winkle. D. "The Man Who Thinks He Can."— *Poems That Live Forever*, comp. Hazel Felleman, p. 310 (1965).

Wedemeyer, C., & Kauther, M.D. (2011, March). Hemipelvectomy- only a salvage therapy?. *Orthopedic Reviews*, *3*(1), 12-19.

Woodson, C.G. (1969). *Miseducation of the negro*. Washington, D.C. The Associated Publishers, Inc.

Made in the USA
Columbia, SC
23 November 2020